FEMINISMS IN MOTION

VOICES FOR JUSTICE, LIBERATION, AND TRANSFORMATION

Edited by Jessica Hoffmann
& Daria Yudacufski

Feminisms in Motion: Voices for Justice, Liberation, and Transformation

© 2018 Jessica Hofmann and Daria Yudacufski
All essays © to the individual authors, as noted
This edition © 2018 AK Press (Chico, Edinburgh)
ISBN-13: 9781849353342
E-ISBN: 9781849353359
Library of Congress Control Number: 2018932237

AK Press   AK Press
370 Ryan Ave. #100   33 Tower St.
Chico, CA 95973   Edinburgh EH6 7BN
United States   Scotland
www.akpress.org   www.akuk.com
akpress@akpress.org   ak@akedin.demon.co.uk

The above addresses would be delighted to provide you with the latest
AK Press distribution catalog, which features books, pamphlets, zines,
and stylish apparel published and/or distributed by AK Press.
Alternatively, visit our websites for the complete catalog, latest news,
and secure ordering

Cover and interior design by Morgan Buck
Printed in the USA

For Sophie and Ruby

"There is no such thing as a single-issue struggle because we do not live single-issue lives."
—Audre Lorde

Contents

Acknowledgments

Thank you to everyone who contributed to, subscribed to, volunteered with, read, or otherwise participated in the conversation of *make/shift*. Thank you to Zach, Andrew, Jeremy, Morgan, and everyone at AK Press for their work on this book and so many others. And thank you to everyone who has made, is making, and will make movements for justice, liberation, and transformation.

Introduction

By Jessica Hoffmann and Daria Yudacufski

We edited and published *make/shift*, a biannual independent magazine of community-based, intersectional feminist art and action, from 2007 to 2017. We mailed out the twentieth and final issue in the summer of a year that felt like a watershed moment for feminism in the U.S. mainstream. It was a year that started with enormous Women's Marches and closed with a social-media outpouring of truths about sexual violence that knocked powerful abusers from their pedestals one after another. A sliver of a 1968 poem by Muriel Rukeyser was being quoted all over: "What would happen if one woman told the truth about her life?" Rukeyser asked. She quickly answered, "The world would split open."

In some ways it does feel like the world is splitting open. But it also feels entirely unsurprising. Even if we weren't editors of a feminist magazine who have had the repeated experience of finding that the majority of submissions to each issue were about sexual violence, we are women in this world. We know pervasive sexual violence is the truth because it is and because we do not have the privilege of rationalizing or denying it. (In other words, and of course, #ustoo.)

And: that Rukeyser poem is actually about a different kind of war. It's called "Käthe Kollwitz," and it's about an artist and the world wars she lived through, and economic inequality, and the gendered experience of these, and motherhood, and art, and yes the body (simultaneously individual and social), too.

But what can that mean, "one woman"? We know #metoo, the social-media hashtag that is threading together stories of sexual violence, is true because we are women in this world, but the second we think that, we hear Sojourner Truth asking "Ain't I a woman?" at a women's rights convention in 1851, insisting on the inextricableness of gender and race in her identity—and arguing for the linking of nineteenth-century struggles for women's rights and for the abolition of slavery. We hear the Black feminist group the Combahee River Collective saying, in 1977, "We are actively committed to struggling against racial, sexual, heterosexual, and class oppression, and see as our particular task the development of integrated analysis and practice based upon the fact that the major systems of oppression are interlocking. The synthesis of these oppressions creates the conditions of our lives." We hear Kimberlé Crenshaw synthesizing these ideas—ideas born from lives—in the term "intersectionality" in the 1980s. And we hear queer feminism asking what this word "woman" means *while* knowing that if violence against women were taken seriously, at large, addressing it would mitigate other violences (as Courtney Desiree Morris argues in her widely shared 2010 essay originally published in *make/shift*, "Why Misogynists Make Great Informants: How Gender Violence on the Left Enables State Violence in Radical Movements"). By now we've all read the stories about how many of the men behind recent mass shootings have a history as domestic abusers. We know violences, and the systems of power they enforce, are connected.

It is true, this idea that if one woman told the truth about her life, the world would split open, *and* it is an idea ripe for questioning, challenging, expanding, refracting. To keep pushing at it: What should we make of a split, or several? Is the world already split open along multiple seams? What do these splits feel like? What do they do? What could they do? What would it take for the world to heal?

The Combahee River Collective, again in their 1977 statement, suggested an answer: "If Black women were free, it would mean that everyone else would have to be free since our freedom would necessitate the destruction of all the systems of oppression."

There are multiple feminisms, and we think the most promising of them keep asking questions, keep feeling the truths of interconnectedness, keep pushing to get at the roots, to expand the field of what to care about (everything) and what is possible. In a world structured on hierarchies enforced by violence by way of disconnection, we believe intersectional feminism offers the best views—and examples—of ways of living based on the reality of interdependence, ways that would allow everyone to thrive.

A decade ago, after a few years of working together on a smaller zine called *LOUDmouth*, we and our friend Stephanie Abraham founded *make/shift* magazine to document, critique, and participate in the feminisms of our time, with a specific mission to amplify antiracist, queer, and transnational voices—that is, voices that challenge and create alternatives to systems of oppression in an interconnected, interdisciplinary, multi-issue way. While other feminist media outlets were offering feminist critiques of dominant culture or looking at the effects of current events on women, we wanted to document *feminist* cultures— the actions and ideas that were emerging from lives and communities to uproot violences and transform hierarchies, to create something more like freedom and sustenance for everyone.

With backgrounds as organizers, educators, activists, writers, and independent media makers, we started *make/shift* to cover the movements we were part of, spotlighting community-based art and action, the kind of work that pushes feminisms to grow, usually from the margins. We wanted to publish voices speaking in the tradition of Audre Lorde, Gloria Anzaldúa, Angela Davis, bell hooks, Trinh T. Minh-ha, Mujeres Creando, and so many other feminists of color who have insisted on complexity, pointed out the connections, and refused to separate the intimate from the public, the cultural from the political, the creative from the critical. That is the tradition we believe is most likely to build a world in which everyone can be whole and free.

Of course, a media outlet that represents these values should be made with a process that reflects these values. That meant, among other things, committing to collaborative editing and to sharing media skills;

publishing a majority of women of color in each issue; paying writers at least *something* for their contributions (even if we never had enough money to pay what they deserved for their work); editing and publishing the magazine in a way that was sustainable for us to do, as volunteers, on top of busy jobs and lives; and valuing critique, accountability, multiplicity, and complexity. Conventional magazine wisdom is that there should be a consistent voice and style from cover to cover; *make/shift* deliberately flouted that, putting different forms, styles, and voices in conversation (the way they actually are).

In 2007, when we had just published our first issue, we tabled for *make/shift* in the lobby of a museum where longtime activist and author Angela Davis was speaking at an exhibition of feminist art from 1965 to 1980. "[I think about] how capitalism constitutes our intimate lives, our dreams . . . forces us to dream as individuals, to dream for ourselves, maybe for our families. Why can't we dream for our communities? Why can't we dream beyond the nation?" she asked.

In some ways, brownfemipower's essay from *make/shift*'s second issue, "Immigration at the Front: Challenging the 'Every Woman' Myth in Online Media," is from a different time. We talked about "the feminist blogosphere" then; it was a burgeoning thing that got big fast and that preceded but could not quite anticipate today's social-media landscape. There was a clear hierarchy of power and popularity in then-emerging online feminist media, and it fell along conventional lines (white women at the front). As brownfemipower's essay shows, it was a time when "intersectionality" was not at all widely embraced by feminist media, and there was a massive disconnect between what prominent white feminists perceived to be feminist issues (things like reproductive rights, body image, violence against women) and issues such as immigration, climate change, prisons, and policing. It is because of women-of-color bloggers like brownfemipower (who took a lot of shit for it) that those issues are weaved through today's feminist media. Likewise, it is because of queer and trans activists that there is an entirely different awareness of gender now across mainstream society than there was when Dean Spade and Sam Feder were talking about trans documentaries in *make/shift* ten years ago.

Yet when feminist discourse hits the mainstream—as in the 2017 and 2018 Women's Marches across the United States, and #metoo—the most visible threads still often center white women voicing a feminism that is binary in its understanding of gender and oblivious to the relationship between violence and power. Again that myth surfaces: the one woman, the "every woman." A poem about two world wars, poverty, motherhood, and several other things is reduced to a one-note quote about sexual violence that fails to recognize all forms of violence and hierarchy as pieces of interlocking systems that are not natural but wholly challengeable, and changeable. Are we watching the world split open right now, or are we watching familiar binaries and reactions as some category called "women" splits open a brief window in which to punish some category called "men," with a backlash looming around the corner?

Once again, intersectional feminism has already opened up this conversation, has not only imagined but begun practicing ways of addressing violence that are not punitive but rather transformative. We offer a peek of this vast conversation in "The Power We Have: Things that Worked in Transformative Justice This Year" by Leah Lakshmi Piepzna-Samarasinha, "'Love' Is on Everyone's Lips: A Roundtable of Women of Color Organizing in Detroit" facilitated by Adela Nieves, "Bring the Troops Home?" by Jessi Lee Jackson, and basically every other piece in this book.

In making make/shift, we wanted to share the wisdom of our contemporaries nearby and around the world, from Tiny aka Lisa Gray-Garcia in San Francisco to Trifa Shakely in Sweden to Manshi Asher in India, alongside the wisdom of our elders, including Ida McCray, Emma Torres, Loretta J. Ross, Silvia Federici, and many others. They offer varied answers to the question of what it means to live in this world while bringing forth a different one. For ten years, we published creative and critical writing by people actively engaged in transformative work in their own communities, and we documented and critiqued works published elsewhere in a reviews section edited by author and activist Mattilda Bernstein Sycamore that featured multititle reviews of projects across mediums, mostly from small presses. We have been able to include in this book just a few of the dozens of excellent and unparalleled reviews that Mattilda edited across twenty issues of make/shift.

If we start with an oft-quoted line from a poem written by a white woman at the height of another generation's attempts to transform the world, register the truths of that poem, and then push at it and question it, place it in dialogue with a legacy of women-of-color-centered feminism that precedes and exceeds it, those are ways of dreaming together beyond received limits, of expanding the conversation and opening up the set of possibilities for our shared world. We think those are ways of doing feminism and making media rooted in hope and love.

Intersectional feminism didn't appear a few years ago. It has roots that go back forever, and it has been voiced and otherwise nurtured by women of color for generations. It is like a river moving through time, communities, and other contexts, full of differences and always changing. We have always envisioned *make/shift* as dipping into, reflecting on, and contributing to this river, putting into print a few of its moments and voices from a particular time. From 2007 to 2017, we published work by about 350 people who have added to the burbling of that river. It started flowing way before us and will continue long after us, and it is always bigger and more full of possibility than any one of us. It is multifaceted, simultaneous, and constantly shifting, a space where past, present, and future voices and actions flow together, overlap, diverge, and keep moving to make a world where everyone can be free.

A Note from the Editors

The pieces in this book were published in *make/shift* magazine over a ten-year period, from 2007 to 2017. During and since that time, movements for justice and liberation have continued to challenge, expand, and change the language we use to describe our world, our communities, and our lives. For instance, nobody was saying "non-binary" in 2007. The terms "genderqueer," "trans," and "gender-variant" were commonly used at that time to describe genders that exceeded or did not fit within the gender binary. And you'll see that writers in this volume tended to use "Latina/o" or "Latin@" in instances where today they would likely write "Latinx." In these and other cases, we decided to leave the texts as originally written rather than copyediting to reflect the vocabulary of 2018. We have chosen to document rather than erase the evolution of language because it is one of the many ways social movements critically and creatively transform the world.

And we hope it goes without saying, but just in case: because *make/shift*'s vision and politic is deliberately and decidedly heterogeneous, and because feminisms are constantly in motion, the views expressed here are those of their respective authors at the time they wrote them, not necessarily those of the editors, and not even necessarily those of the writers today or tomorrow.

"Without You Who Understand"

Letters from Radical Womyn of Color

Edited by Alexis Pauline Gumbs, with letters by
Lisa Factora-Borchers, Alexis Pauline Gumbs, and Lailan Huen

Dear Reader,

1.

In 1979, Barbara and Beverly Smith published "Letters from Black Feminists" in *Conditions,* a predominantly white-operated feminist journal. The Smith sisters, who were participants in a Black-lesbian-feminist-socialist group called the Combahee River Collective and who went on to play an instrumental role in the founding of Kitchen Table: Women of Color Press, made a number of crucial interventions into feminist history-making in this groundbreaking article.

First, they asserted that there was such a thing as a Black feminist, and even a Black feminist *movement,* to be documented in the letters they presented. They explained that letter writing was the way that Black feminists combated their isolation and tokenization within academic and activist spaces. Each letter writer was often the "only Black feminist in town." Their letters were lifelines, reminders that "Black feminist" was a possible way of being alive.

One thing we know as Black feminists is how important it is for us to recognize our own lives as herstory.
—Barbara and Beverly Smith in "'I Am Not Meant to Be Alone and Without You Who Understand': Letters from Black Feminists 1972–1978"

Originally published in make/shift no. 4 (fall/winter 2008/2009)

The Black feminists who edited and contributed to that series of letters did it to validate each other and to amplify an audience of participants in their own time, but they also did it as an offering to a future they wanted to create. Knowing that exclusion from archives and academic records serves to hide traditions of resistance from warriors to come, the Smith sisters collected these letters as evidence, medicine, and resources for those of us who would come along later to live in the future their words made possible.

Now, we are living in that future. A world where an understanding of multiple simultaneous oppressions is widely available if underused, a world where I can fill an altar on my mantel with classic works created and published by radical womyn of color. Now, in the future we borrow from the feminists who came before us, we are still tokenized, we are still often far away from each other, and the word "feminist" is often deployed in a way that ignores the work of our elders and ancestors and pretends we do not exist.

Right now, we need each other as much as ever.

2.

Building on the work of radical Black feminists and many other feminists of color, the collection of letters you are about to read says there is such a thing as a community of Radical Womyn of Color. This community is not based on a specific cultural heritage but rather grows through an intense and vigilant desire for *each other*, and the faith that there is a way to be alive that contradicts gendered and racialized oppression and the homophobia, ableism, economic violence, and imperialism that threaten our survival and disrespect our love. Radical Womyn of Color live in doorways, the crowded spaces between abbreviated text messages, gardens, long e-mails on group lists, blog comments, love notes, online statuses, hands held and backs gotten, glances thrown and caught. "Radical Womyn of Color" is not an identity, it is a promise. This means we identify *with* each other. This means we will struggle together and not turn away. This means we will fight for each other, and demand everything. This means we will expect more than we know how to give, we will push and support until our chrysalis explodes. This means we love each other enough to make the world that we deserve out of our words, our bodies, our breath and our need, our histories and our futures.

3.

The letters included here are addressed to different audiences, written in different styles, and interested in different issues. However, all three letters are evidence of our hope. Each letter says that the answers to all of our needs are written in each other's hands and waiting in each other's faces. Each letter explains that we need each other, we want each other, and we are ready to risk everything that means.

How do we reclaim our healing after colonization and in the midst of a culture that has appropriated all of our traditions and is selling them at prices that we cannot afford? *We turn to each other.* Lailan Huen's "Notes on Spiritual Genocide" is a poetic love letter and a plea to all womyn of color to build sustainable resources for holistic spiritual and physical well-being together in our own communities.

How do we grow into dream? *We turn to each other.* Lisa Factora-Borchers trusts her growing late-night revelations, possible creations, and potential tomorrows to a beloved friend, reminding us how personal our politics are and how crucial our intimate faith is to our collective transformation.

How do we get free? *We turn to each other.* My letter was written in desperation as a call for help when two of my loved ones and a number of queer and trans activists of color were victims of police brutality. The people who read the letter responded with passion and moved to action to demand their freedom, and freedom for all of us.

Please read these letters knowing that they carry our histories and our futures and all of our faith. Please know that these letters are meant for you. The intimacy of these letters is not exclusive. It is the intentional way we build our desire and longing into a place to live. Welcome.

Love Always,
Alexis Pauline Gumbs

P.S. We would like to lift up Zachari Curtis, Rosa Cabrera, and Kameelah Rasheed, who corresponded with us in this process and inspired us with their bravery and their insight. Cyber pen pals for life!

Notes on Spiritual Genocide
(a love letter to my sisters in struggle)

Here, in this land taken through genocide, rape, and conquest,
we presently find ourselves in a moment of vast spiritual death.

They cut up our beautiful continent and sold off her limbs.
They put our bodies on display for the white men and
women's gaze.
They stole our children, desecrated our bodies, and poisoned
our lands and foods.

We now read magazines filled with bodies that are not our own.
We watch television with white faces, white speech, white ways
of being.
We buy and buy until we feel better about ourselves.

Who has access to the resources needed to survive capitalism?
Who has the time to take care of their bodies?
Why are our medical systems set up to make us more sick?

We have become disembodied.
Our spirits suffer without ritual.
Our bodies hold the pain of centuries.

Mis Compañeras,

This is a love letter to myself and all the women of color who have been severed from their own bodies and spirits. As an Asian American woman whose family lost its cultural traditions in the leap of faith from our small village to this land of uncertainty, I have been left with no choice but to create my own spirituality, one grounded in the mother earth around me, grounded in my own breath, grounded in the communities around me that fight for justice, dignity, and love. I slowly learned to trust my body's instincts to know what foods were good for it. I finally learned the importance of slowing down, of forging the time to take care of my body and spirit. But now, as I look for spiritual guidance, I face a limitation of resources for healing my body and spirit from the trauma of racism, sexism, capitalism, and imperialism without encountering those same forces in the "spiritual" spaces that exist and becoming retraumatized and redisempowered.

Searching for some way to keep my body healthy, I recently took up yoga. I had been to a class a long time ago taught by a big white man with long blond hair, and never went back. But my body was beginning to fall apart, my joints were starting to give up on me, and I was only twenty-five. A friend took me to a new yoga studio in Oakland, California, where we were among the few people of color in the whole class, taught by a white woman who chanted in Hindi but failed to translate the meaning of what she had everyone repeat. I have tried other studios since then, and although I was able to find a few classes taught by women of color, the vast majority of teachers and students are white. It astounds me that in the teachings, there is such consciousness of body and breath, but so little consciousness of race or class. It baffles me that so many hordes of privileged white people can take up this practice with such entitlement, co-opting this centuries-long spiritual tradition, owning it, and selling it to others for profit. Everywhere I went to look for spiritual guidance, whether it was a Hindu, Buddhist, or Taoist space, I encountered similar whitewashing and cultural rape.

It is from this anger that I write to you all in solidarity with your processes of self-love, because I know that it is a difficult journey that takes a lot of strength in this world that teaches us to hate ourselves. For those who come after us, I write to share my lessons in humility, as someone who has burnt myself out many times over in the fight for justice, as someone who spread my energies all around while neglecting my own spirit, and as someone who is recovering from the workaholic culture that we live in. I write in the hope that we will create the time and space for healing, rejuvenation, and strengthening one another, rather than being swallowed by this beast. I look to all the freedom fighters who have died early of cancer and other ailments, who tell me that these diseases can be prevented by slowing down, learning to listen to and take care of our bodies, reconnecting to the earth, reconnecting to one another, laughing more, finding joy in each moment, releasing the pain and trauma from our bodies, making time to rest and be still, screaming when we need to, forgiving those we love and who love us, and learning to breathe deeply.

I write to you all in this crucial moment because I know that only together can we spiritually and physically survive in the present situation of global war, destruction, and militarization. Only in community can we find our breath, and create rituals that help us connect to our pasts and ancestors. Only by looking into one another's truths can we recognize the trauma present and find healing. Only by coming together can we build a future that will be able to hold and nurture the dreams of our children. Let us build healing centers in our communities. Let us find the medicine in one another, in our songs, dance, and prayer. Let us move past the fears that we hold in our shoulders, and release the anger when it no longer is useful to us. Let us all become one another's healers. Let us make space to receive our ancestors' wisdom. Let us know that we are not and have never been alone.

With Hope,
and Love,
Lailan

Dear Amanda,

It's 11:28 p.m. and I have a headache.

Lying next to him, I kissed his forearm and rubbed his skin against my face, pretending it was a magic balm, maybe from Gilead, and the throbbing would ease. It didn't.

I'm on some wild ride and each night it slows to a close and I think about what happened, the whirlwind of my day, the colors I didn't appreciate. Each night I walk over each person, each interaction, and marvel at the small and incredible thought that if I did not take that one minute before sleep to think about that interaction, it likely would be forgotten already, like a trillion earlier encounters that I can no longer recall.

A deep ache to create something beautiful pains me daily. Onto a page, a table, a plate, glass, or T-shirts, I want something to spill out of me and to see a piece of myself outside of myself. It's almost an obsession to see how round I can get the paintbrush to bend or how perfectly two words can fit together in description. I ripped a sweatshirt at the neck just so it felt different against my skin. I ran through the park wearing it and my shoulders gasped at the exposure. Each morning I wake, full of hope and ready for light. The sidewalks are salty, the city beeps and quakes, and the people are scarves and gloves. Winter is here and it presses against my chest.

Each day I jot down words that I hope will lead me into a deep canvas of untapped stories and creativity. Where lost becomes found and zebras are red, the world in my mind remains unwritten. It is perhaps in that silence, the unwritten portion of my life, that the long funeral procession continues. The unwritten. It's almost a tragedy, and yet each time I try and write it to life, a spool of masking tape funnels around my mind, knotting my ideas together, impossible to pass, impossible to flourish.

Instead, I write you this letter, hoping that the image of you as my reader will let me tap into what I fear most, hoping that, because it is you, I will be able to trust my mind to loosen its tight muscles and simply flow in the freedom of probable acceptance.

I received your letter yesterday and waited until I was still to read it. As we age, it's becoming far too easy to multitask and pretend we absorb all the minuscule particles of experiences. We absorb less as we age; we need more time to center ourselves, I've found.

You write in paradox, did you know that? You write with regret. You write in deep love of me yet with the knowledge that we likely won't connect for a while. The paper feels like love and misses, and handprints. The words sound full but imperfect, catching and disappointed. What I am saying is I miss you, too.

Too many dreams may trip my life, I've discovered. There are so many desires, all of them genuine, and so deserving of effort. The quiet trance of writing. The drive to perform. To rest my palm on a pulpit. I always wanted to preach. Travels beckon during my dry spells. I simply want all of these things with a capacity that is almost breaking. I desire so much, I cover my face with my hands. I am confused, or no, maybe I'm just shamefully uncertain. Knowing the truest desires of the heart is difficult, but also signals that I am treading in waters too deep. I may have not always known the destination, but I've always known direction. That intuition has quieted. Roaring in its place has been money, family, time, plans, body, demand, and age. They scream into every canal of my ears, asserting their power. Intuition quiets, unnaturally.

Are you happy? I mean, pretend you and I were just born and, in this pretend world, you could be born at twenty-eight and twenty-nine with no previous knowledge of clichés, and think about that question.

Because I keep coming back to this wide view of life, the one where we see ourselves typing, slaving away for someone else, thinking it'll all be for a greater good when really in our hearts, a different beat is sounding, but we're too far gone to realize what that is anymore.

That is scaring me. I feel frightened that my life is becoming round, soft, comfortable, and irrelevant. The space between my sense of self and who I am is being negotiated and I don't even know if I'm there for the negotiating. Sometimes I feel like life and choices come to the table for you, ready to take you into a tomorrow that you aren't sure you even want. I want to want again.

There was a time when I had no trouble falling asleep. Now, there is a small part of me that fears the four minutes between lying down and becoming unconscious. The day's memory floods my bed and the drowning begins again.

I miss my sister so much it hurts.

This entire year can be described in one word: striving. Striving for peace, striving for spirit, excellence, recognition, community, understanding, and meaning.

My headache has stopped. It's 12:03 a.m.

I love you,
Lisa Factora-Borchers

To You Who Understand:

Two loved ones of mine have had their names added to the long list of victims of the New York Police Department's everyday, every-night brutality. And every time this happens it is an assault against my people, whoever they are. People of color, queer people, young people, transgender people, activists, sex workers, immigrants. Every time this happens it is my people, locked away.

But these two. These are my people. This is who I have cried with after breakups, eaten ice cream with when I should have been studying; this is who sat with me in limbo every semester, unregistered and undocumented because no one believed we'd be able to keep paying for school, least of all us. This is who brought me lemonade and sandwiches when I couldn't get out of bed and couldn't say why, and most importantly these are the people who stayed up all night with me too many times to count, like Pinky and the Brain in Pumas with wild hair, plotting and believing in another world. Projecting and practicing freedom. These are the ones who said, Yes, we can build that. And we should paint it purple, not blue. And if someone had been tracing our hands as we punctuated every detail about what playgrounds to make out of the rubble of prisons, what mosaics to glue to the empty U.S. Mint . . . if you had been tracing our hands you would have seen that we were spelling *blood and water* and *water and blood*. This is what I mean when I say, These are my people.

They are the ones I have trusted to hold my youth and to hand it back to me with a firm nudge if I ever consider selling out. These are the ones I have trusted to sell their vintage sneakers and stolen accessories to hire a lawyer when the state finally notices. We have agreed that this is morally and strategically better than actually becoming lawyers ourselves. So these are the ones I trust to break me out of prison, to never forget where I am. To prove the lie of the state when it says no one loves you, you little Black girl. You are nothing. No one cares where you are right now. And they have trusted me too, to pawn, to plead, to risk, to witness, to remember. I have agreed to the same.

But I didn't think it would be today.

As I write this, my people are locked down for keeping their part of the agreement. After months of planning a fundraiser for the Sylvia Rivera Law (Liberation) Project, my people were ready to celebrate. After gathering queer and trans people of color and allies from all over the tri-state area, my people, these two, deserved the peace of bass and the release of rhythm. Late Wednesday night, like every night, my people were dancing. But late Wednesday night, like every night, the state was on the prowl. And right in front of the bright loud colors, right in front of the opening sounds (you see, my people dress like confetti parades, my people move like new memories), the NYPD was doing the state, forcing the power of one Black man into a space too small for dignity. And my people—though practicing the celebration, though air-traffic-hailing the future that night—my people do not forget the moment. This is why my people wear sneakers and flat shoes. They remember what we agreed. So early Thursday morning they stopped the dancing to witness this arrest, one of millions of arrests (these too my people). And they said with their eyes what we promised we would say. They said:

We see you. We remember what you deserve. And when the lie comes out that you are not human, that who you are does not matter, we will stand up in that moment with the truth. We see you.

And the officers could not tell who my people addressed with their eyes from the reasonable distance of the sidewalk. The policemen did not know if by "you" their brown eyes meant the person in the handcuffs or the one clanking them shut. So while their brightly clad feet and their hair awake with dancing did not get in anyone's way, the policemen found their gazes too wide and too loud. So the policemen grabbed them. And closed their own eyes.

These two. My people. And shoved them in the car without warning. And what I got then was a 2:00 a.m. text message indecipherable and cut short. And twelve hours later an e-mail. They have not been charged. They have not been arraigned.

Because there is no such crime as love in excess. There is no such crime as too bright for 1984. There is no crime called smarter and braver than what day it is. There is no such crime as wanting more.

But they have not been released yet either. Because to place your soul firmly against the blunt edge of lawfulness is to share terror on measured and socialist terms. And police officers cannot afford to remember the neighborhoods they come from and who is now missing, lest their hearts beat and break against the tight armor of the state. And dreamers cannot afford fancy lawyers. So what I got then was a 2:00 a.m. text message, and twelve hours later an e-mail.

And what I have now is a promise to keep.

(Note: At the end of my original letter I pasted the details of which juridical and police offices people should call to demand the immediate release of and the dropping of all charges against my people. Radical women of color all over the world posted this on their blogs, and called the district attorney's office so many times that they stopped answering the phone. And so many people from UBUNTU in Durham, North Carolina, called that the district attorney's rep felt pressed to explain that this was a "local" issue.

And my loved ones were released. And all charges were dropped. A coalition led by queer people of color in New York City is crafting a long-term, holistic response to this [ongoing] violence.)

So our promise lives on.

Love always,
Lex

"Love" Is on Everyone's Lips

A Roundtable of Women of Color Organizing in Detroit

By Adela Nieves

On September 10, 2010, Adela Nieves sat down with Detroit activists Oya Amakisi, Grace Lee Boggs, adrienne maree brown, and Jenny Lee to discuss leadership and activism in Detroit, and twenty-first-century feminisms.

Oya Amakisi (thirty-nine) is a filmmaker, former teacher at Detroit's Aisha Shule / W. E. B. Du Bois Preparatory Academy, and director of the Detroit Women of Color International Film Festival. She served as culture and programming coordinator for the U.S. Social Forum (USSF) in Detroit in July 2010. Grace Lee Boggs (ninety-five) has been working on a wide range of issues for decades, including Black Power, labor, inner-city violence, and education. She is the author of *Living for Change* and coauthor, with her husband, the late James (Jimmy) Boggs, of *Revolution and Evolution in the 20th Century*; founder of the Boggs Center to Nurture Community Leadership in Detroit; cofounder of the multiracial, intergenerational, neighborhood-focused collective Detroit Summer; and an

Originally published in *make/shift* no. 9 (spring/summer 2011)

active participant with Detroiters for Dignity and Democracy. adrienne maree brown (thirty-two) is an organizational healer, facilitator, singer, artist, and doula-in-training. She is the former director and a current board member of the Ruckus Society and was a national cocoordinator for the 2010 USSF. She sits on the boards of Allied Media Projects, the Third Wave Foundation, and the Common Fire Foundation and on the advisory board of the East Michigan Environmental Action Council. Jenny Lee (twenty-eight) is the program director for Allied Media Projects, which supports media-based organizing, and a founder of the Detroit Digital Justice Coalition. She was an early member of Detroit Summer, and eventually one of its leaders. Adela Nieves (thirty-seven) is a community organizer, independent journalist, and media activist. She is on the advisory board of Allied Media Projects and on the board of the East Michigan Environmental Action Council. She wrote and edited for the collectively run southeast Michigan magazine *Critical Moment* and was the national communications coordinator for the 2010 USSF. In 2007, she was *Essence of Motown's* "Writer of the Year."

AN: Detroit has been getting a lot of attention in the press. Let's talk about what is happening here on the ground.

OA: Honestly, I didn't recognize all the powerful things happening here until the USSF, when I began working with different organizations doing amazing work: [resisting] environmental racism and terrorism in the city, the youth movement, artists who are also activists, intergenerational organizing, and religious institutions, too. Detroit is an amazing place; how we work together is another conversation.

AMB: I see so many amazing people with amazing ideas doing the work. But they haven't figured out how to talk to each other in a way that mobilizes clear action, or how to get out and talk with community members, despite the huge desire to do so.

JL: Actually, I found Detroit to be one of the least competitive organizing environments. In part it's because people here *have* to collaborate and work together. I think Detroit has thrived off incredible collaboration and lack of ego.

With Detroit Summer we've had to acknowledge that reaching people involves more than communicating a message about what's wrong. It's about forming meaningful relationships over a lifetime, and committing to supporting each other in a transformative process that will have ripple effects on your interactions. Our vision of growth is based around the depth of relationships, and creating really practicable models of youth leadership. But our weakness is we're unable to stay focused on that particular task because of the compulsion to address some massive issue, or respond to something that happens.

We need to look at all this work as pieces of an ecosystem, where one isn't struggling for superiority over another. Our weakness has been a lack of choreography, and the ability to give those pieces the attention they need to be successful.

Grace, you recently wrote that we should stop marching and protesting, and start working to make King's "radical revolution of values" a reality. Can you identify negative or destructive aspects of past activism, and what we should do differently today?

GLB: I'd have to start with what was going on in Detroit in the 1980s. Following the 1967 rebellion, there was a lot of unrest in the city. Young people were asking, why continue going to school based on the idea that one day you could make a lot of money, when you could make a lot of money right now rolling? So we had a huge dropout of young people from school, and a huge upsurge of violence in the city. That was met with two actions, led primarily by women: Save Our Sons and Daughters (SOSAD), organized by Clementine Barfield, and We the People Reclaim Our Streets (WE-PROS), where the prime organizer was Dorothy Garner. Both got quite a bit of attention but were not resolving the issue.

When Mayor Coleman Young said, "We have to have jobs, and the auto industry is not going to solve our problems . . . so we're going to have a casino industry," we said, "No." And he said, "You're nothing but a bunch of naysayers. What's your alternative?" And in response, we formed Detroit Summer in 1992 with the idea of enlisting young people to begin rebuilding, redefining, and respiriting the city.

King said we need to engage young people in direct actions that would transform themselves and their surroundings at the same time. That's what Detroit Summer was doing: transformative organizing, actually engaging young people. They began planting community gardens, painting public murals, and the elders came and worked with the young people. And connections were made between city and country, and between youngsters and oldsters. It began creating whole new connections and relationships between people. It was a transformative shift, a paradigm shift, from marching to beginning to create the new.

We have survived throughout the ages by helping one another. People think economics and income are the main things driving people. But what has really driven people is the maintenance of relationships with one another. Each of the previous ways people looked at revolution was narrow—focusing on jobs, or women. We're being forced from one society to another kind of society, and each one of us, no matter where we are, are trying to grow our souls.

Jenny, as an organizer for Detroit Summer, can you speak about the practice of this transformation?

JL: It was a shift that was happening nationally. People had gone through similar experiences organizing protests against corporate globalization in the mid-1990s and early 2000s. There were a lot of contradictions coming up, including leadership dynamics in those movements [relating to] race, gender, sexual identity, and disability.

There were also big paradigm shifts away from the idea that change happens in mass mobilization, and the idea that change happens by focusing our energy on opposing a certain power structure with a particular worldview. So a lot of people began to focus on their own communities.

When I got involved with Detroit Summer, the emphasis was on building community that reflected a vision we wanted to see ripple throughout the globe. It would subvert the policies and practices of institutions like the World Trade Organization, but be grounded in people's commitment to different kinds of relationships with each other, with the earth, with their cities. Like Grace was saying, Detroit Summer was part of a lineage of movements that had taken place here in Detroit, and part of the paradigm shift in how people view our ability to create power, rather than just taking or directly confronting power.

OA: I was a part of the generation in the 1980s where we had life before crack—BC—and then life after crack, when our world changed. A large number of my friends were killed, incarcerated, or affected in some way by drugs in our community, as well as the lack of jobs and the deterioration of education. So the average brother and sister in the community weren't interested in the World Trade Organization or the International Monetary Fund . . . none of that meant anything to them. It was about trying to survive.

One of the mistakes I found in organizing across the board is the idea that there is only one right way. We're all working for one common goal, for people to have a decent life. When you take away all the fancy names, people want their children to be educated, they want a home, to be able to provide for their families, to be safe, and they want to be productive.

I've worked with many different organizations, with many people from different backgrounds [who have] common goals, trying to find what fits for me. When I came back to Detroit in the 1990s, after living in Birmingham, Alabama, I found solace in the African American Community Center community, and became a teacher at Aisha Shule. There was a whole community of people trying to connect with our ancestral roots, and a belief that we needed to save ourselves instead of waiting for the government to save us.

I've also worked with the feminist movement, with young people, older folks from the civil rights movement, ministers, activists in the Black Power movement, and people working on environmental justice. Those backgrounds helped strengthen my perspective, and I realize there's no one solution. We need protesting, beautiful gardens, murals, transformative justice. We need people to cut up and make them scared. We need all of it.

AMB: What Oya just said really resonated with me: there's no one perfect form of organizing. When Grace wrote about [not participating in] the protest, I wrote back, and said, "I feel you, except I want to be careful not to throw protest off the boat completely."

To me it's not so much what people are doing, but how they are doing it. In Detroit, a lot of people are doing gardens. Some are doing them in a transformative way; some are not. A lot of people are doing marches, some of it in a transformative way, a lot of it not. That's a problem worldwide. People are doing marches, and the people coming are tired; it's not filling them up with hope, and the person they are protesting isn't even there and doesn't even know about the protest. At the same time there are actions and rallies that are extremely important, vibrant, and timely.

What I'm excited to see grow is the question of what holistic organizing looks like. We need to localize our political attention.

Detroit hasn't yet grown the capacity to come together and say to the mayor, "We have incredible alternatives. We have agricultural alternatives, young independent entrepreneurs ready with a different vision for how the economy can work, different ways of managing conflict than what the police are offering. We have all these viable alternatives for Detroit." We haven't figured out how to respect the different kinds of organizing in Detroit in order to come together and present a united front.

I want to shift focus to feminism in Detroit. There's feminist work happening, but it's not identified as "feminism."

GLB: When Clementine Barfield formed SOSAD, she challenged her preacher. She just stood up, said what she wanted to do, and if he didn't like it, to hell with him. [In] Detroit, women just move in and take over and do what they want to do. They don't do it the way NOW or feminists try to do it; they don't fight for equality, they just [*hits table hard with her fist*].

That's why you don't hear the word "feminism," because feminism is associated with fighting for equality. And I think Black women don't think they should be fighting for equality; they just say, "This is who we are, and this is the role we are going to be playing."

OA: I don't want to be equal to a man. In some cases, we're superior. So the fight for equality with men, I couldn't relate to it. I was around strong, powerful women who made things happen, like Grace said.

When I worked in the feminist movement, it was primarily white and racist. They were very condescending toward me. There was this energy almost encouraging us to hate men. Then we were confronted by the Black Power movement in our community, which said if you stood up for women's rights, then you hated men. And neither is true. I don't have to hate you to love myself.

I force myself to take leadership roles, even when I'm uncomfortable. It's not just for myself, but for the women who struggled to make these changes for me, and the ones who'll come after me. It's not an option of you giving me power; it's mine to take. We all create the world we want. That's different from feminism, to me.

AMB: I've seen a lot of situations where women are in charge, but they still do patriarchal, capitalist, competitive things. Their leadership style is "I'm strong like a man, and I can manipulate, dominate, and take over." I don't consider that feminist leadership.

I've come up in a generation where I've disconnected "feminist" from having a vagina. When I see strong feminist leadership, I'm seeing someone being strong because they are vulnerable, they are learning as they are going, they are growing together and creating a sustainable space that people want to come to.

On a grand scale, we've had a century of masculine leadership, and we're ready for a century of feminine leadership. The person recording us now is a feminist-supportive man. It's exciting to me to see men, women, and trans folks being able to hold a different energy in their leadership. It's very present in a lot of spaces in Detroit, but we need more. That will be the make-or-break thing about whether Detroit does grow into this new city—if we don't have new ways of holding leadership, we'll easily fall back into old practices.

JL: My experience with feminism has definitely been as a practice and not as a struggle for equality, which is a benefit of coming up after the earlier movements where that shift took place. For me, feminist practices, which I think define Detroit Summer and Allied Media Projects, are what adrienne mentioned. It's about facilitative leadership, where the role of a leader is to facilitate contributions of multiple people in a collective, rather than driving their own agendas and herding the masses along. It's about deep listening, and the idea that solutions emerge from listening to people's experiences, and generating movement from there. And it's about relationship-based organizing—the idea that the personal is political, and all of our relationships are just as important as the meta-level structures we're trying to change.

The other strand of feminism I inherited, beyond these practices of leadership, is women-of-color feminism, and intersectionality, which is more of an analysis, a way of looking at problems. I think we could use more of that in Detroit.

Consider how state violence happens in Detroit, for example. The Coalition Against Police Brutality does incredible work and makes these immediate interventions by projecting alternative visions of how to solve problems without police. But police violence primarily impacts young Black men. A women-of-color-feminist analysis would look at all the different forms of state violence that are invisible through just the lens of police violence: the domestic violence women experience, the violence sex workers experience, the violence transgender women experience. All those different levels of violence get obscured, and therefore are left out of the solution.

So if feminism were prefaced, like "women-of-color feminism" or "radical-women-of-color feminism," would that make a difference?

AMB: I think it's a moot question. I feel similarly about "socialism" at this point. If you break down everything about that word, you probably would agree with it. But the early practitioners make it impossible to take on that label. My generation, I feel, doesn't want the labels. We've been practicing feminism for how long? We still haven't figured it out. Calling it womanism or something else doesn't seem to make a difference in the practice at this point.

JL: In other cities, people cling to labels that are irrelevant or useless in Detroit. That defines Detroit's approach to feminism in a lot of ways. It's not about creating a community separate from all the other dynamics and people that are part of our communities, or whether they have the perfect radical analysis. What we go through here is much more out of necessity for community, regardless of it being women, men, trans people, queer people, disabled, radical people, or apolitical people . . . it's really holistic.

AMB: I think there's also an economic component to it. We still don't have equal pay, right? But in a city like Detroit where very few of us have jobs, we are less likely to measure power that way.

JL: Like patriarchy has less of a stronghold here because of the economy?

AMB: Yeah, I think so. When it's all about who is getting hired and how much you're making, that's how you measure your worth. But I can't look at Oya and go, "Girl, what are you making? Here's what I'm making . . . " You know, we don't have jobs right now! [*laughter*] So we have to be like, "Okay, we don't 'make' anything, but who do you know? Who is in your network? Who can you connect with?" Our income range here is below what anyone in any other part of the country would respect, or consider a living wage, and yet I'm living better than I've ever lived in my life and learning more than I've ever learned before.

If we look at the movements of the '60s and '70s in Detroit, we had male-dominated movements then, while today we have many more women of color in leadership. Why?

GLB: Oya, I want to ask you, do you think men in the movement in Detroit have learned?

OA: Yes, even when they're uncomfortable with it, even when they have to check themselves, and even when others check them. That's the difference I've found between here and the South. In the USSF process, there were challenges with some of the men, but there was a greater force saying, "This is unacceptable, and this is what we're going to do because it's better for the collective."

JL: Many organizers in Detroit began talking about humanity, and that idea became a point of organizing. With that, the identity politics that resonate in other cities fell away. With Grace and Jimmy in particular, talking about dialectical humanism and the question of what is the value of humans if not for our labor in these industries, that's been the opening through which this kind of organizing can grow.

AMB: I've been told and I can see that Detroit is not a nonprofit city or a foundation city, and it's not about organizations. . . . It really is about people and communities. In Detroit, challenges have been borne out of love. The word *love* is on everyone's lips when you talk about what is unique about organizing here; people have kindness as a basis for how they behave.

When you talk about feminist leadership, we need to build our organizing from that place, from what can we do out of compassion, kindness, and love for each other as organizers and as members of our community?

AMB

River

By Jessica Trimbath

1.

We're sitting by the river and he's telling me a story about his boyhood. He was thirteen. He went with a friend to the Youghiogheny and they spent the whole day building a raft from driftwood they found along the shore. They rode it downriver, but it eventually fell apart, crashing them into the bank.

"Little Huck Finns," I say, laughing.

This story was his answer to my question, "What was it like to be a boy?" He doesn't ask me what it was like to be a girl. I listen to his story and I like it because I love him, but I kind of hate him, too. When we were thirteen, my friends and I weren't building rafts. We were fucking and getting raped and getting molested and binging and purging and falling apart, much like their raft. It's kind of ironic, considering they'd learn their roles well and ride the backs of women their entire lives—mothers, lovers, wives. Just like we learned to be pretty at any cost and we're facing our own rivers. We're fighting them

Originally published in *make/shift* no. 4 (fall/winter 2008/2009)

tooth and polished nail. We're sometimes drowning, sometimes swimming, but we're in our bodies and our bodies are in the water so when all is said and done we knew the river better. We survived.

2.

"Do you remember that time . . . " she starts to ask.

I already know what "time" she's talking about. Maybe it's the way her eyes are kind of stunned as she delicately approaches this taboo memory of shared humiliation while we lie on my living-room floor surrounded by her sleeping babies. We smoked a joint and something about being together and being older has given us the strength to confront all the forgotten monsters. We've already talked about her brother raping her when she was little. We've lit a candle for her older sister Marcy, who committed suicide when we were in elementary school. We've taken down shoeboxes full of pictures and old letters. We're ready.

"Yeah," I say, cutting her off, looking away, "I remember those guys in that car."

She laughs bitterly and looks into my eyes, "That fucking car."

There's a literal heat in the trajectory of pain and love between our eyes. I can feel her so distinctly because I know her so well. Twenty years and counting. We fought once at a party in first grade. She scratched my arm with her long nails and made me cry. We've already covered that base tonight. She apologized so sincerely and we both burst into laughter.

I smile and look up at the ceiling, consciously keeping my face joyful because I know she's so sensitive and I can see she's scared of this one. "That car was so fucking dorky," I say. "Remember the neon purple license plate?"

We laugh again. I love her laugh. It's a laugh of knowing. A laugh that has survived so much shit and can still shake her entire body.

She grows serious.

"Every time I see an electric license plate like that, I remember it."

"Me, too," I say, feeling strange about the déjà vu sensation. It seems I am anticipating every word of this conversation, like it all happened before, lifetimes ago or, at least, over and over again privately in both of our minds throughout the years when we just couldn't bring it up. She looks at me and her eyes are calm. She sees I am okay with talking about it and she feels safe.

Without asking, I know she remembers this in her body in the same way I do—with that sick feeling of shame and embarrassment localized in the solar plexus chakra, where people store power and self-worth. Those guys took us for a ride, literally. We were only fourteen years old.

"I feel like I made you do it," she says, biting her lips nervously.

"No fucking way, Jen." I grab her hand under the blanket. "We both decided to do it."

I know why she feels that way. She was *that girl*. Everyone knows that girl: the one who was getting molested pretty early on, although nobody understood that part of it. The girl giver of forbidden secrets; the little broken girl playing it big by bragging to all the other little girls on the playground about all the dirty things she knew about sex. And we listened uncomfortably, unable to walk away because she was giving secret teachings. We felt her pain, but we couldn't name it or console it.

"I need a cigarette," she says, sitting up. She pulls a pack of menthols from under the table behind us.

"I'll share it with you."

We sit with our bare legs stretched out in front of us and I see we haven't changed that much physically. Jen's legs are still so girlish, although the rest of her is womanly and mature. She sees me looking and laughs, kicking her heels together playfully. The smile fades.

She lights up and takes a long drag and hands it to me. How many cigarettes have we shared in the dark, stealing menthols from Jackie's mom while she was asleep on prescription meds in that secluded trailer in the woods where we were coming of age in a very dangerous place? We'd all crowd into Jackie's tiny bathroom and pretend we knew what we were doing. We'd talk about who we liked, who we were gonna fight, how to get a ride to go drink. We'd cover our cigarettes with toothpaste, believing it got us high. We'd do stick-'n'-poke tattoos with crusty safety pins and ink from broken pens. Now Jackie's in jail and were we ever children? I thought about it all day while Jen and I watched her kids play in the fountain downtown. As you get older, kids become smaller and smaller and you are hit with it one day—that blunt realization that you were once that little and, when you were, people were fucking you up in so many different ways, obliterating your innocence with their own fears and fucked desires.

Jen's legs are smooth and skinny. Together, stretched out from under her nightgown with one foot over the other, they are a timepiece, taking me back to places and memories I can't forget. They are innocent.

"We were so young. Do you realize how young we were?"

"Yeah." She takes a drag and nods, letting the smoke out slowly. "Ain't that fucked-up?"

"It's real fucked-up. They were at least twenty-one because, remember, one of them went into a bar and bought beer?"

"Yeah."

She's in a daze. I watch her eyes glide down the length of her body toward her seven-year-old daughter sleeping at our feet. Dezmarie. I can read Jen's thoughts through her eyes and I know she's doing exactly what I was doing all day by the water: she's measuring her own losses against Dezmarie's sweet age. *Dezmarie's seven*, she's thinking. Seven years old. That's how old Jen was when her older brother started molesting her. Now she's thinking about how small and beautiful and vulnerable little Dezzie is and she's being flooded with that out-of-her-body feeling—a symptom of her post-traumatic stress disorder, a survival mechanism that kicks in for us when things are just too horrible to comprehend or be present for. She's realizing that, at the time, because no one protected her, she felt like she deserved it. She's seeing Dezmarie's small frame and how it radiates love and spontaneity and childhood and she's realizing that, despite the distorted memory of being ugly and damaged and dirty (the way molestation makes you see yourself), she was just a little girl— as little as Dezmarie is now.

She just stares ahead. She's ready to lose touch and fade out on me. She closes her eyes and tears stream down her cheeks. I pull her hand into my lap and my own tears start stinging. She digs into her purse and pulls out an orange prescription bottle full of downers. Ativans and Klonopins. She doesn't take one, but she holds the bottle in her lap like a rosary, a talisman against the potential freak-out of this painful moment.

I think of my own losses. When I was seven I was lucky. I wasn't being molested. I was being beaten with leather belts by my father. Everyone was. It was called discipline. I didn't even know it was fucked-up until I left and met people who had never been hit, had never lived with violence. I listened to these armchair anarchists fresh from suburbia and upper-middle-class childhoods talk about their successful friends and siblings. They were on the front page of the city paper for buying and fixing up their own houses. Poor was the new cool, but real poor means growing up that way and there is no getting over the damage it does to you then. It isn't an act of resistance and it isn't adventurous. It's depression and post-traumatic stress and never feeling good enough. It's the dark, deep-seated things that happen within stressed families for generations. I'd hang out with these kids and think about my own siblings, all addicted and overmedicated and fucked-up from seeing too many things no one should ever be exposed to.

We sit in silence for a long time, passing the cigarette back and forth. It's been a strange week. This is the third conversation I've had of this nature. My friend Dee and I walked through a cemetery swapping stories of creepy uncles and neighbors. When she was a little girl her uncle used to wake her up at night saying, "It's so hot, Dee. Isn't it hot tonight? Let me cool you off."

He'd wipe her down with a wet rag, wiping her legs slowly, then under her arms, and then he'd lift her little nightgown and go over her belly and chest. She'd lie there paralyzed in bed, trying not to breathe, trying not to be. She couldn't tell anyone. At Christmas dinners he'd come up behind her and push his hard-on against her little back, pretending it was just a hug. She still can't sleep straight through the night and it's hard for her to come without feeling dirty.

I told her my uncle Joe used to always say fucked-up things. When I was five or six I had a nightgown with a puffy-paint city map on the front of it. Uncle Joe would say, "I want to go here, here, and here," pointing to my nipples and between my legs. I'd pretend it didn't happen, walking to my bedroom feeling ashamed.

"Every woman I know," Dee said, sitting down in the grass. "Every woman I know has been fucked up in some way."

"Every girl taken from the rainbow."

Jen pulls her hair back into a ponytail and leans over to take Dezmarie's thumb out of her sleeping mouth. "She's too old to be doing that."

"Jen, what are you thinking about? Are you okay?"

"Yeah. I'm just thinking about what happened."

What happened.

We were fourteen and all made up like whores, standing behind the mall smoking cigarettes, waiting for any chance we could get to be bad, to be grown-up. We had already internalized the idea that to be a woman meant to be pretty and learning your role meant knowing your worth was in male approval. We just wanted to fuck. We didn't even really know what it meant, but we wanted to do it because it made us badass.

Before the guys showed up we were joking and dancing, being little girls. Somewhere in the not-too-distant past we were in the twilight age of not giving a damn about anything but the next sleepover, the next game of hide-and-seek, the next summer vacation. Back then we were completely in touch with our bodies and we were animals, just loving the bliss of running full speed through cornfields, climbing trees, swimming in the river. We felt whole.

But by fourteen we were forced to endure daily sexual harassment from boys our age who were ruthless predators. In school we'd get our asses slapped, our hair pulled. We'd be constantly asked, "Can I hit it? Can I get some head?" The teachers would excuse it: "Just ignore them. Boys will be boys."

Boys will be boys. Boys will become men.

Jackie, Jen, Brandi, and I stood behind a dumpster. Brandi was showing us how to make ourselves pass out.

"Breathe in and out real fast and then stand against the wall and I'm gonna push on your chest."

Jackie flicked her cigarette to the ground and gave Brandi this sassy, what-the-fuck kind of look. You should have seen her. She was fully developed at thirteen and had the mouth of a trucker. Her swear words were exquisite and she was the funniest, brightest star of our circle. She also had the hardest life. Her home was broken and war-torn. Her mom used to load us all into her car at night to be her little accomplices in routine acts of vandalism against her husband's lovers. We'd throw eggs at houses, bricks into car windows; we'd make lots of threatening phone calls. Jackie's mom found boxes full of kiddie-porn magazines in his car and she showed us all, saying, "Look what kind of man your father is." Jackie never recovered.

She ended up pregnant at fifteen and by twenty-one she was serving time for selling cocaine. Last time I saw her she was all sketched-out at a bar and her teeth were blackened from crack.

But back then, that night at the mall, she was still ours. She was still young and beautiful and full of potential. Brandi moved toward her.

"Okay, but don't hurt me," Jackie said and started breathing.

She stopped and Brandi shook her head. "No, just keep doing it. I'll tell you when."

Jackie looked like she was gonna explode. Brandi pushed her into the wall and leaned forward, putting all her weight on Jackie's chest. Brandi was a big girl. She had tattooed knuckles and her head was shaved on one side. She was our pit bull, the big girl we'd call on when we couldn't hold our own or when we just needed to scare the shit out of someone. Jackie's head grew limp and she crumbled to the ground.

"Oh shit," we yelled, moving to pull her up.

She came to, laughing. "That's crazy."

"Do me next," I said.

Brandi and I moved into position while Jen held Jackie up next to us.

Suddenly a car pulled up and it was shining its high beams directly at us. We threw the cigarettes to the ground thinking it was Jackie's mom. It pulled up closer and that's when we saw that obnoxious license plate rimmed with electric-neon purple.

Two guys stepped out of the car, smiling two shit-eating grins like they knew what we were all about and they had our home phone numbers in their back pockets.

"What are you girls doing back here?" the taller, uglier one asked.

We just kind of looked at them.

"Is this a party?" said the other, shorter one.

I can't even remember how to describe them. They wore ugly dress shirts and had too much gel in their hair. They were looking us up and down with that hungry, body-sweeping stare that every girl learns to put up with eventually.

Somehow it happened. They told us to get in, but they only had room for two of us. Jen looked at me and I looked at her and we just knew we were going for it. Jackie and Brandi told us not to. The guys called them sluts and Jackie tried to fight one of them. We ended up telling her to just calm down, to leave her mom's door open, and then we got in.

I don't remember much after that. I remember riding with the windows down, smoking cigarettes and not talking. I remember the guys passing glances back and forth and smiling like they were just so damn cool and we were so damn stupid. I remember the digital green numbers of the dashboard clock flashing noon as if the time had never been set. Their ashtrays were full and there were plastic bottles on the floor, Mountain Dews and empty cans of shaving gel. I had no idea what time it was and I was full of anxiety, feeling like I shouldn't be there, but the world around me hadn't equipped me with enough fuck-you to force the night to a safe conclusion. Boys will be boys and girls will let them do it.

They told me to switch seats with the taller one as Jennifer took her pants down and he climbed on top of her. I remember Jennifer's face, enduring, twisted in pain and acceptance, her head banging against the ashtray with his quick and hungry thrusts.

I remember switching places and the shorter one took off my skirt. I remember him pushing into me and the pain lit a fire up my entire body. I remember screaming and telling him, "No, get the fuck off of me, stop, it hurts." He kept going, breathing like an animal. I remember pushing him with all of my strength and he just wouldn't budge. I heard Jennifer screaming and pulling him by his hair, digging those deadly nails into his face.

"Get off of her!" she yelled, and he finally got up and I remember I could see in his eyes that he was confused and ashamed. He was bleeding. His friend told us to get the fuck out of the car and they left us there alone, fourteen, on a dirt road miles away from any houses.

We walked and walked, without talking. We got to Jackie's trailer in the early morning and we went into the bathroom where we swore not to tell anyone. I went to pee and saw my underwear were full of blood. I was terrified. Jen told me not to worry; it was my hymen.

"My what?" I asked, completely scared.

"He broke your hymen," she said, fiddling with her hair in the mirror. "It's a little piece of skin that covers your hole. That's what happens. It means you're not a virgin anymore."

I looked down at the blood in disbelief. At once I felt disgusted and ashamed, but I also felt a sense of pride and accomplishment. I felt like a woman.

Somewhere in the back of my mind there was that lingering sense of injustice. *Is this it?* I thought. *Is this what it is to be a woman?*

I remembered Jennifer's face and her head hitting the side door. I remembered the pain and the complete absence of pleasure. I didn't think about the way Jen and Jackie and I were pleasing each other with our secret girl games in Jackie's bedroom when her mom was away. The way we would kiss and touch and dry-hump until we were coming. We didn't know what any of that was, but we liked doing it and it was just good. But we were told it wasn't healthy. It stopped when Jackie heard her mom talking about gay people and Jackie didn't want to be gay. It scared her half to death. So we had to learn the rules: pain and shameful acceptance is good. Pleasure and discovery is bad. *What a raw fucking deal,* I thought to myself, still sitting on the toilet, kind of wondering where I would go from there if all my girlfriends were afraid to be gay and this was the only alternative. I had yet to begin to disentangle the utter mindfuck of feeling humiliated and initiated in one night. I probably never did. I'm probably still swimming in the psychic repercussions of that one.

"Jen," I say after some time, breaking the silence in my living room. The CD has played to its finish and we're out of cigarettes. The windows are open and the babies are breathing softly into the cool air.

"Yeah," she answers. Her eyes are transfixed on the wall.

"Was that rape?"

A bitter, cynical half smile spreads across her face. It says to me that she's right where I am; she recognizes the cruel irony of the situation: that a woman's boundaries are so constantly and systematically violated, she can't even clearly define what has happened to her, let alone tell someone who wasn't there.

"Yeah, it was," she decides for both of us.

Dezmarie stirs and turns over, opening her tiny eyes. "Mommy, are we going swimming today?" she asks in a sleepy voice just coming out of a dream.

"Yeah, baby," Jen answers, only half-aware of what she's saying. She's still letting it all sink in. She's letting it sink. She's sinking in to the truth of our situation: we were born and we will live until death in these dangerous, girl-poisoning waters, and all we can really do is teach each other to swim and hope that, together, we will find our way back to the sea, where our tails will return to us and we will be little girls again, innocent and free, playing mermaids under a full moon in the summer.

3.

Downtown stands electric and alive with its light-root reflections chiming silently in the water. We're sitting on the dock with our legs dangling over the edge. He's still talking about his boyhood and I'm not listening. I can only hear so many tales of privilege before I realize what two different worlds we occupy and, so, retreat into mine and leave him to his, no Charon to bring us back to each other.

I'm remembering Jen, my lifelong friend, my sweet country girl with the biggest heart and the deepest pain. I'm thinking about all the women I've known and loved. I'm thinking about all the ways we deep-sea dive like Isises through the underworld of sexual trauma to save each other from the fire, pulling each other up and out constantly. I've heard men say that female friendships are too damn complicated, that we're always fighting about something, and it's true, but it's only because we get so close and so real. We pull each other up, even if we're pulling hair. We pull each other down, too, but that's just the way it goes when you're in over your head and fighting for breath.

"Girls and boys grow up so differently," I say, cutting off his soliloquy. "We live in two totally different worlds."

"Girls don't grow up that differently," he says, immediately dismissing me, a habit of his gender conditioning. Traditional masculinity depends on a constant repudiation of the feminine to remind men where their balls end and our cunts begin, so what can I say? There isn't enough energy or time in my body to change this for him.

"I know how girls grow up," he says. "I have two sisters, remember?"

I stand up, wiping my hands on my jeans, and I jump down from the dock, landing on the rocky embankment. I turn up to him and he's dumbfounded. He has no idea what he did wrong. But the funny thing is, I'm not even angry. I just don't have patience for invisibility, not anymore.

The bus stop isn't far and I decided a long time ago that I wouldn't live in fear of walking alone at night because I need night walks as much as I need food and water. I need the cool air and the sleeping houses. I need the shadows and the fat spiders up in the arches of the old bridges. I figure it's a toss-up between possible rape and eternal house arrest, another nice double bind for me to negotiate my way through. Again, something he doesn't need to worry about.

Two different worlds.

"You don't know shit," I yell over my shoulder, walking away slowly, because, really, I'm not angry. I'm just done.

The moon shines pregnant-fat above the water and the river knows me. She watches silently, full of dark secrets and life-sustaining treasures, waiting patiently for the right diver to come and bring them up.

Why Misogynists Make Great Informants

How Gender Violence on the Left Enables State Violence in Radical Movements

By Courtney Desiree Morris

In January 2009, activists in Austin, Texas, learned that one of their own, a white activist named Brandon Darby, had infiltrated groups protesting the Republican National Convention (RNC) as an FBI informant. Darby later admitted to wearing recording devices at planning meetings and during the convention. He testified on behalf of the government in the February 2009 trial of two Texas activists who were arrested at the RNC on charges of making and possessing Molotov cocktails, after Darby encouraged them to do so. The two young men, David McKay and Bradley Crowder, each faced up to fifteen years in prison. Crowder accepted a plea bargain to serve three years in a federal prison; under pressure from federal prosecutors, McKay also pled guilty to being in possession of "unregistered Molotov cocktails" and was sentenced to four years in prison. Information gathered by Darby may also have contributed to the case against the RNC 8, activists from around the country charged with "conspiracy to riot and conspiracy

Originally published in *make/shift* no. 7 (spring/summer 2010)

to damage property in the furtherance of terrorism." Austin activists were particularly stunned by the revelation that Darby had served as an informant because he had been a part of various leftist projects and was a leader at Common Ground Relief, a New Orleans–based organization committed to meeting the short-term needs of community members displaced by natural disasters in the Gulf Coast region and dedicated to rebuilding the region and ensuring Katrina evacuees' right to return.

I was surprised but not shocked by this news. I had learned as an undergrad at the University of Texas that the campus police department routinely placed plainclothes police officers in the meetings of radical student groups—you know, just to keep an eye on them. That was in fall 2001. We saw the creation of the Department of Homeland Security, watched a cowboy president wage war on terror, and, in the middle of it all, tried to figure out what we could do to challenge the fascist state transformations taking place before our eyes. At the time, however, it seemed silly that there were cops in our meetings—we weren't the Panthers or the Brown Berets or even some of the rowdier direct-action antiglobalization activists on campus (although we admired them all); we were just young people who didn't believe war was the best response to the 9/11 attacks. But it wasn't silly; the FBI does not dismiss political work. Any organization, be it large or small, can provoke the scrutiny of the state. Perhaps your organization poses a large threat, or maybe you're small now but one day you'll grow up and be too big to rein in. The state usually opts to kill the movement before it grows.

And informants and provocateurs are the state's hired gunmen. Government agencies pick people that no one will notice. Often it's impossible to prove that they're informants because they appear to be completely dedicated to social justice. They establish intimate relationships with activists, becoming friends and lovers, often serving in leadership roles in organizations. A cursory reading of the literature on social movements and organizations in the 1960s and 1970s reveals this fact. The leadership of the American Indian Movement was rife with informants; it is suspected that informants were also largely responsible for the downfall of the Black Panther Party, and the same can be surmised about the antiwar movement of the 1960s and 1970s. Not surprisingly, these movements that were toppled by informants and provocateurs were also sites where women and queer activists often experienced intense gender violence, as the autobiographies of activists such as Assata Shakur, Elaine Brown, and Roxanne Dunbar-Ortiz demonstrate.

Maybe it isn't that informants are difficult to spot but rather that we have collectively ignored the signs that give them away. To save our movements, we need to come to terms with the connections between gender violence, male privilege, and the strategies that informants (and people who just act like them) use to destabilize radical movements. Time and again, heterosexual men in radical movements have been allowed to assert their privilege and subordinate others. Despite all that we say to the contrary, the fact is that radical social movements and organizations in the United States have refused to seriously address gender violence[1] as a threat to the survival of our struggles. We've treated misogyny, homophobia, and heterosexism as lesser evils—secondary issues—that will eventually take care of themselves or fade into the background once the "real" issues—racism, the police, class inequality, U.S. wars of aggression—are resolved. There are serious consequences for choosing ignorance. Misogyny and homophobia are central to the reproduction of violence in radical activist communities. Scratch a misogynist and you'll find a homophobe. Scratch a little deeper and you might find the makings of a future informant (or someone who just destabilizes movements like informants do).

THE MAKINGS OF AN INFORMANT: BRANDON DARBY AND COMMON GROUND

On *Democracy Now!* Malik Rahim, former Black Panther and cofounder of Common Ground in New Orleans, spoke about how devastated he was by Darby's revelation that he was an FBI informant. Several times Rahim stated that his heart had been broken. He especially lamented all of the "young ladies" who left Common Ground as a result of Darby's domineering, aggressive style of organizing. And when

---

1. I use the term "gender violence" to refer to the ways in which homophobia and misogyny are rooted in heteronormative understandings of gender identity and gender roles. Heterosexism not only polices nonnormative sexualities but also reproduces normative gender roles and identities that reinforce the logic of patriarchy and male privilege.

those "young ladies" complained? Well, their concerns likely fell on sympathetic but ultimately unresponsive ears—everything may have been true, and after the fact everyone admits how disruptive Darby was, quick to suggest violent, ill-conceived direct-action schemes that endangered everyone he worked with. There were even claims that Darby sexually assaulted female organizers at Common Ground and, in general, was dismissive of women working in the organization.[2] Darby created conflict in all of the organizations he worked with, yet people were hesitant to hold him accountable because of his history and reputation as an organizer and his "dedication" to "the work." People continued to defend him until he outed himself as an FBI informant. Even Rahim, for all of his guilt and angst, chose to leave Darby in charge of Common Ground although every time there was conflict in the organization it seemed to involve Darby.

Maybe if organizers made collective accountability around gender violence a central part of our practices we could neutralize people who are working on behalf of the state to undermine our struggles. I'm not talking about witch hunts; I'm talking about organizing in such a way that we nip a potential Brandon Darby in the bud before he can hurt more people. Informants are hard to spot, but my guess is that where there is smoke there is fire, and someone who creates chaos wherever he goes is either an informant or an irresponsible, unaccountable time bomb who can be unintentionally as effective at undermining social-justice organizing as an informant. Ultimately, they both do the work of the state and need to be held accountable.

A BRIEF HISTORICAL REFLECTION ON
GENDER VIOLENCE IN RADICAL MOVEMENTS

Reflecting on the radical organizations and social movements of the 1960s and 1970s provides an important historical context for this discussion. Memoirs by women who were actively involved in these

2. I learned this from informal conversations with women who had organized with Darby in Austin and New Orleans while participating in the Austin Informants Working Group, which was formed by people who had worked with Darby and were stunned by his revelation that he was an FBI informant.

struggles reveal the pervasiveness of tolerance (and in some cases advocacy) of gender violence. Angela Davis, Assata Shakur, and Elaine Brown, each at different points in their experiences organizing with the Black Panther Party (BPP), cited sexism and the exploitation of women (and their organizing labor) in the BPP as one of their primary reasons for either leaving the group (in the cases of Brown and Shakur) or refusing to ever formally join (in Davis's case). Although women were often expected to make significant personal sacrifices to support the movement, when women found themselves victimized by male comrades there was no support for them or channels to seek redress. Whether it was BPP organizers ignoring the fact that Eldridge Cleaver beat his wife, noted activist Kathleen Cleaver; men coercing women into sex; or just men treating women organizers as subordinated sexual playthings, the BPP and similar organizations tended not to take seriously the corrosive effects of gender violence on liberation struggle. In many ways, Elaine Brown's autobiography, *A Taste of Power: A Black Woman's Story*, has gone the furthest in laying bare the ugly realities of misogyny in the movement and the various ways in which both men and women reproduced and reinforced male privilege and gender violence in these organizations. Her experience as the only woman to ever lead the BPP did not exempt her from the brutal misogyny of the organization. She recounts being assaulted by various male comrades (including Huey Newton) as well as being beaten and terrorized by Eldridge Cleaver, who threatened to "bury her in Algeria" during a delegation to China. Her biography demonstrates more explicitly than either Davis's or Shakur's how the masculinist posturing of the BPP (and, by extension, many radical organizations at the time) created a culture of violence and misogyny that ultimately proved to be the organization's undoing.

These narratives demystify the legacy of gender violence of the very organizations that many of us look up to. They demonstrate how misogyny was normalized in these spaces, dismissed as "personal" or not as important as the more serious struggles against racism or class inequality. Gender violence has historically been deeply entrenched in the political practices of the Left and constituted one of the greatest (if largely unacknowledged) threats to the survival of these organizations.

However, if we pay attention to the work of Davis, Shakur, Brown, and others, we can avoid the mistakes of the past and create different kinds of political community.

THE RACIAL POLITICS OF GENDER VIOLENCE

Race further complicates the ways in which gender violence unfolds in our communities. In "Looking for Common Ground: Relief Work in Post-Katrina New Orleans as an American Parable of Race and Gender Violence," Rachel Luft explores the disturbing pattern of sexual assault against white female volunteers by white male volunteers doing rebuilding work in the Upper Ninth Ward in 2006. She points out how Common Ground failed to address white men's assaults on their co-organizers and instead shifted the blame to the surrounding Black community, warning white women activists that they needed to be careful because New Orleans was a dangerous place. Ultimately, it proved easier to criminalize Black men from the neighborhood than to acknowledge that white women and transgender organizers were most likely to be assaulted by white men they worked with. In one case, a white male volunteer was turned over to the police only after he sexually assaulted at least three women in one week. The privilege that white men enjoyed in Common Ground, an organization ostensibly committed to racial justice, meant that they could be violent toward women and queer activists, enact destructive behaviors that undermined the organization's work, and know that the movement would not hold them accountable in the same way that it did Black men in the community where they worked.

Of course, male privilege is not uniform—white men and men of color are unequal participants in and beneficiaries of patriarchy, although they both can and do reproduce gender violence. This disparity in the distribution of patriarchy's benefits is not lost on women and queer organizers when we attempt to confront men of color who enact gender violence in our communities. We often worry about reproducing particular kinds of racist violence that disproportionately target men of color. We are understandably loath to call the police, involve the state in any way, or place men of color at the mercy of a historically racist criminal (in)justice system; yet our communities (political and otherwise) often do not step up to demand justice on our behalf. We don't feel comfortable talking to therapists who just reaffirm stereotypes about how fucked-up and exceptionally violent our home communities are. The Left often offers even less support. Our victimization is unfortunate, problematic, but ultimately less important to "the work" than the men of all races who reproduce gender violence in our communities.

ENCOUNTERING MISOGYNY ON THE LEFT: A PERSONAL REFLECTION

In the first community group I was actively involved in, I encountered a level of misogyny that I would never have imagined existed in what was supposed to be a radical-people-of-color organization. I was sexually/romantically involved with an older Chicano activist in the group. I was nineteen, an inexperienced young Black activist; he was thirty. He asked me to keep our relationship a secret, and I reluctantly agreed. Later, after he ended the relationship and I was reeling from depression, I discovered that he had been sleeping with at least two other women while we were together. One of them was a friend of mine, another young woman we organized with. Unaware of the nature of our relationship, which he had failed to disclose to her, she slept with him until he disappeared, refusing to answer her calls or explain the abrupt end of their relationship. She and I, after sharing our experiences, began to trade stories with other women who knew and had organized with this man.

We heard of the women who had left a Chicana/o student group and never came back after his lies and secrets blew up while the group was participating in a Zapatista action in Mexico City. The queer, radical, white organizer who left Austin to get away from his abuse. Another white woman, a social worker who thought they might get married only to come to his apartment one evening and find me there. And then there were the ones who came after me. I always wondered if they knew who he really was. The women he dated were amazing, beautiful, kick-ass, radical women that he used as shields to get himself into places he knew would never be open to such a misogynist. I mean, if that cool woman who worked in Chiapas, spoke Spanish, and worked with undocumented immigrants was dating him, he must be down, right? Wrong.

But his misogyny didn't end there; it was also reflected in his style of organizing. In meetings he always spoke the loudest and longest, using academic jargon that made any discussion excruciatingly more complex than necessary. The academic-speak intimidated people less educated than him because he seemed to know more about radical politics than anyone else. He would talk down to other men in the group, especially those he perceived to be less intelligent than him, which was basically everybody. Then he'd switch gears, apologize for dominating the space, and acknowledge his need to check his male privilege. Ironically, when people did attempt to call him out on his shit, he would feign ignorance—what could they mean, saying that his behavior was masculinist and sexist? He'd complain of being infantilized, refusing to see how he infantilized people *all* the time. The fact that he was a man of color who could talk a good game about racism and racial-justice struggles masked his abusive behaviors in both radical organizations and his personal relationships. As one of his former partners shared with me, "His radical race analysis allowed people (mostly men but occasionally women as well) to forgive him for being dominating and abusive in his relationships. Womyn had to check their critique of his behavior at the door, lest we lose a man of color in the movement." One of the reasons it is so difficult to hold men of color accountable for reproducing gender violence is that women of color and white activists continue to be invested in the idea that men of color have it harder than anyone else. How do you hold someone accountable when you believe he is target number one for the state?

Unfortunately, he wasn't the only man like this I encountered in radical spaces—just one of the smarter ones. Reviewing old e-mails, I am shocked at the number of e-mails from men I organized with that were abusive in tone and content, how easily they would talk down to others for minor mistakes. I am more surprised at my meek, diplomatic responses—like an abuse survivor—as I attempted to placate compañeros who saw nothing wrong with yelling at their partners, friends, and other organizers. There were men like this in various organizations I worked with. The one who called his girlfriend a bitch in front of a group of youth of color during a summer *encuentro* we were hosting. The one who sexually harassed a queer Chicana couple during a trip to Mexico, trying to pressure them into a threesome. The guys who said they would complete a task, didn't do it, brushed off their compañeras' demands for accountability, let those women take over the task, and when it was finished took all the credit for someone else's hard work. The graduate student who hit his partner—and everyone knew he'd done it, but whenever anyone asked, people would just look ashamed and embarrassed and mumble, "It's complicated." The ones who constantly demeaned queer folks, even people they organized with. Especially the one who thought it would be a revolutionary act to "kill all these faggots, these niggas on the down low, who are fucking up our children, fucking up our homes, fucking up our world, and fucking up our lives!" The one who would shout you down in a meeting or tell you that you couldn't be a feminist because you were too pretty. Or the one who thought homosexuality was a disease from Europe.

Yeah, that guy.

Most of those guys probably weren't informants. Which is a pity because it means they are not getting paid a dime for all the destructive work they do. We might think of these misogynists as inadvertent agents of the state. Regardless of whether they are actually informants or not, the work that they do supports the state's ongoing campaign of terror against social movements and the people who create them. When queer organizers are humiliated and their political struggles sidelined, that is part of an ongoing state project of violence against radicals. When women are knowingly given STIs, physically abused, dismissed in meetings, pushed aside, and forced out of radical organizing spaces while our allies defend known misogynists, organizers collude in the state's efforts to destroy us.

The state has already understood a fact that the Left has struggled to accept: misogynists make great informants. Before or regardless of whether they are ever recruited by the state to disrupt a movement or destabilize an organization, they've likely become well versed in practices of disruptive behavior. They require almost no training and can start the work immediately. What's more paralyzing to our work than when women and/or queer folks leave our movements because they have been repeatedly lied to, humiliated, physically/verbally/emotionally/sexually abused? Or when you have to postpone conversations about the work so that you can devote group meetings to addressing an individual member's most recent offense? Or when that person spreads misinformation, creating confusion and friction among radical groups? Nothing slows down movement building like a misogynist.

What the FBI gets is that when there are people in activist spaces who are committed to taking power and who understand power as domination, our movements will never realize their potential to remake this world. If our energies are absorbed recuperating from the messes that informants (and people who just act like them) create, we will never be able to focus on the real work of getting free and building the kinds of life-affirming, people-centered communities that we want to live in. To paraphrase bell hooks, where there is a will to dominate there can be no justice because we will inevitably continue reproducing the same kinds of injustice we claim to be struggling against. It is time for our movements to undergo a radical change from the inside out.

LOOKING FORWARD:
CREATING GENDER JUSTICE IN OUR MOVEMENTS

Radical movements cannot afford the destruction that gender violence creates. If we underestimate the political implications of patriarchal behaviors in our communities, the work will not survive.

Lately I've been turning to the work of queers/feminists of color to think through how to challenge these behaviors in our movements. I've been reading the autobiographies of women who lived through the chaos of social movements debilitated by machismo. I'm revisiting the work of bell hooks, Roxanne Dunbar-Ortiz, Toni Cade Bambara, Alice Walker, Audre Lorde, Gioconda Belli, Margaret Randall, Elaine Brown, Pearl Cleage, Ntozake Shange, and Gloria Anzaldúa to see how other women negotiated gender violence in these spaces and to problematize neat or easy answers about how violence is reproduced in our communities. Newer work by radical feminists of color has also been incredibly helpful, especially the zine *Revolution Starts at Home: Confronting Partner Abuse in Activist Communities*, edited by Ching-In Chen, Jai Dulani, and Leah Lakshmi Piepzna-Samarasinha.

But there are many resources for confronting this dilemma beyond books. The simple act of speaking and sharing our truths is one of the most powerful tools we have. I've been speaking to my elders, older women of color in struggle who have experienced the things I'm struggling against, and swapping survival stories with other women. In summer 2008 I began doing workshops on ending misogyny and building collective forms of accountability with Cristina Tzintzún, an Austin-based labor organizer and author of the essay "Killing Misogyny: A Personal Story of Love, Violence, and Strategies for Survival." We have also begun the even more liberating practice of naming our experiences publicly and calling on our communities to address what we and so many others have experienced.

Dismantling misogyny cannot be work that only women do. We *all* must do the work because the survival of our movements depends on it. Until we make radical feminist and queer political ethics that directly challenge heteropatriarchal forms of organizing central to our political practice, radical movements will continue to be devastated by the antics of Brandon Darbys (and folks who aren't informants but just act like them). A queer, radical, feminist ethic of accountability would challenge us to recognize how gender violence is reproduced in our communities, relationships, and organizing practices. Although there are many ways to do this, I want to suggest that there are three key steps that we can take to begin. First, we must support women and queer people in our movements who have experienced interpersonal violence and engage in a collective process of healing. Second, we must initiate a collective dialogue about how we want our communities to look and how to make them safe for everyone. Third, we must develop a model for collective accountability that truly treats the personal as political and helps us to begin practicing justice in our communities. When we allow women/ queer organizers to leave activist spaces, and protect people whose violence provoked their departure, we are saying we value these de facto state agents who disrupt the work more than we value people whose labor builds and sustains movements.

As angry as gender violence on the Left makes me, I am hopeful. I believe we have the capacity to change and to create more justice in our movements. We don't have to start witch hunts to reveal misogynists and informants. They out themselves every time they refuse to apologize, take ownership of their actions, start conflicts and refuse to work them out through consensus, mistreat their compañer@s. We don't have to look for them, but when we are presented with their destructive behaviors we have to hold them accountable. Our strategies don't have to be punitive; people are entitled to their mistakes. But we should expect that people will own those actions and not allow them to become a pattern.

We have a right to be angry when the communities we build—communities that are supposed to be the model for a better, more just world—harbor the same kinds of antiqueer, antiwoman, racist violence that pervades society. As radical organizers we must hold each other accountable and not enable misogynists to assert so much power in these spaces. Not allow them to be the faces, voices, and leaders of these movements. Not allow them to rape a compañera and then be on the fucking five o'clock news. In Brandon Darby's case, even if no one suspected he was an informant, his domineering and macho behavior should have been all that was needed to call his leadership into question. By not allowing misogyny to take root in our communities and movements, we not only protect ourselves from the efforts of the state to destroy our work but also create stronger movements that cannot be destroyed from within.

Pieces of Us

The Telling of Our Transformation

By the Azolla Story,[1] featuring writing by Stacey Milbern,
Mia Mingus, and Leah Lakshmi Piepzna-Samarasinha

This is for you, for us. We are more than the bodies we have been told to hide. We have found each other, somehow. And we are fighting to stay connected with everything we have. Together, we are here.

As three physically disabled, queer, east and south asian women of color, we believe wholeheartedly that what Audre Lorde said is true: "The visibility which makes us most vulnerable is that which also is the source of our greatest strength." Writing by disabled queer people of color—whether they would have identified with us or not—has been what has kept us continuously looking for each other. Each of our stories has sustained the others. We write them out of survival and resiliency; we offer them with love, and hope you find what you are looking for in them.

Originally published in *make/shift* no. 9 (spring/summer 2011)

1. The Azolla Story is an interdependent, multiracial, fierce community for queer and trans disabled people of color. *Make/shift* featured writing from different members of the Azolla Story over two issues.

The first time I recognized you—the me in you—I remember catching my breath. A rush of blood from an embarrassing crush-like state from being so close and yet so far away; a sweat, a slight flush. Do you recognize me? Do you recognize me recognizing you?

In the beginning, I was a little afraid that you would see through me and know that I am still so afraid of myself. I never had any teachers, just the silence of my own longing and the shortness of my breath. And yet, I knew there was no other way to quell the fear than to move into it, to keep moving toward you. Feeling the anxiety that you could be someone who might be able to recognize me, someone who could choose to turn away, the pain—so close and risky—that you may not be able to recognize yourself in me.

And yet, still, moving against fear, pulled by desire and curiosity: *It's you. You are here. You have survived, just like me. So many things I ache to ask you, so many things I need to tell you. So many things I want for us. Do you know how amazing you are?*

You are the kind of beauty I could never see inside myself. You are the kind of connection I have been terrified of and craving ever since I can remember forgetting. Did you forget too? How did you remember?

Pouring the kind of love I never had over you, not caring about how outlandish it sounds: I love the way you move, the way you swing and shake and need, the way you look. Feeling the places of you in me become more settled, more emboldened, more fierce. Turning corners inside of who I am now, crossing over imagined borders, crashing through time and space.

Bursting with the truth of: tell me, tell me, how could I have ever lived any other way than this?

—Mia

My love for you took me by surprise because I had never lusted after you. Student-council girl always working so hard to win over the affection of able-bodied people, I was the girl who laughed with you on the disability bus and then ignored you in school. You drooled. You stimmed. You had scars all over your wrists but said you rode the bus because your brother had a heart condition. Everything you did made you so blatant and the way you couldn't control the space you took up disgusted me. I thought if I pretended not to see you, others wouldn't notice all the ways that I was blatant, too.

When I heard about a youth leadership conference that would pay for my crip self to travel to Washington, D.C., I immediately wanted to go. Even though the event was *for* and *by* disabled youth, it didn't really sink in that I'd be submerged in disability. I arrived, shocked to see this throng of people signing, rocking back and forth, and using service dogs. Being blatant. No one got mad when the girl with Tourette's had an outburst. People did not rush to finish each other's sentences. When the ice-cream shop wasn't accessible to wheelchair users, the group insisted on staying—said we even had a right to be there—and swarmed the sidewalk, shoving disability in the faces of people who stared. I felt like I lost my voice, like my gut had crawled up my throat and was lodged there. I never knew I could crave something so much, and I spent that whole weekend silent, overwhelmed by my desire to be with you.

Between that weekend and the next time I would be in disability space, I had a fight with death. This time I literally lost my voice. I was so mad at God—I had gained all this confidence from that conference and as soon as I was getting "disabled and proud me" down pat, I got sick and the disabled self I knew changed. I started having a trach and using a ventilator. The conference had made me feel like I could pull off independence. It had me thinking I could make disability cute. Trach and nurses . . . not so much. I spent a month with therapists learning how to breathe and speak again. I withdrew from the college I was going to attend in the fall. My parents moved my bed into the living room, and I started having nurses in my house all the time. I had no idea how to live with a trach. It was to the point where every time I took a shower, I thought I would drown. I was so scared of this new body, so scared at how fast it was swinging out of my control.

My parents promised that if I made it through that hell, they'd take me to the conference again (I got accepted to go a second year). The only way I could make it was if I had someone around the clock with me. My whole family came and stuffed themselves into the hotel room the conference gave us. My brother and sister took turns sitting in workshops with me, and my parents lifted me in and out of bed together. Instead of shunning me as the weirdly disabled trach girl, other disabled people invited me to dinner with them. Told my parents they could help me. Promised I would be okay because they wouldn't leave me. Made it sound like being with me wasn't even a burden. It was the first time I felt like I could really speak. I found my voice in community.

I describe those two summers as the first deep breaths I ever had. Shoulders letting loose. Tightened muscles becoming free. Deep breath. In. Out. Here.

—Stacey

CRIP SUPERPOWERS

Sick hit me like a hurricane when I was twenty-two, the same time remembering childhood sexual abuse, working off the books waiting for a visa to come through, and being in an activist-of-color abusive relationship did. When my fibro flares hit, I was sore. Confused. Tired to the bone. Trapped at the top of three flights of stairs. I limped slowly to the corner store and back, carrying one small bag of groceries, resting for a long time after. Asking for help was weak and girl and vulnerable. Everything my whole life had taught me was that to be a working-class femme of color was to never be vulnerable, to never ask for help. My kind of femme wasn't a delicate flower. She was tough, reliable, show-up, a bottom liner, effortless, fierce, fast, impenetrable. That's how you were valued, not just as a boring *girl*. That's how you survived when you were living without a net. When I was between flares, I tried to forget and keep up with everyone else. When they hit, I clutched myself, at the top of the stairs with no care plan, no frozen food in the fridge, no community. Like many queer women of color, I figured I had enough identities to deal with already. Why add this one?

When I went back to Toronto this year, ten years after sick touched down like a hurricane, I tried to talk to queer women of color I knew who were chronically ill. Tried saying that I felt so much better, not because of the California sunshine but because I knew that I could ask for accommodation. Because I had a web of folks who helped each other.

I tried to tell them about how good it felt to ask for help. About using my '92 Honda Accord with its disabled parking pass to ferry all my crip friends to sliding-scale acupuncture and the grocery store. About using Facebook as an adaptive device when I can't get out of bed. I tried to tell them about us dancing at the queer club, me next to a pole I can grab for my shaky balance, my friend sitting on the edge of the stage to rest her leg prostheses, enough room for folks in wheelchairs, waving the heavily perfumed away. I wanted to tell them about the joy.

A friend of mine did this amazing piece for a queer crip sexuality performance night once. It was a Choose Your Own Adventure of queer crips trying to survive a zombie apocalypse! The audience watched as the crips helped each other; used our canes, tinctures, meds, and assistive devices to fend off the walking dead; chose not to abandon each other; and had hot sex while we did it!

I want our bodies and minds to be seen as more than a liability. I want our bodies and minds not to be something that makes us a problem, a flake, taking up too much space in our movements and communities. I want our communities and movements to see our broken beautiful selves as assets. Smart. Genius, even. To see our smarts—the way we can community-organize flat on our ass in bed—as what the movement needs most.

I want to tell my chronically ill women of color friends about our time in Detroit, with that magic Creating Collective Access posse on the fourth floor of the Allied Media Conference dorms. About all of us at the crip table. About how nobody was ever alone at the top of three flights of stairs.

—Leah

Some physically disabled women of color I know say that their great mental willpower to control their bodies is how they survived so long. I would never want my autistic friends to shut off their brains in order to be more neurotypical. I'm not sure why I keep trying to mimic able-bodiedness when it hurts so much.

Just like my body has managed to shuck off every cold metal device the medical industrial complex has created to tame it, my body has begun to revolt against me when I do not meet its needs. If I want to be in harmony with my body and not think of it as just a shell for my spirit, I have to do what it says. I am forced to rest when my body says it's exhausted, leave the room when it's time to get up, and run when my body says it's going to cause a scene. I often resent the way my body controls my actions—the way it forces me to be *in* it—but I also know that it is wise and that there is so much that I can learn from it.

Perhaps sustainability starts with obeying our bodies?

—Stacey

TIP ON THE TIGHTROPE

I live on the edge. It has become my home. I have learned to find a sense of comfort there, limping and balancing carefully, never knowing if today will be the day I fall off the other side. Sometimes it is the edge between hope and despair, usual pain and unusual pain, love and hate. Sometimes it is the edge between disability and queerness, adoptee and korean. But most times it is the edge between wholeness and connection, silence and isolation, exhaustion and fear.

There are some things that you just don't talk about, some things that no one knows what to do with. Things that will make people angry at you for bringing out the angry in them, hate you for bringing out the hate in them.

I wish I could hold it more gently and not be yet another woman of color who loathes her body and questions the very fibers that make up desire; yet another disabled woman cast to the side by her own cutting glance. I wish I could be more fierce and fight it back down into its dwelling, shut the lid tight on it and never look back. I wish I was stronger. I eat the shame and guilt like they were my punishment for dinner every night, feeling sure that I deserve it. *Who is a bigger lie than me? Everything silences me.*

What to do with a body that has been smuggled off the operating table and hidden away from the brace makers, yet still not loved by the very one who set it free? What to do with the nagging, haunting feelings and voices that have stayed and made their home inside of me? The fear of "no one wants this rejected adoptee queer disabled body" and the quiet shame of "not even me." How to talk about loneliness? How to talk about suicide and anger and the gnawing silly bristling resentment of legs and feet and backs and movement and fun?

When I fall, I drown. Are you not drowning too, with the ache and exhaustion that you will never learn the language of love, that the initial great escape was all for nothing because maybe they were right, maybe we are wrong? Because what good is escaping if we can't even run into each other's arms, if we are still miles away from ourselves and from any semblance of getting free?

—Mia

THESE WARRIOR (CRIP) BONES ACHE FOR REVOLUTION / BUT THE PEOPLE AIN'T READY.[2]

This is not cute. I'm not rocking my cane today, navigating the treacherous and making it seem effortless. I'm in my lime green booty shorts and an ill-fitting T-shirt I slept in, armpits stinky, lying out on the couch. Everything hurts: my wrists, ass, hips, lower back, but most of all my energy and cognitive abilities, and today, I am a chronic-pain zombie girl. I keep saying I'll do some yoga, make an acupuncture appointment, make some more nettle tea, take a Soma. I can't get up.

It's not an all-powerful empowerment moment when my best friend has been hurting for ten days now. He calls me crying from the bus stop and I pick him up because I know what it's like to have a one-block walk be an epic journey. His house has a pantry-moth infestation and we have to throw out all the gluten-free food bought with food stamps. The nontoxic cleaner is so much more heavily scented than we thought it would be and it makes both of us sick. He is losing it, and I can't scrub the kitchen 'cause my body hurts too; it's one of those landslide stupid crip POC queer/trans poverty moments where nothing is going well. His roommate's lover is staring at him uncomprehendingly, and I get hit with rage where I feel like both of us could die and the QTPOC movements we have both been a part of for so long will either be shocked or not get it because they cannot wrap their minds around our crip queer brown bodies being something they know how to fight for.

2. This is a riff on Tamar Kali's song "Warrior Bones."

How come it's only other crips, who also sometimes all can't fucking get out of bed because of the pollution, atmospheric pressure, tumor resurgence, the fact that the two goddamn wheelchair-accessible cabs are both booked, etcetera, who show up?

What is it gonna take for the movements to get the memo that this is important, that it is about you, that you could be a crip, or you could never be, but you should give a fuck?

—Leah

We are here. We are here, we are here, we are here. Writing to hold on to each other. These stories are pieces of us: bold, scared, full of rage, mournful, and hesitant. We will find each other among these pages as we never have before, ready to risk our fear for the promise of each other. Ready to give in to our bodies, give up the facade, and give to each other everything we never had, everything we can possibly dream of.

Photo by Ashley Inguanta

The Power We Have

Things that Worked in Transformative Justice This Past Year

By Leah Lakshmi Piepzna-Samarasinha

This is part 1 of an occasional series of notes from the field.

Some days, things seem rough. I want to feel on fire, on the verge of an earthshift, but I'm just going to the grocery store. A year and a half ago, we shut down the Port of Oakland.[1] Today, end of the world notwithstanding, it is quiet. Two years ago, we were cresting a wave of optimism, excitement, and possibility in the movement for transformative justice. Right now, things are quiet; some things are not working or are challenging; it's not that same big movement-excitement moment.

But if movements have twenty-five-year life cycles, if our bodies' cells die and replace themselves every seven years, it makes sense

Excerpted from a piece originally published in *make/shift* no. 13 (spring/summer 2013)

---

1. Editors' note: On November 2, 2011, in the midst of the Occupy movement, activists organized a general strike in the city of Oakland, California. As part of it, we (a very heterogeneous "we," including, among others, the author of this article and one of the editors of this book) walked into the Port of Oakland and, in solidarity with several port workers, who raised the arms of their massive cranes, shut it down. We danced, talked, strolled around, and were fairly incredulous at the mix of calm, enthusiasm, and lack of police reaction as the sun set on the port, and we just stayed there for a few hours that night.

that we don't always grow at the same rate. There is the moment where we get our fabulous new world-changing idea, and there is—maybe—the win. And in between, there is the long haul. Maybe this is a moment to examine how we sit with the times not of big disaster or big optimism, but of small victories. I wrote this piece to capture some small moments of brilliant, successful defiance.

NOT-SO-SECRET SURVIVOR:
AMITA SWADHIN'S STRUGGLE FOR LONG-TERM ACCOUNTABILITY

In July 2012, I received an e-mail from my friend and comrade Amita Swadhin. A longtime writer and organizer in queer and South Asian communities and creator of Secret Survivors, a theatrical project about surviving childhood sexual abuse, Swadhin had just found out that her father, Vashisht Vaid, had been booked as a speaker at an event called the New World Fair outside the Queens Museum.

Vaid repeatedly raped Swadhin during her childhood, from ages four to twelve. She attempted to prosecute him as a teenager, but, because of pressure from family members, prosecutors, police officers, and social workers, he received only five years' probation and no jail time. Two cousins, an aunt, and a childhood friend all disclosed being sexually assaulted by Vaid to Swadhin, who wrote last summer in an e-mail to her friends:

> My father is now in his early 60's, and has never been held accountable in any way by his own ethnic and/or religious community (or any community, for that matter). The fact that he has now published books purporting to use "Hindu knowledge" (under the broad umbrella of "new age" and "liberation" philosophy) for social change and communal enlightenment is more than I can stand. that his books have been published by a website that seems in some way linked to the Occupy Wall Street movement is ridiculous, and that this event is taking place in front of the Queens Museum of Art, a space that has served as a cultural home base for me and for many of us is salt in the wound to say the least.

Many survivors of childhood sexual abuse—myself included—would, understandably, freeze when faced with this news. I'm sure Swadhin froze in her way. But she also asked her friends and comrades what kind of accountability action we might be willing to facilitate on the day of the event. She wrote,

> I would really love to see this man be called out publicly and be prevented from gaining more credibility as a community/spiritual leader than he has already managed to create for himself. People should know about the violence he has inflicted on generations of girls in his family and community.

Swadhin's friends and comrades responded with courage and creativity. Swadhin and supporters (including Queens Museum staff) sent an e-mail to the organizers of the New World Fair, informing them of Vaid's history of sexually assaulting women and girls in his family and asking them to remove him from the lineup with a transparent explanation of why he was removed. They also suggested screening the documentary about Secret Survivors. The e-mail was met with a frustrating response from an organizer who said that Vaid was "doing US [the festival] a favor by speaking about such fantastic esoteric knowledge which will still continue to be a part of this event, as this event is all about Evolution," and that he "[did] not know . . . what your family issues are nor do I want to be involved."

Swadhin and her supporters crowdsourced a response in days. Our wide-ranging conversation examined how, to quote Swadhin, "this case was as much about Hindu nationalism and white American racism/exotification of 'Hindu' and 'Indian' knowledge . . . and how that elevates violent opportunists like my father" as it was about how common denial and minimization of childhood sexual abuse is.

In the end, beauty was created by us. Not easily. But possibilities were expanded with everything from Amita's crisp response to the fair's organizers as they tried to backpedal:

I'm not sure I would classify this as a misunderstanding, as much as a case of The New World Fair unknowingly endorsing a convicted sex offender as the bearer of "esoteric" and "healing" knowledge, and then being unwilling to publicly admit that an egregious mistake was made.

to her assertion:

> I do not think that [the organizers] are "bad people" . . . far from it. I understand that we live in a world in which our neighbors, colleagues, spiritual guides, friends, and even family members are sometimes, unbeknownst to us, people who rape and otherwise sexually assault children. What matters most to me is not that you didn't know the truth about my father and that you fell for his presentation as a "guru" or holder of "esoteric knowledge." What matters to me is what you do now that you know.

And, small but big, people created a simple flyer. We posted it on the Facebook wall of the event and on Tumblr. We used the moment not only to prevent Vaid from speaking, but also to have open, real-time conversations with many bystanders about childhood sexual abuse. On Facebook and e-mail and in person, people engaged. Many folks' automatic response to childhood-sexual-abuse storytelling is to deny, but many folks also don't like the idea of children and adults being raped. What was crisis also became opportunity to engage, tell stories, and ask people to think about what change, accountability, and justice could look like.

In an article written about these events by Bushra Rehman for *The Feminist Wire*, Swadhin said,

> I hope other survivors of Child Sexual Assault are encouraged to speak up and speak out after seeing my example. Yet I am also conscious it's taken me 20 years (the past three of which have been spent publicly performing my survivorship) to gain the personal power, courage, and

network of support to feel safe taking this kind of public step. And even now, I struggle with very real anxiety about retaliation from my father against me or other members of my family.

I'm writing this months after all this occurred. I'm exhausted after a twenty-hour journey back home across the ocean after visiting the place where my grandparents are buried. It took me twenty years to get there. I'm thinking about how slow and huge this work of crafting our own justice is. How these campaigns occur—organized in a flash through Facebook and e-mails, through relationships, networks, and love—and how easy it is for them to disappear when the event's page gets archived. How powerful and important it is to record these journeys, the small and huge pebbles of which will add up to a pathway that will lead us home.

Everyday Actions

By Sharon Hoshida

I have marched, chanted, organized, died-in, carried banners, CODEPINKed, lobbied legislators, fasted, and editorialized for peace since 1968. As my sixtieth birthday approached, I thought about how others mark the culmination of a decade by throwing lavish parties or attempting heart-stopping feats like skydiving. I decided to shed my hair as an overt gesture for peace.

Fortuitously, Genevieve Erin O'Brien, a queer Vietnamese Irish American performance artist, e-mailed me asking for support for an upcoming performance. Her latest one-woman show, *The Monk Who Licked Me*, which evolved from her visit to Vietnam, would end as she shaved her head as a commitment to peace. She needed a location for a "durational performance" where she would offer others the opportunity to become warriors for peace, shaving their heads in this public space.

At first I thought shaving my head would be an interesting way to demonstrate my personal commitment to peace. Then I

Originally published in *make/shift* no. 3 (spring/summer 2008)

thought of a thousand reasons *not* to take this action. *What if I don't like the shape of my head? Hmm, my driver's license expires next week—what about my new picture?* The shedding of one's hair is a significant way to demonstrate a humbling of one's public self. I started taking small steps to eliminate the excuses.

Soon I was in the audience at Erin's show, traveling with her on her homecoming through the countryside, cities, and temples of Vietnam. My work for peace began with the war that devastated her motherland, destroying the people and defoliating the earth. While she described how the resurgence of life and spirit and greenery has transformed the landscape, I couldn't help but think of the pattern of death and destruction being repeated today in Iraq and Afghanistan and, all too soon, if the madmen continue their reign, worldwide.

The next morning, Erin asked me, "Are you going to shave your head?" I hedged, shrugged my shoulders. Yet, in my heart I knew I would say yes. Yes to solidarity with Erin, this inspired and serious artist. Yes to peace, Gandhi, the Tibetan nuns who sang their sacred music at sunset, the Dalai Lama, monks who immolated themselves in the name of peace. Yes in solidarity with my sisters of survival: we survived bouts of cancer; some fought and lost every hair on their heads in the process. Yes in solidarity with transgender folk who face harassment and danger for the audacity of presenting themselves in nonconforming ways. Yes, I stepped up to the chair, let my locks fall to the ground.

Now I wonder: Is it enough to shave and let grow, or do I keep it shorn until the war ends? If so, I hope that by the time I am laid to rest, my hair will drape down to my shoulders, so that I might truly rest in peace.

What's Pink Got to Do with It?

Articulating Feminist Resistance to War and Militarism

By Christine E. Petit

In the summer of 2005, I found myself strutting down a runway wearing little more than lingerie. Written on the front of my light-pink ensemble was "give Bush the pink slip." The audience clapped, but the real crowd pleasers were the "no peace, no pussy" pink slip that followed, a Spirit of Justice costume that included peace-sign nipple pasties, and the "detain this!" undies flashed by a model/activist as she did her little turn on the catwalk. The theme of this "progressive fashion show"? Women are just too sexy for war.

I spent a year volunteering for and researching the women-initiated and -led peace and social-justice group CODEPINK: Women for Peace.[1] And although I found myself inspired by the creative work of the women involved with the group, I was simultaneously put off by the fact that their

Originally published in *make/shift* no. 1 (spring/summer 2007)

1. CODEPINK's brand of women's peace organizing was the focus of my master's thesis, "Feminist Activism or Feminine Activism? CODEPINK and the Politics of Femininity," completed in the fall of 2005.

actions often highlighted women's traditional roles as mothers, caretakers, sex objects, and consumers.

The tactics used by CODEPINK and these articulations of women's resistance to war are by no means new. Biological and cultural explanations for women's pacifism have been around for as long as women have been resisting war. And that's a long time, according to professor and former *National Women's Studies Association Journal* editor Maggie McFadden, who in "Women and War, Women and Peace" traces this trajectory from the actions of women in ancient Sumer, Egypt, and Greece to the women's peace organizations of today. But the feminist in me gets squeamish at the suggestion that women are somehow innately more peaceful than men or that it's the job of women to clean up after "their" bellicose men.

In "The Truth about Women and Peace," Jodi York articulates some of the critiques of these approaches. Biological explanations make working for peace just another manifestation of "women's work"—something women *should* be doing because as mothers or potential mothers it is in their interest to preserve life. Cultural explanations focus more on gender socialization and call for a revaluation of traits associated with women (for example, being cooperative and nurturing). But this approach reinforces the dichotomous gender relations that underpin patriarchy and its partner in crime, heterosexism.

While the women-and-peace narrative has some cultural cachet—indeed, when the antiwar movement does get any play, mainstream media outlets love to show the CODEPINK ladies donning their pink attire—is this a *feminist* response to war? CODEPINK and other women's antiwar projects certainly have feminist elements, but a feminist analysis of war and militarism is often missing.

Take the Nobel Women's Initiative and the Lysistrata Project, for example. The Nobel Women's Initiative began last year when six female Nobel Peace laureates came together to promote women's rights and peace. So far, it seems that their main mechanisms for achieving these goals are a series of UN resolutions and plans for a biyearly conference to "ensure meaningful dialogue and networking by women's rights activists around the world."

The theater-based Lysistrata Project, on the other hand, is a much more grassroots way of interjecting women's voices into the debate around war. The project encourages people to do readings of *Lysistrata*, a Greek comedy in which women on both sides of the Peloponnesian War unite for peace by refusing sexual relations with men until they stop the war. Sounds kind of clever, right? I suppose. That is, if you are willing to accept that only men enjoy sex, that sex is the only means of power available to women, that sex only happens between women and men, and, of course (again), that men are to war as women are to peace.

So, while these modes of women's peace organizing are feminist in that they center women as political actors, the feminisms that interest me go beyond narrow political processes and normativity to challenge the systems of oppression that propel us into one war after another. The good news is that many feminists are doing just that.

Just look at Idan Halili. Faced with the compulsory military service mandated to all Israelis, Halili asked for an exemption based on a rejection of militarism informed by her feminist beliefs. In her letter to the Israeli army, Halili emphasized how the military—through its hierarchical and male-dominated structure, distortion of gender roles, culture of sexual harassment, and connection with domestic violence—contributes to the marginalization of and violence against women. After serving two weeks in a military prison, Halili was excused from conscription, but not because she was given conscientious-objector status. Instead, the committee deciding on her case ruled that her feminist values made her "unfit" to serve.

In her essay "The Eagle Has Talons: One Queer Soldier's Peek at Life in the Trenches," in *We Don't Need Another Wave: Dispatches from the Next Generation of Feminists*, Jessica A. Stein writes, "The feminist struggle [within the U.S. military] isn't only about something as simple as women in combat, promotions, sexual harassment, or 'don't ask, don't tell.' It's not only about missiles and bombs. It's about the foundations of power those weapons defend: houses formed around the belief that some people have more value than others and so have the right to exploit them until each person is subsequently militarized." Stein asserts that cohesiveness within the military is forged through "racism, sexism, classism, ecological degradation, and the debasement of every one of us."

INCITE! Women of Color Against Violence, a national organization of U.S. feminists of color, makes connections between sexism, racism, and militarism in its campaign against war, occupation, and colonization: "Soldiers are seen as 'manly' and the third world people under attack as 'womanly.' This breeds sexist and racist hatred and violence against people living under invasion and anybody that is not 'super-aggressive manly.'"

Even when war is waged in the name of ideals such as "democracy" and "women's liberation," we see the devastating effects of militarism on the most marginalized sectors of society. Zoya, a member of the Revolutionary Association of the Women of Afghanistan, wonders: "When the entire nation is living under the shadow of guns and warlordism, how can its women enjoy their basic freedoms?"

If I were to conclude this piece by saying there's no room for pink lingerie in the peace movement, then I'd be no better (well, not much, anyway) than those who are constantly devaluing anything "womanly." That's not what I'm advocating. The antiwar movement needs creativity. But our creative performances need to upset rather than reinscribe the norms of capitalism, white supremacy, and patriarchy that drive war. Now that's something my pussy can get on board with.

How That Poetry Is Also about Us

By Heather Bowlan

It's easy to conflate identity in poetry with narrative, with story—but to say poetry that investigates identity is "about" its author, implying ties to that writer's biography or sense of self, keeps us safe as readers from asking how that poetry is also about us. Identity is necessarily constructed, in part, by stories, the ones we've lived, the ones shared as memories by loved ones, the ones given to and imposed on us by the larger communities and cultures we inhabit. Some of these are similar, almost the same if we don't look closely, but they layer up inside of us, and we wear their delicate mesh of visible, invisible layers as we navigate the world. The theme of identity links several new collections by poets who blend craft, culture, and experience, and who offer their readers a textured, often fragmented, often violent, and still very beautiful world.

Religion, mythology, and archetypes populate these poems, although these ancient and venerated stories are often revised, interrupted, and, in some cases, rejected. In the surreal, sutured space of Vi Khi Nao's

Originally published in *make/shift* no. 20 (summer/fall 2017)

The Old Philosopher, the speaker inhabits the world of the Bible with as much authority as Jeremiah or Mary Magdalene, and Canaan's fields, rural Vietnam, and the painted trees housed in a modern-art museum are equally likely to serve as landscape. God is an active presence, even a character, in these poems, who "superimposes his imagination" onto the speaker's body ("Snow"), and the speaker, in response, is full of irreverence as well as belief. As the poem's title might suggest, sex is the subject of "Biblical Flesh," but Nao pushes past the easy clichés and crafts a hallucinogenic orgy: "Your toes shake their heads like guests at a one-star hotel You book one night in the Promised Land of the Israelites and wait for your 3rd lover to arrive."

Placing the poem in what is now Israel and Palestine, and beginning with "What is torture?" Nao raises, but doesn't answer, the questions of consent and complicity that inform the necessary tension for her speaker's kink, and simultaneously raises them on a larger scale, posing them to her readers. She ends the poem, "Then you turn to Lot's wife and ask, 'Was the view worth it? Is it still gorgeous?'"

In her collection *(A)Live Heart*, Imani Sims also explores the tensions and pleasures of reclaimed knowledge and story from western narratives. These lyric poems don't shy from naming the sources of Black queer women's pain and anger (prison, hunger, violence), and they evoke transformation and magic as sources of resilience. Sims revisions the Medusa myth, which, as she indicates in a footnote, was itself repurposed by the Greeks, who incorporated and subordinated older traditions' goddess worship into their culture. In "Medusa Bone," it's the speaker's heart that turns to stone for survival:

> Original medusa, turned goddess,
> All snaked ventricles swinging
> Between ribs,
>
> Writhing fortress.

Women's bodies in these poems, often portrayed in fragmented syntax, are both "chest / full of fists / and uninterrupted tears" ("Little Red") and "unflowered bud, dry smoke / high, rolling laughter"

("Kumquat"). For these witches, the very things that break them, rebuild them; their lives provide the necessary ingredients for spell-casting.

Language often edges toward incantation in Kimberly Alidio's expansive book *After projects the resound*. Alidio investigates both the cultural history and the lived experience of her speakers' queer Filipina identity through etymology, politics, and pop culture. The language of these poems carries a frenetic energy—this poetry does not aim to engage readers, it confronts us. Take "AKA" and "Fermented AKA ferment," list poems of different words for annatto (typically used for seasoning and food coloring) and ketchup, respectively, which appear early in the collection. Organized by country of origin and/or ingredient lists, the poems wind their way through colonization, submerging the dominant word or recipe in a cacophony of difference.

Throughout *After projects the resound*, the poems' speakers challenge the legacy of western colonial practices with humor and anguish. This is most arresting when the poems address the speakers' complicated positions as women who are aware of institutional oppression but unable to operate outside of it:

> LOL YOUR PINAY SELF
> LOL YOUR SUBCONSCIOUS DECOLONIAL
>   INDIGENEITY
> LOL RECOVERY AS AN ESCAPE HATCH FROM REAL
>   NEGOTIATIONS
> LOL CARING THAT WHITE PEOPLE THINK OUR
>   BODIES ARE CHEAP
> LOL THINKING ONLY WHITE PEOPLE THINK OUR
>   BODIES ARE CHEAP
> LOL THINKING WHITE POETS MATTER AT ALL

These lines, part of a much longer list in "All the Pinays are straight, all the queers are Pinoy, but some of us," are powerful because of their self-directed anxiety, heightened by the text-speak and all caps, which builds with every scorned emotional and intellectual defense against oppressive violence.

The very fact of whiteness as the assumed dominant racial identity is taken to task in Vivek Shraya's *even this page is white*. Here, skin is the subject, and the speaker explores the reality of living brown and queer in western culture, while pointing out the limitations of white identity. Some poems incorporate found language from book titles, social media, online petitions, and celebrity quotes to touch on everything from #oscarssowhite to the literary canon to Kanye West.

"The Origins of Skin," a long poem in the book's second half, uses the frame of a creation myth for human skin to mark the divisions between a brown speaker and a white "you," who sometimes reads as one person, sometimes as any and all white readers of the poem. From the opening lines, "would you believe me if i told you the purpose of skin / is not utility but unity?" the speaker attempts to connect with "you," but the awareness of physical difference always marks a boundary: "you said the word *my* followed by *skin* / you felt nearest and furthest from / me."

Shraya makes a similar move, grounded in contemporary questions on the "invisibility" of whiteness and cultural appropriation, in "the one thing you can do." The poem is dedicated to Yi-Fen Chou, the pseudonym of Michael Derrick Hudson, a white man whose work was published in 2015's *Best American Poetry* and who claimed to use the pseudonym to improve his chances for publication. "use your name / name your colour / over and over," the speaker instructs; "white is not poison / just your disavowal of it / over and over."

Christopher Soto's poems deftly chart personal longing and grief and the connections and losses shared by those labeled as outsiders— by family, by the police, by well-meaning allies. In his chapbook *Sad Girl Poems*, the speaker mourns the suicide of his lover Rory while mapping the larger landscape of his life as a queer latin@. Backslashes and brackets erupt throughout these poems, drawing attention to punctuation as a boundary and simultaneously interrupting and emphasizing the language that overflows its limits:

The night he died // I went to the beach. Waves beat statically
Against the fins of mermaids.

I tried to call his cellphone [but he didn't answer]. My body was
A match // His memory was a flame. ("Crush a Pearl [Its
    Powder]")

The implied, painful redaction of "[but he didn't answer]"—the potential for this loss to disappear from the world—is echoed in Soto's use
of brackets across the collection. In "Home [Chaos Theory]," brackets
denote blunt truths from the speaker's experience of homelessness, an
experience that is rendered invisible within the category of "the homeless," even to his friends, "As if I had never been homeless. / [As if I were
not sitting // directly beside them]." When the speaker observes San
Francisco police harassing a woman they believe to be homeless, the
brackets reinforce the danger of silence in that moment:

& the tourists watched

> [As the police walked towards her]
> [As the police went to grab her]
> [As the woman continued yelling]

Soto builds a forceful refusal of invisibility crafted in a hypervisible
text. Elizabeth J. Colen employs a similar strategy in her claustrophobic
novel in prose poems, *What Weaponry*. The book catalogs the destruction
of a couple's relationship in a town whose inhabitants aren't welcoming of
the couple's fluid sexuality. Like Soto, Colen draws attention to her text
to render the unsaid, said. Bolded text appears throughout the poems, a
kind of ghost poem that forms slowly and heightens the tension building
between the lovers. Through these fragments, Colen maps the internalized violence of alienation and othering: "And it takes me a minute to
remember what we've talked about. *The dead*. It's always the dead. I don't
know why any of this should make you smile, but **your face breaks open**
like a crowd at a sporting event" ("Shot-Silk Effect, No. 3").
    These interruptions are most jarring when the words in bolded text
are themselves fragmented, built by half words and letters that form an

insistent undercurrent within a poem. In "Inside the Night Museum," this emerges as a disjointed, strangled repetition of the word "still":

> Century-old storefronts explode like Roman candles, white smoke lines townie lungs, water flows uphill from spent hoses, slickening the streets, throwing street light back at the sky . . . How to spread even after everyone's seen. How to **still** warm. Coffee circle over one yellow square. Stain on grape applique, auburn oblong like blood or chocolate or mud from some tiny fist . . . Scream in the woods like some rush to forgiveness. Creak in your arm, pulling splinters.

This broken language, straining toward meaning, occurs most often when the couple is directly confronted by their hostile environment, and as that hostility becomes so pervasive it infects every living and nonliving thing around them. The attempt to push through and find connection asserts itself again and again in this novel of dissolution—something that can be said of all the collections reviewed here. In this moment, when it's clearer than ever that our identities, when framed by others, can be used as weapons against us, this group of writers shows us a different way, creating their own narratives around identity, building community where it's been denied.

This Might Be the First Time

An Installment of the Column "Nobody Passes"

By Mattilda Bernstein Sycamore

I don't know what's possible, as my mother and I drive through pitch-dark suburbs that I don't even recognize until we get right near their house—did they always have those same lights at the end of the driveway? The trees are even bigger than I remember, driveway cracked in even more places.

In the family room with my father in his hospital bed, I stand there kind of frozen with my hand on my hip. I can see myself seeing him, looking at him like I'm daring everything. Every now and then, my father gets agitated and his hands move around like they're part of a different person, my sister Lauren asks: are you okay? Do you need something to drink? Lauren, her boyfriend, and the attendant are watching *Survivor* and I glance over occasionally to glimpse various almost-naked athletic male bodies and women in bikinis—someone just lost something, and I guess people like this show because it's like porn.

If I'm trying to establish some form of narrative here, crying is that narrative and everything else is around it—crying is

Originally published in *make/shift* no. 1 (spring/summer 2007)

elemental, the rest is important too but I can't reestablish the order with all this crying. I say to my father: what did you think of my letter? He says I don't think I got it. I say would you like me to read it to you now? He says yes.

Can I say something about my father's voice? Feeble is not the word I would use, though I can see others invoking it. Can I possibly choose innocent? Softer and more childish than before. I say to my mother: could you get the letter?

My mother, standing at the head of the bed, her eyes almost squinting from panicked determination: that is not possible. Me, standing at the foot of the bed: Karin thinks I'm going to give you a stroke. My mother: there are other things to talk about besides the letter. Is this when I start sobbing? It makes more sense here, if here is about sense. This is the moment made for the movies, I can feel my chest arching forward, head back—this is the fight-or-flight reflex, I mean the fight part. I say: you're just trying to control his death because you couldn't control your life with him. And the tears are pouring down my face like armor. This is the moment when I'm cold like the way I survived them except that I'm also crying—it's both at the same time and my father looks up at my mother and says: is that true, Karin?

But what are the words? Once my mother, my sister, my sister's boyfriend, and the attendant finally leave, I'm crying and my father's crying and are we crying together? I'm saying: when I first heard that you had cancer, it surprised me because for so long I had wanted any trace of you to disappear from my life, but I found myself wishing that I could save you. I realized that I still had some hope that you'd come to terms with sexually abusing me, that you would acknowledge it and then we could have some mundane conversation about publishers or something else from my life I thought you might be interested in.

I see his face tense up into a grimace when I say sexually abuse, but where I'm really crying, probably the most except for at the beginning, is when I'm saying: I wish you could acknowledge sexually abusing me, because it would make it easier for me to go on living. I'm asking for something that he could give me. A few tears drip down his face and he says thank you for sharing your letter and then there are so many layers to my sobbing: there's holding the chest while spasming anyway; there's tears gliding smoothly down skin; there's speaking with tears in eyes, in face, in vision, inside everything.

What I want to do is to touch his arm, softly, his skin. It feels intimate and nurturing and dangerous and right now I'm okay with all of these sensations. At some point I say that I've learned there are other ways to be strong besides holding everything in—and of course here there is more sobbing, sobbing is the texture of the air, sobbing is the feeling of this room, sobbing here it feels like strength.

My father says something that I don't understand, it sounds like: you're a very compelling liar. But he doesn't look like that's what he's saying, I ask him to repeat himself but he doesn't—talking is difficult for him, a lot of the time we're together his eyes are closed and I ask him if he's tired, he says no. I say is it because of the drugs, and he doesn't say anything. I say your eyes are closed, but you're listening, right? He nods. This might be the first time he's ever listened to me.

At one point, there's a single tear dripping down his cheek—I touch it with my finger, then brush his hand softly again. It's almost sexual in this moment, even if it's scary to say that. When I leave the room, I don't feel afraid of the house anymore—that chimney where I'd imagine myself floating away, away from him splitting me open, right now it just looks like a chimney, I mean a fireplace leading to a chimney.

Bring the Troops Home?

On Family Violence, Economic Fear, and War

By Jessi Lee Jackson

"Support our troops. Bring them home!"

When I hear the familiar antiwar chant, I think about my enlisted brother and the home we shared growing up. I never know how to tell the story of his involvement in this war. In one version, my brother is a pawn in a bigger game, choosing to go into the Army because it was the only economic option. In another version, my brother is a perpetrator who has turned to violent acts and institutions as a way to feel powerful. Both stories are true, and both connect to experiences we shared growing up together in small, poor, rural towns—experiences of economic despair and violence.

THE ECONOMIC NARRATIVE

I grew up in the 1980s and 1990s in the Upper Peninsula of Michigan, moving from one rural town to another each time the factory my father worked in closed or downsized. In 1991, when I was twelve, we settled down in Iron River, a small town that had been steadily shrinking since the last

Originally published in *make/shift* no. 5 (spring/summer 2009)

iron mines closed in the 1970s. My father worked in a small factory that contracted with the Defense Department. Besides the ones at this factory, pretty much the only other jobs were in logging, at the prison outside of town, and in the public schools. When I graduated from high school, I fled to college out of state.

Unlike me, my brother Jim[1] didn't leave northern Michigan. He got into a college in the U.P. but drank too much, skipped all of his classes, and got kicked out. He worked long hours for cash at an "adult bookstore." The guy who worked the job before him committed suicide in the upstairs apartment. It was a part of Jim's job to clean up the mess. He washed the blood off the walls, hauled the splattered mattress to the dump, and moved into the apartment.

My parents took out loans to pay for another try at college for my brother, but he continued failing until reenrolling wasn't an option. Jim's girlfriend Mary got pregnant, and they decided to have the baby and get married.

The responsibility of a child sent my brother looking for legitimate work. He wanted to stay in the U.P., but in 2001 it had some of the worst unemployment rates in Michigan. He worked at Wal-Mart on the overnight shift. In 2002, after a year and a half of negotiating welfare benefits, working full-time, and borrowing money from our parents, Jim started getting pursued by a military recruiter. He was drawn to the idea of family health-insurance benefits and better pay. He enlisted in the spring of 2003, just days after the beginning of the Iraq war. Mary and Jim told their son, "Daddy's going away for a little bit. He's going to be a soldier." After nine weeks of basic training, the whole family moved onto Jim's base in upstate New York.

For a long time, Jim didn't get deployed. He got promoted, moved his way up through the ranks, enjoyed base housing, and bought a big TV. Jim and his family moved to a base in Germany. They drove to Paris and visited German castles. My parents, despite their ambivalence about his choice to join up, were proud that their son was traveling. He reenlisted, worrying that to leave would be to fall back into the same bitter economic situation he had escaped. In the fall of 2007, my brother was deployed to the war in Iraq.

---

1. I've changed some names for this essay.

By that time, most of the boys I grew up with, and a fair number of the girls, had already done a tour in Iraq. My father's friends swap stories about their kids at war—stories about enduring the heat in fatigues or staying in demolished mansions. There are also things they don't talk about: Abu Ghraib, imperialism, and violence.

THE VIOLENCE NARRATIVE

My older brother was violent toward me. Maybe every younger sibling could say those words. Because violence between siblings is such a typical family dynamic, I have a hard time knowing how to understand my experience. For a long time, I believed that it wasn't a big deal. My family had dismissed me as a "whiner," and I thought that talking about the violence was complaining. However, as I've grown older, I've been able to take the violence more seriously.

When I talk about the dynamics of violence, it's difficult to walk the tightrope between sensationalizing it and downplaying it. If I try to make my case that the violence was "real" and counted, I may be overemphasizing my fear or the extent of the physical damage. If I simply state that my older brother "picked on me," I ignore moments when I was terrified for my life. Tied up in the impossibility of telling the truth, sometimes I can't stand to speak about it at all.

My brother's violence ranged from spontaneous to calculated. He studied both karate and aikido, and I never knew when I might suddenly be swept into a painful hold. When he was a teenager, he began holding knives to my throat. When he was angry, he would act out with quick force, pushing me down the stairs or twisting my arm until I cried in pain. At other times, he was dead calm. Then it felt more like torture—like he was playing with his power.

I remember his attacks, how I would flatten my voice: "That hurts. You're hurting me and you need to stop." I wouldn't fight back, fearing I'd provoke more violence. I told myself that it wasn't as bad as what many of my friends were experiencing—I wasn't being raped, I wasn't being beaten with belts. It wasn't my father doing it. I didn't count the violence as real.

My parents never recognized the violence as real, either. Instead, they dealt with the problem in a way they probably considered evenhanded—instructing me not to whine and Jim not to "be mean." I don't think they purposely decided to leave me at risk—it was just too painful to see the violence. They didn't have any tools for loving their son and still holding him accountable for his violence. Perhaps they blamed themselves: when we followed my dad's job around the U.P., my brother (the shy computer geek) suffered from intense bullying in each new town. My mom, depressed and disconnected from her friends and family, didn't feel powerful enough to act. My father, a survivor of violence at the hands of his own father, now tried to avoid anger and conflict.

I understand some of the reasons my family didn't deal with the violence. Still, it was painful to be in an environment where I didn't feel safe. It took me years to develop a language for the ways I had been hurt. When I turn toward my family, the words I searched for years to find still soften and slip from my mind. To them, I am an oxymoron: a survivor of family violence from a family that didn't have any. My experience is unintelligible.

When my brother was deployed to Iraq, I found myself uncomfortably inside the demographic of "soldiers' families." The language of concern for my brother's safety is easily accessible, so familiar that it is simply assumed in every social interaction. Most of the people I encounter in my community and friendship circles are working with the understanding that we want to "support the troops by bringing them home." They check in with me in their serious voices: "How is your brother?"

I never know what to say. At times, I leverage his status for radical or class credibility. It gives me a certain weight in antiwar discussions to have a brother in Iraq. All the while, though, I wonder if my "family member" opinion would hold as much weight if people knew about the violence. Complicated circumstances make people less convenient as tokens.

At other times, I'm annoyed by the assumption that we should all be so concerned about my brother's safety. The lack of concern about my safety as a child feels even worse when I contrast it with the current focus on my brother's safety. People I haven't talked with about my family history can be shocked by my cold response to their concern. To them, my brother is just some kid who got suckered into a pointless war. We have a cultural understanding of what that means, and an antiwar script that paints him as a helpless victim.

But even when I'm angry, I'm concerned. I want my brother to live through this war. I want this for him so that he might someday have the opportunity to unlearn violence. I also want this for myself so that I can have years to work through what happened without feeling pressured to attempt confrontations or reconciliations before I'm ready. I want to believe that my life can eventually transcend the violence. I want my brother to live.

ON SAFETY AND SHAME

My family is a case example of the connection between state violence and family violence. Participation in both is one way to respond to fear and shame. My brother was the target of intense bullying, and his victimization of me was related to his own experience of feeling powerless. Later, ashamed of not succeeding in a limited economy, Jim chose to make himself available to fight other people's wars. These things were supposed to prove that he was powerful and successful.

Unfortunately for my brother, none of these choices addressed that underlying fear of being poor, weak, wrong, or powerless. In most cases, they layered more shame over the top. Jim cannot be proud of spending his teenage years beating up a girl. He's also skeptical about the war in Iraq, aware that he's risking his life for someone else's profits. In each instance, his responses give him more reasons to feel foolish, leaving him angrier at himself and the world.

He's a sucker in this story—it's not primarily his wealth that he's building by putting his life at risk. But he's the sucker who's pulling the trigger, and I won't bind him too tightly to the economic narrative that erases his agency. Violence is more than an economic act. Jim had a choice. He chose the Army because he was afraid and ashamed to remain poor. Ignoring that choice erases the possibility that, in the future, he will make a different choice.

I know the odds are slim. My brother has been at war, in one way or another, for most of his life. He has been willing to respond to his fear and shame by becoming the victimizer, participating in family violence as well as state-sanctioned violence. This war provides a language about my brother's safety, while there is still little that can be said in casual conversation to recognize the people he has hurt. He needs to be encouraged to find alternatives to violence. Coming home could be the first step on a nonviolent path for soldiers like my brother, but for that to happen they will have to think of themselves as more than victims or heroes. They will have to question their choices and learn new ways of responding to economic and interpersonal shame. Creating peace is going to take much more than simply bringing my brother home.

Beyond Borders
Haneen Maikey of alQaws

By Jessica Hoffmann

Haneen Maikey is a cofounder and director of alQaws[1] for Sexual and Gender Diversity in Palestinian Society, a group of LGBTQ Palestinian activists working to transform ideas around gender and sexual diversity and aiming for broad social justice—which inherently includes resisting and challenging the occupation of Palestine. Maikey is based in Jerusalem, and I was lucky enough to speak with her in November 2015 while she was in Los Angeles for a few speaking engagements.

—Jessica Hoffmann

JH: Can you talk about your own political development?

HM: What is really interesting is that I politicized my Palestinian identity way after I started to understand my sexual identity as a political issue. I grew up in a tiny village at the Lebanese border. It was your high school, your friends, your family, that's it. I had no

Originally published in *make/shift* no. 17 (summer/fall 2015)

1. "alQaws" means "the rainbow."

interaction with Israelis. Identity is by definition reactionary, because you define it according to how the other perceives you.

I moved to Jerusalem when I was eighteen. Jerusalem is complex and full of contradictions. It's full of settlers and Zionists—you face the occupation and settler colonialism and separation on a daily basis. I went during the "good years"—late Oslo. It was only when the second intifada took place [starting in 2000] that the dots were really connected for me. Before that, I was exploring my sexuality sort of parallel to, separate from, understanding my Palestinian identity.

AlQaws first existed as a sort of LGBT support group within a Jewish organization. AlQaws started to separate from Jewish organizations parallel to what happened on the personal level. We all dated Jewish women back then—Israelis—and suddenly on the personal level of relationships, and also on the community, social, and political levels, things were moving apart. It's a broader political process. We have to see queer organizing in the context of what happened to civil society in Palestine and what happened to my generation, which is the second-intifada generation.

Our radical politics were shaped by these political, personal, community interactions on a daily basis. It's not like we were just happy and drunk and wrote this radical manifesto. It came out of ten years of repeated experience. In this learning process, sometimes our analysis wasn't radical and was problematic politically. Sometimes we made mistakes, sometimes we normalized,[2] sometimes we didn't understand our bodies as colonized.

What is the radical politic you all developed?

AlQaws is a group of Palestinian LGBTQ activists who came together to work to dismantle sexual and gender hierarchy, and open a broader

2. The Palestinian Campaign for the Academic and Cultural Boycott of Israel (PACBI) has defined "normalization" specifically in a Palestinian and Arab context as "the participation in any project, initiative or activity, in Palestine or internationally, that aims (implicitly or explicitly) to bring together Palestinians (and/or Arabs) and Israelis (people or institutions) without placing as its goal resistance to and exposure of the Israeli occupation and all forms of discrimination and oppression against the Palestinian people." This is the definition endorsed by the BDS National Committee (BNC).

discussion about sexuality in Palestine. AlQaws is not a "gay" organization. There is a tension between a global gay-rights movement that says we are one big pink family and groups who work on sexual oppression and focus on local contexts. We also believe that discussing gender and sexual oppression in isolation instead of in the context of Israeli occupation, apartheid structure, Nakba strategies, and displacement is unethical. All of these things are materialized oppressions in the daily life of any Palestinian, and you cannot separate sexuality from this.

We also have an anti-normalization policy. AlQaws doesn't cooperate with people who don't have any clear position on the occupation, apartheid, and Jewish supremacy.

And we believe that current political analysis needs to be queered up. We need a new lens about sexuality and gender. The international community and political powers are using gay rights to divide the world into who's progressive and who's not, who's modern and who's not. We think that sexual analysis is really important to any liberation struggle now and in the future.

How does alQaws make the connection between sexual and gender oppression and colonial oppression?

We are focusing on the dialectic relationship between these: what it means to be colonized bodies, colonized queers, or a colonized society. The colonizer is working hard to erase any progressive forces in our society, including how much we are an open society, inclusive, open enough and free enough to discuss controversial issues. It's not random that it's hard to talk about these issues. I'm not saying that objectively Palestinian society is so open, but the construct of homophobia and un-acceptance of LGBTQ issues, minorities, and sexual and gender diversity—it's also fed by colonial structures.

We are based and started in Jerusalem, and it's an ideological decision to stay in Jerusalem, because it's the most marginalized socially, economically, and politically. Palestinians from Jerusalem are facing real economic and access challenges, starting with high unemployment and displacement threats by house demolitions and more. We deal with these issues on a daily basis. We are the only

Palestinian organization working in historical Palestine. We work in different parts of Palestine, divided by checkpoints, the apartheid wall, borders. How do you build a community that can have local leadership but also a strong national leadership with the understanding that these borders are impacting our lives, dividing our families, impacting our mobility?

And we recognize pinkwashing as a colonial strategy. Pinkwashing is a PR campaign funded and coordinated by the Israeli government in cooperation with a lot of U.S.-based right-wing Zionist organizations and Israeli LGBT organizations. It uses gay rights to promote a progressive, fun, fabulous image of Israel, and actually aims to divert attention from Israel's war crimes and violation of international law. It aims to dehumanize and undermine the Palestinian people and Arabs in general, promoting them as homophobic, barbaric, and backwards. It aims to make people forget that this is a colonized/colonizer dynamic, and it becomes instead, you're progressive and I'm killing my gays.

Palestinian queers also internalize this. It's a very powerful means of making Zionism—which is a racist ethnic ideology—more appealing to gay people. Pinkwashing not only promotes racist ideas about Palestinians to the world but also relies on the fact that racism and Islamophobia already exist in this world and in other gay communities. We need to talk about why gay communities are embracing the Israeli campaign of gay people coming to their international Pride parade. It's based on gay rights and a western framework, reinforcing the isolation of gay identity from other identities and concealing the structure of inequalities and injustice that makes certain bodies—Jewish bodies—more accepted and more valued than other bodies. This is why we need to deconstruct this western hegemony and gay-rights approach, because a lot of oppression is happening in the name of this single-politics approach.

Rights as an approach is not something I personally and alQaws as a collective relate to. Israel was based on a right of self-determination. So we should reject this framework. And what does it even mean to demand gay rights—from whom? From the occupier? Or the occupier arm in the West Bank? What does that mean to get your gay rights without getting your human rights, or dignity, or basic food, work, basic conditions of being a human being? We think in Palestinian society and without a broader critique, "gay rights" is an unethical approach.

What is a more ethical, locally determined approach?

We have our bubbles of radical Palestinian queer activists, but most things are happening outside of our bubbles. People are living their lives, and they don't need alQaws or NGOs or movements. People are impacted firsthand by issues relating to colonization *and* sexuality.

We are also not taking ourselves outside of this square. We say LGBTQs in Palestine are inside a society and impacted by everything the society as a whole is impacted by. We also have another thing [queerness], but we think this is a thing that also should be owned by the society. We all should talk about how we are oppressed sexually, how our gender as a social construct is controlling our bodies and our roles in the society, dividing us, and how we all as individuals are oppressing each other in terms of gender and sexuality. This feminist approach makes sense to people. It puts them in a position that they have responsibility, and they can have a moment of talking about what is our collective responsibility as a society. We are not saying it's easy to change, but we are opening these spaces so people can think with us about solutions.

In your lecture you discussed how the globalized gay model is based on a very individualistic narrative and notion of identity— I'm ashamed, I come out, now I'm proud—and how that is actually not universally applicable.

For many LGBT groups and organizations, the global gay model is clear, easy, and accessible. The focus on a single issue (homophobia) is tempting, because it is easier than thinking about the complexity of our experiences and how our bodies and sexualities are used and abused by different layers of power. This is why we see events like IDAHO [the International Day Against Homophobia] becoming popular among Arab queer groups that instead of exploring local models were pushed into framing their struggle as against homophobia.

Homophobia is one of the social attitudes or expressions that we need to deal with and counter all the time, but this is not the struggle. There is homophobia in Palestine as everywhere. It's not a rooted sickness in our society like the Israeli government loves to threaten the western world with. Homophobia is a visible attitude. How can you discuss homophobia in a society that doesn't discuss sexuality? The homophobia framework doesn't work in Palestine, which doesn't mean we don't fight it as part of a deeper and more holistic cultural and social-change strategy.

Also, what does it mean to come out, or to have individual visibility? We can see with different parts of Palestinian society—women will not tell their parents they are sleeping with men, or lesbians will not even be visible in feminist organizations, but they will be activists and have a lot of impact and power. In a collective society, your name is your family's name, and as long as you don't touch it, you can do whatever you want (with the right privileges). Your society, your family, is a big thing. For many people it is the base. People love to live in their village and be close to their families. It's not something I or the movement should or can take from them, or provide an alternative to. I can't provide these strong communities that can also support, be warm, give you money, be with you.

"Gay rights" has become the new global measure of whether different nation-states and peoples are progressive or not. It's the new "women's rights." It's a colonized/colonizer dynamic, this savior complex where LGBT activists go to "save" people in other places. In order for me to convince you to be saved, I need to convince you to hate your own community. This disconnects people from their own communities and societies, and it is really risky.

You said the other night, "We are privileged to have no government to work with."

I see other groups in the Middle East all the time working with ministries and holding governments accountable and all of this shit. It's like, who's accountable to who? What is this relationship? Because working under two governments that we perceive as illegitimate—Israel and the

Palestinian Authority—made us free to think about other strategies. We are not busy doing policy change and forgetting the grassroots and community building. A lot of people would critique us: you should work with government, you should work with religious institutions, you should work with these big figures. And I'm like, we are not interested. We are not even interested to work with the old Left or the old generation of civil society. We are really interested to work with new progressive forces, young and new activists, student groups—we are modest enough to say this is the capacity we have, and the things we know we're strong at, and we want to focus there.

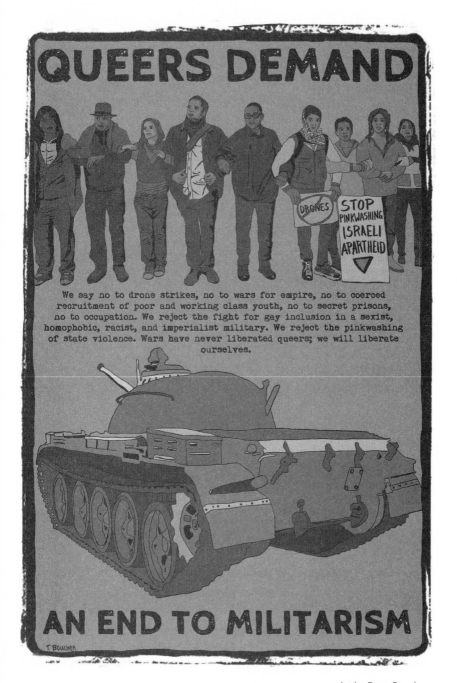

Art by Roan Boucher

Bathing Beneath the Lebanese Sky

By Stephanie Abraham

In *The Day Nina Simone Stopped Singing*, Darina Al-Joundi's memoir about growing up in Lebanon during the civil war, Al-Joundi remembers dramatic events in surprisingly matter-of-fact ways, which is what makes the story so palpable. My mind keeps going back to what happened in 1982, after the intense bombings and a four-week blockade, when Al-Joundi and her family were finally able to leave an underground shelter.

> The alleys strewn with cooking stoves and refrigerators hurled out by the blast of the explosions. . . . in the distance I heard the barking of dogs that now ran around in packs, human thigh bones between their teeth. I followed my sisters and at the end of an alley we saw a bombed-out old house with a big garden and a large pond of stagnant water. All three of us jumped in, to

Originally published in *make/shift* no. 10 (fall/winter 2011/2012)

drink, to wash. We were naked and green, splashing about among the frogs, our hair covered with algae, but happy as larks beneath the sky of Beirut. It was the most wonderful bath of my life.

Refrigerators, thighbones, and that bath have allowed me to understand war and survival more concretely and intimately than ever.

Al-Joundi knows violence in ways most of us can't imagine. As teenagers, she and her sisters wanted to do something to combat their feelings of helplessness, but their father forbade taking up arms and pointed them to the Red Cross. Shortly afterward, at a village that had experienced a massacre, Al-Joundi saw families literally cut up into pieces. She observes, "What frightened me most in Sabra weren't the dead but what could be read on the faces of the living. I had just turned fourteen." As she grew older, her firsthand experience of brutality increased. Partly that was beyond her control—the war would not let up, nightly conversations revolved around how one had managed to dodge death that day, and physical abuse, including rape and domestic violence, became a personal reality. But partly it was self-inflicted: "I was convinced that I was going to die at any moment, so hungry for everything, for sex, drugs, and alcohol, I doubled my efforts . . . with a brutality that left no room for desire and even less for any feeling."

This book, however, is about so much more than war and survival. Al-Joundi addresses the complex intricacies of Lebanese society with true-life simplicity, often shown through her relationship with her father. The honesty between them feels truly exceptional. So when he asked her to honor his lifelong wish to prohibit the reading of the Koran at his funeral, she saw to it. He was a secular man who devoted his life to intellectual pursuits and *hated* religion, and he wanted jazz. Al-Joundi interrupted the prayers and played Nina Simone. As a result, shortly after the funeral, she was beaten terribly by men who had been in attendance, and then she received the ultimate punishment: her family had her institutionalized at a "mental hospital"—for talking, drinking, dancing, going out, and smoking too much, behaviors that were perceived as immoral for women. Living in a time of madness, those around her decided she was mad.

Al-Joundi's story has helped me to contextualize my own. The shared experiences between the Lebanese in the homeland and those in the diaspora seem clearer than ever, in particular when it comes to questions of mental health, language, and memory. My Lebanese grandmother was locked up in a mental institution for ten years in Detroit, starting in the late 1950s. Although my family never talks about it, from the bits of info I've gathered, it was for raging and speaking out more than people thought appropriate. The question of who gets to define what is rational is something Lebanese women and their descendants know too well.

My Christian great-grandparents left Hasroun as teenagers a century ago. The story goes that they sailed to the New World for love. They may have, but there were massacres taking place against Christians at that time, which may have influenced their decision to leave their homeland at such a young age. In 1948, when my pops came home from kindergarten, he declared to his *sitto*, "Speak to me in English! I am an American!" As a result, I carry the shame that comes with growing up assimilated, without knowledge of one's language or customs. Learning that Al-Joundi was punished in school in Lebanon for speaking Arabic reminded me that anti-Arab racism and oppression is *that bad*; it's a global phenomenon. When I read that the way people decided to handle the war was to turn the page and pretend it didn't happen, "with a wave of the magic wand called amnesia," I understood that erasing memories is a cultural pattern developed in resistance to oppression, in hopes that the next generation will not have to experience it. Unfortunately, trying to forget the pain often leads to forgetting Lebanon, forgetting your people, and forgetting yourself. In Al-Joundi's refusal to forget, she helps me remember.

Immigration at the Front

Challenging the "Every Woman" Myth in Online Media

By brownfemipower

By brownfemipower

THE NEW BEDFORD RAID

As the editor of *Women of Color Blog*, I've spent the last two years online. In fact, these days I spend most of my time online rather than participating in "real world" organizing. Although many activists still vehemently deny that the Internet is a site where essential activist work occurs (with reasons ranging from "it's just a computer/just a screen; you're not really talking to a real person" to "the communities I care about do not have access to the Internet" to "it's too expensive"), I have found the Internet to be a vital space in my feminist organizing. I am Chicana—which means that while I myself am not an immigrant, many members of my family are, as are large portions of my community. The Internet has provided a tool for those of us who are living in isolated communities to "hook up" with other people like us and to share information we couldn't find in other places.

The Internet is not without its problems, however. The Internet is a site of violence for

Originally published in *make/shift* no. 2 (fall/winter 2007/2008)

many people—online threats of violence are common against women in particular, and many people (including big bloggers) have had their sites hijacked by angry readers.

Many times, however, the problems of the Internet speak of something much deeper and more nuanced than outright violence (which most people willingly stand against). The Internet can and does replicate the problems present in real-world organizing—problems that marginalize the women I most care about, the women of my community.

On March 6, federal immigration agents raided Michael Bianco, Inc., a leather company in New Bedford, Massachusetts. In addition to the company's owner and three managers, 361 workers were arrested. This raid, officially called Operation United Front, was a part of the larger Operation Return to Sender, a series of anti-immigrant raids run by U.S. Immigration and Customs Enforcement (ICE).

As news about the raid began to leak out, it quickly became clear that the repercussions of the raids on female workers were severe. The Massachusetts Immigrant and Refugee Advocacy Coalition (MIRA) posted a video on its website featuring the testimony of a mother who was arrested during the raid. The woman testifies that nursing mothers were separated from their babies and/or forced to "prove" that they were lactating by expressing milk in front of male guards. She tells of how one guard told another guard to "pass an Oreo cookie" because they were "milking the cows." Women were given five minutes to eat dinners that were thrown at them by guards "like we were dogs." The woman in the video also alleges that she was in a detention center in a completely different state before she was allowed to contact her child in Massachusetts. And yet, despite the horrific experiences of these women (many of whom are still struggling through the criminal-legal system), there was next to no coverage of the raid in feminist-centered online media.

The Feminist Majority's website made no mention of the raid in their "Feminist News" section. The National Organization for Women did not have a single post on their website about the raid until May 30, in spite of the fact that they have put out timely commentary on decisions by the U.S. Supreme Court as well as the Imus debate. The only mention of the raid on the website of *Ms.* magazine (which is connected to the Feminist Majority's "Feminist News") was an article written by Dolores Huerta for the print magazine. And of four "big" self-identified feminist blogs—*Feministing, Feministe, Amptoons,* and *Pandagon*—only *Pandagon* posted anything about the raid. Even then, one of the editors of *Pandagon*, Ilyka Damen, graciously noted that she was "guilty as charged" after she read an angry post written by Sylvia, a feminist-of-color blogger, who asserted that privilege prevented many "feminists of the paler persuasion" from posting about the raid.[1]

DEFINING THE PROBLEM

The silence of the feminist blogosphere on the New Bedford raid points to a troubling lack of willingness in the online world to mobilize around vast populations of women who are not what feminist of color Beth Richie labels the "every woman." Richie states, "What has happened in this country is the 'every woman' has become a white middle-class woman. . . . The 'every woman' was never us. But she still consumes the greater proportion of attention from the literature. Intervention strategies in this movement are based on her needs. She is featured in public-awareness campaigns except in some very tokenized exceptions. She is reflected in the national recognition and the leadership in the mainstream antiviolence movement."

In other words, throughout the history of offline, grassroots feminist organizing in the United States, white women have attempted to "include" women of color (including marginalized women of color, such as those who are poor, disabled, or imprisoned) in a feminist movement that has largely centered the needs of middle-class white women. In the process, they have further marginalized women of color.

Even if you're not very aware of Internet activism, you've probably heard about the phenomenon of Internet organizing through media coverage of its successes. For instance: the Howard Dean campaign's utilization of the Internet to raise money, or the power of the Internet-

---

1. I define as "big" any blog that ranks as an A-list blog. These are blogs that have more than five hundred links on the blog-search website Technorati, get hundreds of hits an hour (as opposed to the rest of us, who get, if we're lucky, hundreds of hits a *day*), are written by people who have been blogging for two or three years, and have multiple bloggers. The sites listed here call themselves "feminist" sites; most of their posts are about "feminist topics" such as abortion or contraception, or about other topics viewed through a "feminist lens."

based organization MoveOn. Both of these groups have demonstrated that, when properly harnessed, the Internet can facilitate grassroots mobilization without the time-sapping logistical problems of physically going door to door or making phone calls to enlist support. Through the use of Listservs, e-mail lists, and news updates, the Internet is a space where thousands, if not millions, of people can be mobilized within minutes.

Feminist organizations have successfully used online mobilization strategies for feminist-centered actions on numerous occasions. The Feminist Majority, NOW, *Ms.* magazine, and most of the top feminist blogs have used Internet mobilization to intervene against impending antichoice and anti–birth control legislation, to petition for FDA approval for emergency contraception, and to protest sexism and violence in media (including television shows, the blogosphere, films, and music). However, although all of these actions are important and admirable, they have centered the needs of middle-class white feminists while either ignoring or "including" women of color in their organizing.

The online world replicates the centering of the "every woman" in feminist movements in very alarming ways. As an example, while the major feminist blogs either didn't mention the New Bedford raid or mentioned it well after the fact, *Amptoons*, *Feministing*, and *Feministe* all published posts about an offensive episode of *America's Next Top Model* around the same time the raid happened—and *Amptoons* and *Feministing* both invited their readers to e-mail the producers and sponsors of the show.

Now, of course, the episode, which called for the contestants to pose as dead victims of violence, was extremely offensive and spoke to a horrific glorification of violence against women in advertising. But at the same time, in the absence of substantial coverage on these sites of the New Bedford raid or other immigration raids, it is clear that the issues facing immigrant women do not carry the same urgency for these bloggers as "every woman" issues like media representation. What might have happened if those bloggers had encouraged readers to make emergency donations to MIRA or to flood politicians with calls demanding that the New Bedford mothers be immediately reunited with their children?

Feminist media's lack of interest in immigration has definite consequences for immigrant women. The fact that, at this moment, undocumented immigrant women have no legal say in what happens to their bodies, children, or communities is a devastating problem that affects every aspect of their lives—from their right to birth control to their right to contact their children from prison. As Beth Richie notes, "The consequence of this problem of the 'every woman' is that the victimization of low-income women of color is invisible to the mainstream public, at best—and worse, that women of color are victimized in such a way that the mainstream movement not only can't see, but condones."

HOPEFUL SOLUTIONS

So what is the online solution to this problem of the "every woman"?

First and foremost, it's essential that immigrant women bypass any dependency on feminist media that is more interested in "inclusion" than the protection and empowerment of the women in our communities. We must tap into our own existing communities of support online. We must also create our own feminist media that centers not only our needs, but also the ways in which our community members can organize around those needs.

It's also important for immigrant women to use online feminist media not just as a tool to mobilize for immediate action, but also as a tool for long-term grassroots base building. Specifically, immigrant women must challenge the idea that the only way to use the Internet is to fund-raise and sign petitions. Blogs and websites that detail the historical roots of feminist immigrant organizing along with current organizing and opinions written by and for immigrant women allow the stories and issues of our communities to be used in outreach to other immigrant women and supportive allies. The Zapatistas provide a compelling example: the online publication of their literature in translation by allies and supporters has advanced their outreach campaign to people who wouldn't normally be invested in the liberation of Mexican Indians.

Those established online feminist communities interested in acting as allies to immigrants must begin to address how the politics of inclusion play out in their coverage of immigration. That is, do they post an occasional essay about immigrant women, or do they invest time and resources to convey the need for all women's liberation movements to make the goals of immigrant feminists their own goals?

Bloggers can approach immigration in very exciting ways. Blog editors do not have to work within a system to make organizational changes—they can simply decide to make immigration an important topic on their blogs, and do so. Working through issues in a transparent way happens quite often on blogs. Many times, readers come to blogs solely for those posts that reflect on difficult subjects. I have seen topics as far-ranging as porn, race, and veganism approached by feminist bloggers. In light of the continuing anti-immigrant raids as well as the on-again, off-again congressional debates on immigration, now is the perfect time for feminist bloggers to begin a discussion about immigration. Big bloggers must be careful, however, not to ignore the work smaller bloggers are already doing. *Pandagon* was headed in the right direction with their posts on the New Bedford raid—they linked to multiple smaller blogs that *were* discussing the issue, and they attempted to explain to their readers why feminism can no longer afford to ignore immigration. Unfortunately, many readers responded by posting comments that consistently derailed meaningful discussion, which suggests that many of these blogs' readers were not ready to hear the message. But posts that continue to bring up the topic will eventually force immigration onto the feminist agenda—in, I hope, meaningful and productive ways.

Feminist online media presents many problems for immigrant women. Challenging the "every woman" through the creation of our own media and utilizing the support of committed allies may profoundly improve the quality of lives of not just immigrant women, but all women.

It's about justice.

Now is the time.

On Prisons, Borders, Safety, and Privilege

An Open Letter to White Feminists

By Jessica Hoffmann

In 1983, when I was in kindergarten, white (Jewish) lesbian feminist Adrienne Rich implored a white-led feminist movement: "Without addressing the whiteness of white feminism, our movement will turn in on itself and collapse." Twenty-five years later, I'm dubious about a movement—"ours" or otherwise—that has not only failed to honestly and consistently address its whiteness but has also, in so doing, become something far less than a movement for social change.[1]

My comments here are hugely influenced by critiques of white feminism put forth over generations by women of color,[2] critiques I'm guessing you're familiar with. Maybe you're

There is no role for the white liberal [in social change]; he is our affliction.
—James Baldwin, 1963

Originally published in make/shift no. 3 (spring/summer 2008)

1. In a recent radio interview with Thenmozhi Soundararajan, author Chip Smith talked about critique as a form of mutual support through which privileged people who believe in justice can hold each other accountable. My friend and collaborator Mattilda Bernstein Sycamore, an activist writer, has called critique a form of love. The white-middle-class culture I was educated in frames it, especially among girls, as scary conflict to avoid at all costs. I'm writing this letter in part to unlearn that lesson, to learn instead to critique with love and hope, to put it out there and find out whatever that's worth.

2. Especially, in terms of contemporary critique, *Color of Violence: The INCITE! Anthology* and discussions with feminists of color and white feminists actively engaged in antiracism work.

cause you feel like you've reckoned with them. Maybe
t that past generations of white feminists had such a
/class-privilege problem. Maybe *This Bridge Called My*
d reading in your first women's studies class and you know
ectionality," making a point in your feminist projects to
"include" the voices and issues of women of color, working-class and poor
white women, and maybe even trans folks and members of other groups
historically marginalized by dominant feminisms. I'm pretty sure about all
this because many of you have told me so—in personal conversations and
workshops, in your books and blogs and . . .

Yet it doesn't look to me like you've really reckoned with those
critiques. It looks more like you appropriate or tokenize them, using their language while continuing to center white, class-privileged
women's experiences in your "feminism" and engaging in political
work that upholds and strengthens white supremacy and economic exploitation—sometimes directly undermining the social-change work
of feminists of color.

And, yes, you deserve some concrete examples of that, which is why
I'm writing. My intention isn't to repeat the critiques of feminists of color,
but to offer some specific instances in which I, a white, class-privileged
feminist who is often privy to your conversations and who can identify with the experiences and perspectives of privilege, have recently seen
this playing out. At this particular historical moment, it seems to happen
frequently around the disconnect between white feminists' notions of
"safety" as an ideal we should organize around, and, on the other side of
the not-so-fun funhouse mirror, organizing by feminists of color around
policing/prisons and immigration/borders—issues that expose the fantasy
of "safety" as a product of privilege, issues that feminists of color have
increasingly centered in their activism while white feminists seem to be
struggling to understand whether they are feminist issues at all.

PRISONS (OR, SAFETY FOR WHOM?)

In recent years, members of INCITE! Women of Color Against
Violence have incisively and repeatedly critiqued the white-feminist-led
antiviolence movement for its reliance on (and thus complicity with)
the U.S. criminal-legal system, which uses the rhetoric of "safety" to de-

stroy communities of color, squash dissent, and create profit for private corporations. Yet the primary macro-level strategies of the white-feminist-led movement against domestic violence and sexual assault continue to rely on this system, with a major focus on legislation such as the Violence Against Women Act and the push for hate-crime laws to include gender and sexual orientation.[3] On the micro/personal level, I have repeatedly seen white, class-privileged feminists unhesitatingly call on police to protect and serve them, have listened to white feminists advise each other on which "authorities" to go to for protection from stalkers and other abusers, and so on.[4]

At both the macro level of feminist movement strategy and the micro/personal level of individual actions, I'm struck by the apparent lack of awareness of the prominent critiques made by feminists of color of law-and-order approaches to ending (or, even, finding "safety" from) violence. To be a self-identified feminist activist apparently unaware of (or, worse, deliberately skirting) the current work of not only INCITE! but also feminist icons like Angela Davis and numerous other voices calling for abolition of the prison industrial complex as a key element of social change seems to me to be part of a movement that is not only disconnected from but also damaging to some of the most vibrant and potentially liberating social-justice organizing happening today.

Yet . . . I know, I know.

One night in the summer of 1996, when I was eighteen, my (white, female, ex-gutter-punk) roommate and I rushed together to call the police when we were startled by a Peeping Tom outside her bedroom window. It was like a reflex, just what you do. We didn't pause to consider other possible responses—and, after two LAPD officers promised to put our apartment on their regular patrol for the next few weeks, we

---

3. An obvious parallel here is the way the rhetoric of "safety" is used in the so-called War on Terror to justify imperialist military violence—which itself is backed by some people who identify as feminists for supposedly "saving" women from the violence of their (in the imperialist reading) especially violent cultures.

4. *Our Enemies in Blue*, Kristian Williams's history of modern U.S. policing, thoroughly documents how U.S. law enforcement has been developed to protect the privileged classes at the expense of poor people and people of color, from slave patrols to vagrancy laws to today's "broken windows" theory.

gave no thought to what that added police presence might mean to our mostly Black neighbors. I was interning with the Feminist Majority that summer, working to defeat an anti–affirmative action state ballot initiative. By the night of the Peeping Tom incident, I had been confused for weeks about why the multiracial coalition of feminist and racial-justice groups that started out in the spring working together to save affirmative action "for women and people of color" had split into two, the (mostly white) feminists in one camp and the racial-justice groups in the other. One of my co-interns had overheard a prominent leftist civil rights attorney, a woman of color who was working with a former coalition organization, say, "The road to hell is paved with feminists." I thought our work at the Feminist Majority was good and just and concerned with racial as well as gender equality; I didn't understand.

On September 26, 2007, the NYPD used excessive force in the absurd (but not atypical) arrests of two members of the Sylvia Rivera Law Project—an organization that works on behalf of low-income people of color who are transgender, gender nonconforming, or intersex—when they questioned police officers' treatment of a young Black man outside an East Village bar where they were celebrating SRLP's fifth anniversary. The next morning, NOW president Kim Gandy released a statement titled "Expansion of Hate Crimes Law Necessary for Women's Safety." NOW's statement that morning was a clear, and tragic, example of the ways privileged so-called feminism is not only disconnected from but sometimes undermines grassroots struggles for social change: Who is made safe by strengthening a violent law-and-order system? And what does strengthening that system have to do with ending violence? Why was a major feminist organization's message that morning about strengthening court/legal/police power rather than supporting the arrestees from the SRLP?

(This seems naive, right? It seems silly—preposterous, almost—to imagine that a huge national organization like NOW would issue a quick public statement in support of those SRLP folks, and of course the hate-crimes announcement was probably long-planned and the timing vis-à-vis the SRLP arrests totally coincidental and etcetera, etcetera, etcetera—but why should it seem silly? That it does is my point: dominant, white-led feminist movement is consistently unresponsive to the grassroots while it works within and strengthens the very structures that violently maintain social hierarchies.)

In the summer and fall of 2007, I found myself invited to participate in a slew of meetings and conference calls organized by small, new majority-white "feminist" groups around the United States; over and over again, members wondered earnestly how they could draw more women of color to participate in their projects. Around the same time, I read and heard a whole lot of white feminist media makers explaining that "we" need to show young women "why feminism matters." Sometimes I asked them why, in the face of a series of egregious and in some cases highly publicized examples of state violence against marginalized people (for instance, the Jena 6 and the New Jersey 4), prominent white feminists are MIA in and largely ignorant of the work and analyses of major, often feminist-of-color-led movements against state violence. And, I wondered, what is *your* feminism for, and why does *it* matter? Because feminists of color don't seem to need convincing on that point—they're engaged in profound, intergenerational, cross-cultural grassroots work that is transforming not only feminist movements but all social-change movements.[5]

BORDERS (OR: WHO CROSSES, AND WHO CARES)

Prominent white feminists often say they are organizing against violence and for safety. So where have they been while working-class immigrant women have been pulled from their homes and workplaces, often separated from their young children, in immigration raids across the United States in recent months?

Brownfemipower of *Women of Color Blog* has written extensively about how popular white feminist bloggers failed to quickly and substantially

---

5. I'm thinking of the radical visioning around healing and social transformation that is being done by groups working to end sexual violence such as UBUNTU; the movement-altering intervention of INCITE!'s critique of the nonprofit industrial complex; Vandana Shiva's call for "another relationship . . . as citizens of the earth . . . not of owning, not of private property, but of caring, of giving, of responsibility"; challenges to the gender binary posed by a prison-abolition movement that thoroughly includes the prison system's enforcement of gender and sex norms in its analysis; and the long-standing work around gender justice in indigenous struggles against global capital such as Zapatismo—just to name a few.

cover the specific damage done to women during a major immigration raid in New Bedford, Massachusetts, early last year. New Bedford was not an anomaly: immigration raids—many of them marked by multiple forms of violence, including surprise attack, immediate separation of parents and their young children, racist and sexist abuse of people held in binary-gender-segregated immigration detention facilities, deportation itself, and the creation of the constant fear that the next one could happen anywhere, anytime—are *happening all the time, all over the United States.*

Immigrant communities are living in near-constant fear, with little "safety"; women and trans and gender-nonconforming people are suffering gender-based violence at the hands of federal immigration officials; *and* the movement for immigration-policy reform is arguably the largest mass movement in the United States today.

Where are white feminists?

As far as I can tell, white feminists' "solidarity" with the immigrants' rights movement amounts to occasionally featuring a woman who works at an immigrants' rights nonprofit in a publication or panel, and occasionally mentioning a sensational case of violence against a particular immigrant woman on a blog. I was at the mass May Day marches for immigrants' rights in 2006 and 2007 in Los Angeles, and I saw no notable presence of any of the major U.S.-based feminist organizations. In 2007, I could find no mention of the upcoming marches, nor report-backs the next day, on popular feminist blogs. Hundreds of thousands—in some places millions—of people were on the streets for social justice. Where were white feminists?

Even coverage of outrageous cases of state violence against immigrant women has been scarce in media created by white feminists. In July 2007, a trans woman named Victoria Arellano died after being denied AIDS medication and proper health care in an immigration detention center for men. White feminist media makers mostly missed the story—though it was reported in the *Washington Post,* the *Los Angeles Times,* and other major media outlets. It seemed simply not to register as a feminist issue.

Confused by this, I mentioned it on an e-mail list where most of the active participants are white, self-identified feminist journalists.

That day, they were discussing the demise of GreenStone Media—a liberal/centrist, white-, rich-, celebrity-dominated "women's" radio network founded by Jane Fonda, Gloria Steinem, and a few others. The conversation, which started as a call for a moment of silence to collectively grieve GreenStone's short life, broadened into a discussion of the scarcity of funding for feminist media, which led to a few mentions of *The Revolution Will Not Be Funded*, the incisive, grassroots-organizing-focused anthology by INCITE!. Some folks even expressed interest in forming a reading group to discuss the book. Meanwhile, my questions about feminist media makers' lack of attention to Arellano's story were largely blown off. When a couple of these journalists did eventually mention Arellano's story on their blogs, the focus was on violence against trans women of color (framed as perpetual victims), with no analysis connecting the story to movements to abolish the prison system or defy the legitimacy of national borders.

What, I wondered, is the feminist media they so desperately want funded *for*? That the conversation for a moment veered toward *The Revolution Will Not Be Funded* was only more disturbing: a book by radical feminists of color calling for mass, autonomous movement building as an alternative to the state- and capitalism-based "nonprofit industrial complex" that has co-opted social-change activism was being plucked for possible use (co-optation?) by privileged and powerful advocates of precisely the kind of liberal/reformist so-called feminism that has relied on and actively developed that structure.

No, I thought, the revolution will not be funded. And also: the revolution would not have been broadcast on GreenStone Media.

A CALL TO CHALLENGE PRISONS AND BORDERS OF ALL KINDS (OR: WHAT IS FEMINISM FOR?)

In the fourteenth and fifteenth centuries, class- and skin-privileged French feminists railed against misogynist humanism and worked to demonstrate that women were just as capable of rational, moral thought as men were. But they were ignorant of the lives of most women of their time—and thus managed to put forth a feminist analysis and activism that missed the witch hunts. This is not an anomaly or something I dug up from an obscure corner; this bit of European feminist history was handed to me in an essay by Adrienne Rich, written during my lifetime, still widely in print. Maybe you've even read it?

I thought about calling this an open letter to liberal feminists, or to mainstream feminists, or some other things, but I finally decided on the adjective "white"—not because race is the only defining difference between the liberal/reformist so-called feminism I'm critiquing and more radical social-change-oriented feminisms, but because I see many of the strains of this argument threading together around whiteness—if by "whiteness" I can mean not only skin privilege but also straightness,[6] liberalism,[7] a sense of entitlement to safety (especially within existing social structures), and other markers of an identity and worldview shaped by assimilation to power. Because, of course, whiteness is no essential fact; it is a construct, a lumping together of different people and practices into a dominant, powerful whole.

I'm using "whiteness" here to talk broadly about assimilated identities and assimilationist politics, which undermine movements for social change. As white people in the twenty-first century, we can't undo or deny the skin privilege we have been granted via generations of erasure of cultural differences and assimilation to power. But as white feminists, if we are working toward profound social change, we *can* choose not to engage in political work that is about assimilating to and achieving "safety" or "empowerment" or "freedom" of movement within existing power structures—especially when those structures (such as militaristically enforced national borders and the prison industrial complex) are designed to make others unsafe, and unfree.

I wonder again: What is your feminism *for*? If it is for disruption and redistribution of power across society (that is, not just for women like you), it cannot be so ignorant of, exploitative of, and even counter to the prison-abolition and immigrants' rights movements—not only because marginalized women are involved in and affected by those struggles, but

6. Meaning not any particular sexual identity or type of relationship but rather the binary-gender-dependent norm of "straightness" that suggests that there even, naturally, is such a thing, and including assimilated we're-just-like-you gay politics and identities as distinct from radical-queer politics and identities.

7. As opposed not to conservative but to progressive or radical or liberationist.

because they are where some of the most significant challenges to power are being made today.

Privilege is a kind of poison—insidious, it obscures, misleads, confuses—and this is part of how power is maintained, as well-meaning privileged people miss the mark, can't clearly see what's going on and how we're implicated, are able to comfortably see ourselves as not responsible. Liberalism and assimilationist politics are safe ways for privileged people to believe they are fighting the good fight; liberalism and assimilation, I think, are privilege's—power's—instruments.

When I was in fourth grade, in the fall of 1986, my (mostly white, mostly wealthy) class spent a few weeks debating California ballot initiatives. I was assigned to argue the pro side on an initiative to make English the official state language. I took the sample ballot and voter guides home and studied them dutifully, then presented an argument that included the statement "If I moved to China, I wouldn't expect *them* to speak to me in English." I was a kid whose universe was populated mostly by white liberals. I made this argument knowing nothing about colonialism, the treaty of Guadalupe Hidalgo, global economies, or many other things—and no one, not one of the liberal adults at home or at school, mentioned any of these things in response to my argument. I simply got a good grade, as usual, for following instructions and formulating a coherent argument that fulfilled the debate guidelines I had been taught.

On the afternoon of May 1, 2007, I stood with a friend on the sidewalk outside MacArthur Park in L.A., where immigrant rights advocates had relaxedly gathered after a long day of marching. A cop decked out in riot gear told us—the only white people in sight—"You'd better get out of here; we're gonna clear everyone out." We talked back, asked whether he was gonna tell everyone else and what he was gonna do if we stayed put, rolled our eyes, wondered if these rows of LAPD officers wielding batons and guns were really about to enter the park unprovoked, and stayed where we were. Minutes later, the cops did indeed enter the park, where they brutally shot and shoved to disperse the crowd, injuring many. The next day, my friend and I wondered why we didn't think of calling or texting our friends inside the park to warn them about what appeared increasingly likely to happen. Inexperienced because of privilege, we hadn't thought well on our feet, and we'd been in a certain denial about how bad things might get; we'd been pissed and well meaning, but not useful. ("I'm wearing flip-flops," my friend said to me with sad eyes as we walked away from the park that night, after the violence. We'd shown up feeling that safe. I hope my eyes told her, "I know, I know . . . ")

What keeps me connected to feminism is a radical history of multi-issue, multitactic activism that goes by that name. I know of no other social-justice tradition that has so frequently linked so-called private with so-called public political struggles, art with organizing. And that is why I find politics of privilege that call themselves feminism—those that would work uncritically within existing power structures, even strengthening them; those that co-opt the revolutionary work of feminists of color by superficially "including" them in a movement that leaves privileged women and their priority issues at the center—so frustrating.

And that I could call that frustration heartbreaking has a whole lot to do with my own whiteness. I'm inclined to give white feminism, white feminists, the benefit of the doubt. I know what it's like to mean well and yet fuck up, to not get it when the critique means me, to be on the side of power while I intend to challenge it. And after more than a decade in this movement, I know too well why that civil rights attorney I mentioned earlier said, "The road to hell is paved with . . . "

If feminism is about social change, it is about recognizing that safety in this society is a fantasy afforded only by assimilation to power, and the cost of that fake safety is the safety of those who cannot, or will not, access it. If feminism is about social change, it is about radically challenging prisons and borders of all kinds.

If feminism is about social change, *white feminism*—a feminism of assimilation, of gentle reform and/or strengthening of institutions that are instrumental to economic exploitation and white supremacy, of ignorance and/or appropriation of the work of feminists of color—is an oxymoron. And it is not a thing of some bygone era before everyone read bell hooks in college. It is happening now; you might be part of it.

Arrestable

By Ching-In Chen

1.
Olivia looks
at me soft
eyes
question
I'm scared
she says
I have already made
my decision
up at 5 a.m. tea
and bundle
T-shirt layered
under Palestine
hoodie
then the door
streets empty of all
except the night people

2.
I see J and R
L and M
V and A
the warehouse
dusty floor filled with cold feet

Originally published
in *make/shift* no. 6
(fall/winter 2009/2010)

tactical
meets
in the corner
we huddle with
our people
until the clock
the scouts
walk in twos
Bart
into
pink
sun
city

3.
quickstep
into
gray
street
and
plant
our feet
hold onto
arms
wait for
our cars
to stop
the time
fist
signal
gather we gather
each
other's elbows
don't budge
we're sick of war
we rise up

we can't take it
no more
the whoop of cops
and we off
undocumented
and trans folks
sandwiched
a girl with a cane
struggles to catch
up
and past
we don't look
a line of helmets
almost light
into X
and past
S locked
down
to M on
Market

Learning to Say "Fuck You"
An Interview with Ida McCray

By Iris Brilliant

Ida McCray knows prisons. She has experienced prisons as an inmate, an employee, and a social worker. After serving a ten-year sentence for participating in a 1972 plane hijacking from California to Cuba, McCray became an even stronger and more inspired fighter for prisoners' rights. Having experienced the isolation and degradation of imprisonment, she believes that sustaining a connection with one's family is a key to reclaiming one's humanity within an inhumane institution. She is currently the rehabilitation coordinator at the San Francisco County Jail and the founder of Families with a Future, a nonprofit that aims to unite children with their parents in prison and to support visitations through navigating bureaucratic obstacles and providing transportation.

IB: You were involved in a hijacking from San Francisco to Cuba in 1972 with your then boyfriend. What was going on in the country and in your life at that time?

Originally published in *make/shift* no. 9 (spring/summer 2011)

IM: There were a lot of hijackings going on. People had different reasons for doing them; some went to Algeria after the Algerian revolution. Five or six years before the hijacking was the Watts rebellion [in Los Angeles]. That's when I became involved politically. It was straight war. It's straight war now, it's just we're distracted differently [*laughs*]. At the same time, my husband went to Vietnam, and that was a big division between us. We were probably married a year and then he got drafted to go to service. I used to say, "What the hell is a Black man doing going to fight in Vietnam to go and kill people that he doesn't even know?" And he [said], "My daddy went into the service and I need to go to preserve the family name." I said, "*Family name?* Your name is the name of a slaveholder!" So he went his way and I went mine, and I became more endeared to the movements that I was seeing in California: the US Organization, Black Panther Party, and Republic of New Afrika.

What was it like being a Black woman in radical movements at that time?

The reason I didn't sign my name on the dotted line [with the Black Panther Party] was because of the heavy sexism that was going on in the party. The men would be in a room planning shit, and the women would be in a room with the kids, and the two were never connected. And we allowed it to happen because we, too, were young, not knowing how to help them have their manhood after all the things that had happened in history to Black males. As a female in the Black Panther Party, if you weren't able to go through the political pipe [*gesturing to stroke an imaginary penis*], you couldn't join the party, which is why I never signed my name on the dotted line. And that saved me years later because when the FBI came around they said, "Were you ever part of the Black Panthers?" [I'd say], "Oh no! Me? Noooo . . . " [*laughs*].

How did you get involved in the hijacking?

I didn't know two words that I know very well now, and it's called "fuck you." The day before the hijacking, [my boyfriend] took my car and robbed some woman in [San Francisco], [and] the woman was raped [*He was never charged for this.—IB*]. He wanted to escape the country to flee these charges. So when he said he was going to Los Angeles to meet some of his comrades, and would I come with him, I figured that I could dump him in L.A. 'cause I know damn well I'm coming back home afterwards [*laughs*]. So I accompanied him to get on the [flight]. And when we got on board he told me he was going to grab the stewardess, who had real long, pretty hair, and blow her head off so he could get control of the plane. So I said, "No, don't kill her, let me help you." And that's how I got involved in the hijacking [*gets choked up*]. I got thrown into it. I did what I thought was the best way to preserve life. I thought back to when my mama was killing this mouse one time. And I was crying, "Mama, please don't kill the mouse!" I mean, I always felt life was precious. And I still do. It's very, very precious. . . . When we landed in Cuba, he went out and got arrested on the island and I was there with my baby, and pregnant by him. And he left [me] abandoned in a place where I didn't speak any Spanish or know much about the culture.

You said that while you were in the United States, you believed in the idea of international solidarity—

Yeah, that was a lie [*laughs*].

How was that concept challenged when you moved to Cuba?

I did have in my mind ideas of international solidarity from things I had read about the US Organization—that oppressed people would struggle with other oppressed people to overthrow imperialism and capitalism. But when you go there and you're a Yankee, you know, they look at you like you got money! And I'm like, "Hey, I'm poor," but I'm from the richest country in the world. That doesn't register with poor people of other lands because they feel because we're American, we're a lot richer than they are. We could have deodorant, soap, and slips, which is something very difficult for the women in the Caribbean to have. And we don't think [about] the struggles that most women think about all over the world, which is, what are you gonna eat that day? And a lot of people don't have the time to sit around and intellectualize, oh, what's going on with international solidarity! These experiences helped me think globally at a young age, helped me understand how we in the U.S. are filtered information. Black people aren't the only people that are oppressed. People in the U.S. really need to get uncomfortable in themselves and in their privileged status, and also remember that our blood is red just like everyone else's all over the world.

After living in Cuba for four years, you moved back to the United States and were arrested. It took over a year for you to see your children while you were in prison. How did finally seeing your children impact you?

The impact [was] hope. I didn't have any birth certificates saying that they were my children, so they couldn't get any services, any welfare, anything. I started writing everywhere to try to get to see my children, because when I was in prison my breasts were still leaking from my baby. That was my whole struggle, the whole time, because I really needed to see them. I needed to see how they'd grown. I needed to let them know that I love them, and at the same time, it helped me keep humanity in my heart. The person who had no connection to their children was a scary person to me. And I got a glimpse of her and it scared the shit outta me [*laughs*]. I really believe that the very ugliest of us could be capable of doing the most egregious, draconian things, and the other person, given the right environment, can be the most humane, beautiful human being, if they had that opportunity.

You created Families with a Future almost immediately upon your release in 1997. What would you like to accomplish with Families with a Future?

Opening up visitations. How can you have a visiting list of, say, four people in a jail that has about five hundred people? You could have a herd of people being connected. Maybe these fathers, if they were out and not doing time for petty drug things, could have some control over these kids, and there wouldn't be so much killing, so many angry, hard-hearted hearts. I would like to help those who are not getting out of prison—pay for some tutoring or education of the children that are left behind that don't have a mother or a father. I want them to have the opportunity to be as successful as they can be, and that means taking art classes, not just giving [them] a computer [to] play games, but showing them what they can do with it. They need some empowerment. Otherwise they fall into the same trap. They don't understand the value of having a simple diploma. And the system uses them because they don't have a diploma. The biggest part would be working with children via a school program to help them get some skills they can walk with in life.

Do you identify as a feminist?

Absolutely.

What does that mean to you?

That means I love myself and everything about me. I loved my period because I was able to understand the beauty and the wisdom of bloodletting, of moon changes, of being in tune with the universe. It's interesting: when you're locked up, women bleed together, you get your periods at the same time. And that's very telling about our wisdom and our bodies. Woman is god. What comes out of these beautiful breasts is life-giving, and what comes out of my vagina is an entrance to a temple. We're psyched out by society to not understand our power, the same thing they did to Black people. We have a strength that others don't have. That's why they try to keep us separated. So if they can keep you from getting to know yourself, they've won. That's how oppression continues, when you don't know yourself and you don't know your strengths.

Can you envision a world without prisons?

Yes.

What does it look like?

The majority of people in prison don't need to be there. Do some people need to be locked away? You damn right! Some people don't need to be around other human beings. Do you go in there and treat them bad? No, what you do is you keep them isolated from people they can hurt. We don't know who we're locking up! We don't know if they're gonna have a cure for cancer because we don't give them the opportunity to expand their minds, so society is missing out on what gifts they can give back. 'Cause nobody is just one thing, nobody is only awful, awful, awful, so . . . I can envision a world without prisons.

What inspires you?

It's an honor to live and carry the stories of others. Marilyn Buck, Liz Chagra, Brenda Antone, Sandra Shirley—all these women who got cancer from the toxic environments of the prisons they were in. It's no coincidence [that] women [serve] time and [are] poisoned while doing their sentence. I was at the Federal Correctional Institution in Dublin, California, where you'd see clouds of green and yellow smoke because the [nearby] military base is testing toxic substances. Many women contracted cancer there. When you see people die around you like that, you know you gotta do your best.

How have your politics changed since the '70s?

They haven't changed that much. I'm still fighting for the people. And I take a lot of stress for that. I got written up a month ago for advocating for a prisoner that these girls beat up. I don't like bullies. I don't like people who oppress other human beings, and I put my foot down. I learned how to do it in a way so that I'm not breaking the rules. I'm still a fighter for the people who are voiceless, broken, or traumatized.

Not Alternative
An Interview with Trifa Shakely

By Adela Nieves

Trifa Shakely is a feminist and immigrant rights activist in Sweden, where she migrated from Kurdistan in 1998. She started the campaign Ain't I a Woman to support migrant women in gaining access to domestic-violence shelters, and was recently named editor in chief of the feminist magazine *Bang.* She spoke with Adela Nieves about her work, the struggles facing immigrant women in Sweden, and organizing.

AN: Please tell me about Ain't I a Woman and what inspired you to start this campaign around migrant women in Sweden.

TS: The campaign comes from the network No One Is Illegal (NOII), in which I've been active since 2003.[1] It's a flat network without any chiefs, so we are working autonomously, under a more anarchist structure. Not *alternative*! I don't like that word; it means different from something else, or something

Originally published in *make/shift* no. 10 (fall/winter 2011/2012)

1. NOII is a collective based in Sweden that works to provide practical support to immigrants in Sweden who have been denied asylum by the government.

else is first, and "this" is the alternative. I don't see myself or my work as an alternative; I am the one, the main structure [*laughs*].

In NOII, we have direct contact with people in hiding, and undocumented people. So you are working with people who have no right to exist in this society. They can't have a library card, work, go to the doctor, no place to be, nothing. You are working with people who don't have any possibility to live. So you need to help take care of children, talk with schools, call around to see if anyone will help you. . . . We are having a lot of events to raise money to pay people's rent, provide food, doctor visits, and other things. It's a big network; we're cooperating with many other groups.

I met a lot of women who were being abused by police, and people around them, like lawyers and immigration officers, who were threatening them because they knew the women could not call the police—if they called the police, they'd be deported. In Sweden, when you get your last "no" from the immigration office, you have to go into hiding, and your legal status is that you are a criminal—they have to be hidden from police, as well as the people abusing them, raping them.

Shelters are not getting any resources or money from the community or government to care for these women, and taking care of these women requires more work, including therapy. That's what especially inspired me to work on this campaign.

What is the current climate in Sweden around issues concerning migrants? Has the rightward shift in many European governments been, in part, based on white/European nationalism? And can you talk about how homonationalism (using supposed progressivism around gender and sexual equality to justify Islamophobic antimigrant policies) plays into this?

The climate in Sweden is just like other European countries, getting worse and worse. For the first time in Sweden we have a party in parliament, the Swedish Democratic Party, that is nationalistic and racist.

Since 2005, Swedish police can ask people in the street to show ID. This is incredible; it's like Nazism. They can ask anyone in the street, and if you don't have ID, they put you in an immigration prison, where there is no court, and then they deport you back to where you came from. People are very upset about this, and there have been many actions.

At this year's Stockholm Pride, I'm going to debate the Swedish minister for migration and asylum policy, Tobias Billström. He is the first openly bisexual minister. The immigration ministry often has a presence at the festival. A lot of people wonder why they are participating, especially when the theme of this year's pride is "openness." They aren't open to people seeking asylum because of war, LGBTQI issues, or inhumane conditions. Their policies are the opposite of openness.

It's all about border control, and for immigrants, [it's] making get[ting] a visa or visit[ing] family much harder. Deportations are happening every day, and violently. Swedish immigration officers do not regard Afghanistan and Iraq—where, in recent years, most immigrants come from, along with Somalia and Sudan—as places at war when considering deportations to these countries. It's really bad. But this is where most people emigrating to Sweden are coming from now, because of war and instability.

A lot of people are coming to Sweden to work. Almost all are in "black work," without papers. It's hard to have humane conditions for work. The unions are not working with them, except one syndicalist union. Everybody knows that for women, if you clean, then sex work is also part of your job.

How people think of your nationality plays a role in how you work. If you're from Poland, that means you work hard. If you're from South America, that means you're happy and you work hard. If you're from Russia, you give blow jobs. The terms of racism and sexism play a role in how you get paid, and the jobs you are expected to do. It's all about exploitation.

How did you come to Sweden from Kurdistan?

I came to Sweden [in 1998] by myself. Part of my family was already here. I was twenty-two, from a family of political activists. People grow up fast in societies at war. At twenty-two I was a young woman at the beginning of her life, just finished my degree in law and political science, working at the university and editor of two magazines, so I was already a grown woman. The biggest surprise coming to Sweden was that people saw me as and expected me to act and think as a teenager.

What prompted you to leave?

I was threatened. When I finished my degrees, I was working on abortion rights. One day a teacher came to my classroom and said, "Trifa, people are waiting for you," and they put me in a car with six armed men, and took me to prison. I [had] decided to stay in Kurdistan, [but] after that, I understood that it was better for me to run.

Did that experience influence how you work in Sweden?

Absolutely. My experience makes me the person I am now. And all other experiences of racism, sexism, and fear. . . . I've experienced death many times; it makes it much easier to not buy the idea that everything has to be nice and polished. I don't really care about the circumstances; I have to do the work.

What are your thoughts on global feminism and transnational and transcultural solidarity?

For me, feminism is a global movement for justice. This means antimilitarism, climate justice, anticapitalism, and immigration movements all have a place in feminist movements. When I see pictures and read about the fantastic activism around the world, it's all women! All the people I admire and respect—Arundhati Roy, Malalai Joya, Vandana Shiva. I think we are in a historical moment where people, especially in the West, think we cannot change anything, everything is shit, nationalists have power, capitalism is eating everyone up. . . . I don't believe that. There are always small victories, and people are fighting, even in small ways. If the party running parliament is racist, then forget trying to work in parliament—we can work together in other ways.

If you need and want change, you must also be ready to offer something. It's not like Mondays I go to yoga, Tuesday I'm going to a movie, and Wednesday I'm going to fight. Political work is a way of life.

What does women-of-color-centered feminism look like in Sweden, in the EU?

Sweden is a very small country; everybody who calls themselves feminist knows each other. If you write one article about feminism, then all feminists in the country know about you.

The idea of women-of-color or queer-people-of-color spaces is very new in Sweden. I just started a group in Gothenburg, and others started a group in Stockholm, where people meet and talk about their experiences as women of color and queer people of color. Change has been very hard for white people to accept. Someone always comes in . . . we have to say four or five times, please just respect the space, and they say, "Oh, but I'm married to someone from Congo!" [*Laughs*] It's very difficult for them.

But there have been a lot of changes. In March, Sissela Blanco, a twenty-three-year-old antiracist activist and woman of color, became one of the leaders of Feminist Initiative, the feminist [political] party in Sweden. Also, I was hired as editor in chief of *Bang* magazine. We are becoming much more visible.

Is the term "women of color" used in Sweden?

No, we only say "women of color" when speaking English. There is no term for it here. Up until about five years ago, it was very difficult to say "white" because what's white? Everything is white, it is so normal. You can't say "white" without people seeing it as a threat. So we say "not white" (*inte vit*).

Congratulations on becoming editor in chief of *Bang*. Can you talk about the magazine?

Thank you! *Bang* is the oldest and biggest cultural and feminist magazine [in Sweden]. It's not just a magazine, it's like a school for feminism in Sweden and Scandinavia. The media is always looking at what we're up to and quoting us. It's a powerful name in cultural and political discussions.

I had to quit my job as a social worker in 2008 because if you work with undocumented people, then the government won't pay you. So I was like, "Okay, I'm not working as a social worker, I'm working as a wild activist." [*Laughs*] I learned a lot about media working on the Ain't I a Woman campaign. When I heard *Bang* needed an editor in chief, I thought, "Let's try this," and they picked me up. Lucky them. [*Laughs*]

Are you still able to work as an activist while you're at *Bang*?

Oh yes, of course.

So many of us activists suffer from burnout. Yet at the same time we praise activists who are clearly running themselves into the ground. What are your thoughts about the sustainability of activism as practiced?

A lot of people have asked me how I manage because I always have, like, seven projects running at the same time. I really don't know how to take care of myself; I don't know what it means. I'm sure I do somehow, because I'm not burned out and I'm not crazy, yet [*laughs*]. But the term "healing" is strange for me. I know what it means, but I've never really tried to learn beyond that.

Maybe because middle-class whites have made this something for them? I've been critical because it is very individualistic. Some people only care for themselves, and that's their way to fight, that is their activism—like only buying ecologically safe products, but they don't put any of their energy into work on the ground, they just buy something good for their own health.

I don't represent everyone. Some people have a much better economic situation and a safe place to live. It is very common for people to talk about therapies and psychologists, but I've never been in therapy. There's also the lack of national health care in the U.S. It's very expensive if you don't have insurance, so I understand why activists look for alternative ways to care for themselves. Here we still have a good working health system. So it's easier to not focus on it.

I think I've been taking care of myself by really believing in my ideas/work. I'm good about calling and talking through things with people I'm close to, cooperating with others, going to groups and not isolating myself. I should maybe go to the gym more [*laughs*]. I eat well because I cook my own food.

For people who are not yet active, why should they get involved in this kind of work?

You are rewarded in very unexpected ways. If something interests you, and will give meaning to your life, then go for it. What else is important? I can't say how people should act; I don't know their life situations. But I know courage always pays off in unexpected and fantastic ways.

Sparking Difficult Dialogues

Sam Feder and Dean Spade
on Trans Documentaries

In 2006, *Boy I Am*—a feature-length documentary that looks at the experiences of three young trans people in New York City and features members of queer communities addressing questions not often discussed—began touring the United States. In this conversation, *Boy I Am*'s codirector and executive producer, Sam Feder, and trans activist Dean Spade, who appears in the film, talk about responsibility, representation, and the future of trans activism.

SF: I am eager to hear your thoughts about *Boy I Am*. As the filmmakers, [codirector/coproducer] Julie Hollar and I often hear positive feedback from people, but we don't hear anything critical. Part of our goal in making the doc was to spark difficult dialogues. We're talking about it, but not in the ways that we'd hoped for. So, bring it on.

DS: I saw the finished version of *Boy I Am* at the University of Southern California in fall 2006 when I spoke on a panel about the film

Originally published
in *make/shift* no. 2
(fall/winter 2007/2008)

with Jack Halberstam (who also appears in the film). I really appreciated how you and Julie responded to some of the concerns brought up in early screenings by adding new footage to balance the views in the film.

But seeing the film in its entirety brought up a host of new concerns for me. My biggest concern is how the film centralizes surgery. The three central characters all take testosterone and have chest surgery. The more work I do in the community, the more I feel like the most dangerous myth about trans people is not only that we all have surgery but also that our identities are defined by those surgeries. This misunderstanding is reflected in some of the most discriminatory policies and laws about us, and in day-to-day discriminatory behavior. For example, if we can't prove surgery, we can't change our state-issued identification card; there are policies preventing people from having proper placement in shelters and group homes without surgery; and some employers will not allow trans people to use the right bathroom at work until they have surgery.

As you know, the majority of trans people never have surgery, because many don't want it or need it to express their gender, and most insurance programs will not cover it. The cultural preoccupation with trans people's surgical status, and the general view that surgical status is the most important thing to know about us, is an enormous obstacle to our survival. Because there is so little accurate information about trans people circulating, it disappoints me that this film, made by people who are truly our allies, perpetuates these misrepresentations.

SF: Julie and I agree that centralizing surgery is dangerous. If we could reedit this aspect of the film, we would. However, we think the surgery sequence lends an understanding of the seriousness of the undertaking, which helps dispel the myth that it's done lightly or as part of a trend. Although we knew it might be problematic, we didn't think we could ignore it.

This doc initially came about because, while living in NYC in 2003, we found ourselves going to many benefits to raise money for chest surgery. We wanted to find out why, at that date and time, this issue was becoming more noticeable, and how the queer community was responding to it. As two gender-variant and queer people, we felt personally invested in these issues, and we began uncovering the larger questions that involved harsh judgments toward surgery within the community. We wanted to turn the mirror within the queer community and see what the dialogue was or wasn't about.

During the evolution of production we began to see the guys—Nicco, Norie, and Keegan—as a thread for the larger conversation. We aimed to have a spectrum of trans masculinity represented and worked with the three accordingly, but things changed over the three years, and by the end of production the three all had had surgery and were on hormones. Our project changed as we worked, realities changed, community identity changed. Even in the past year, since production ceased, I've seen a huge shift in acceptance, representation, and celebration of the variance within trans masculinities in the queer communities that I'm a part of.

We're left with the question, do we stop screening it? Is there any relevance for the moments in time that were documented, even if our views and our community have evolved? If we stop screening it, what does it say to the trans youth who thank us for making a doc that they can use as a tool for education when coming out to their parents? What does that say to the people who devoted years of their lives to working with us and being very vulnerable? Is the doc doing more harm than good? Should a media maker even take these risks? These questions are always on our minds.

DS: People have told me that the film represents surgery in a sensationalist way by using "before and after" shots—a typical trope of trans documentary film—that invite the viewer to be surprised and fascinated by our bodies.

SF: I believe this editing decision was based on our lack of education at the time. Most documentaries we'd seen had the "body shots." We are both first-time filmmakers, and we saw this as a how-to formula and emulated it without realizing what exactly we were perpetuating.

On the other hand, trans folks and nontrans folks have told me that they appreciate the variety of images in terms of class, race, sexuality, and style. They've also commented that seeing the guys during their process gives viewers a wider range of images to relate to.

DS: I really appreciated how, as a result of our conversations, you reshot the portion of the film that dealt with trans youth. At first, several important community spokespeople (Jack Halberstam, Carmen Vasquez, and others) said that trans youth are being "pressured" to take hormones and that trans health care is easily accessible to trans youth. In reality, trans youth are routinely denied trans health care because of transphobia and ageism, which results in youth seeking hormones in underground economies, injecting unsafely without medical supervision, and often ending up in the juvenile justice system. While this is far more thoroughly explained now in the film, these false notions are still represented.

Many people I've spoken to feel that having this misperception articulated by multiple speakers in the film, although an alternative view is represented, is potentially damaging to the community because it fuels the all-too-common stigmatization of trans health care and the belief that trans youth cannot self-determine their genders. People feel scared about the effects of that position being circulated widely in the community when policies that deny trans youth health care, even at LGBT health clinics, are still endangering the health and survival of trans youth. Can you talk about your thinking behind this?

SF: The aim of this documentary was to uncover some of the judgments of people within the queer community. The precise reason that some people feel it's dangerous to show this side of the position is why we thought it was important. We wanted to present Halberstam, a theorist on gender studies whose writing about trans people has been highly influential within the queer community, in order to show a pervasive argument that allies often maintain. We intended to, through the juxtaposition of differing points of view within our community, make an argument *for* better access to hormones for youth. We felt that presenting the views that do not support access gave our argument more strength than simply speculating on those ideologies that are currently preventing access to hormones for young people. I do believe that the power of film is that it *shows*, rather than tells. While some say we expose too much and it might harm the community, others say we didn't expose enough. As a media maker, it fascinates me to hear such polar opposite reactions from people who consider themselves part of the same struggle.

People have come forward with this criticism, but I'm surprised at the lack of criticism we hear overall. Why haven't more people come forward with critical feedback? If you don't engage with the media maker and you aren't producing media, how do you expect to influence representation?

DS: For one, this movie was made by nontrans people about trans people, like most documentaries about us are. Trans viewers who feel alienated or misrepresented may reach out to me, a trans person in the film, before they reach out to you if they feel politically distanced from you by what they saw. Also, you have already had your say. Often, when I see a film I'm unhappy with, I know that the ship has already sailed, there is no way that the filmmakers are going to change it or remove it from circulation, so why bother having yet another conversation about transphobia (especially with a nontrans person) when my life is full of those conversations, usually that I don't get to choose to opt out of? Media makers have incredible power, privilege, and responsibility. This is especially true when it comes to representing trans people because misinformation is the norm, documentary is the major tool for representing the community, and many nontrans viewers believe everything they see in a doc to be true.

SF: Yes, the one critique we've received, but don't think applies to this project, is the problem with nontrans folks making films about trans folks. We set out to create a doc that would inspire a dialogue in the queer community that wasn't happening publicly. This dialogue included us, our lives, and our community, and that was precisely our concern and drive in making it. It concerned us on many very intimate and personal levels. This is not an example of an outsider looking in and telling someone else's story. The lives of the three trans men, their thoughts, and their questions were representations of the theory we presented and the struggles we were having—this was part of our personal story. Still, if we crossed the line in *Boy I Am,* we need to see that and be accountable for that.

This brings me back to the questions we're always thinking about. What is the responsibility of the filmmaker and an audience member in getting and giving information? As a media producer and an activist,

I find that there is a delicate balance between creating media that will demand attention, educate, and inspire thought and action while maintaining the boundaries of respect and supporting the evolution of the queer community. One must always be aware and strive to maintain this balance. Fear of media portrayal of the queer community was the original impetus for my involvement in media production. Yet, while the ultimate aim is to open dialogue and understanding, the media maker always risks perpetuating the representation they deem harmful. I want to know how you, as an activist, lawyer, educator, writer, public figure/speaker (and then some), weigh these risks about representation.

DS: In terms of how I want to represent trans communities and see them represented, I do have some new ideas about that recently. I think the thing I'd like to see most is for films, trainings, shows, speeches, panels, and other public-education tools to stop trying to answer the questions, "Why are people trans? How do they feel about themselves? What are they like?" and start focusing just on, "What are the obstacles to trans people's survival and equality? What does discrimination look like? How can it be prevented?" I think that as soon as the first set of questions is in play, trans people are objects of fascination. We're suddenly defending our very existence, participating in the assumption that we are strange, unusual, interesting, and, ultimately, that our humanity has to be proven and defended. When people attend trainings, film screenings, and events that attempt to make trans people human by explaining who we are and why we are this way, we further entrench the objectifying method of viewing us that already indoctrinates people who view us on *Jerry Springer* or *Law & Order*.

What we really want to be training people to do is to stop seeing trans people as rarefied objects; to stop asking trans people inappropriate questions about our bodies, sexualities, and life histories; to stop creating policies that demand trans people disclose genital status when nontrans people are never asked to do so; and to begin to be able to identify obstacles that they are participating in or creating to trans people's equality and survival. This is a totally different framework for trans public education. It would include documentary film where trans people didn't do the usual things, like talk about their childhoods and surgeries and put on makeup or binders in front of the camera, but instead where trans people, never having to explain themselves, talked about their issues with Medicaid, prisons, schools, or shelters. The viewer would not learn the genital status of the trans subjects any more than they would learn it for the "experts" in the documentary. I think that the Sylvia Rivera Law Project's movie, *Toilet Training*, is one such documentary, and I think it is like that because it was made by trans people confronting a specific social issue.

I give this same advice to the hordes of well-meaning "researchers" —usually graduate students—who contact me wanting to conduct surveys about how trans people see our bodies or how we have sex. They are interested in studying us to deconstruct gender and to demonstrate how we think about ourselves. I beg them to stop studying us and our existence and start studying the institutional obstacles and systemic oppression we face that is so underdescribed and underdiscussed. Similarly, for people trying to sensitize their institutions to trans people, I beg them to stop creating panels where trans people speak about our life stories, and instead create meaningful training curricula that help trainees analyze the specific obstacles to trans access within the institution. It's about moving away from defining and describing trans people, and toward defining and describing the concrete changes we need to end gender oppression.

Seeing *Boy I Am* again, and dialoguing with you about it, has helped me get at this paradigm shift for trans public-education materials that I'm hoping for. I think it is the next step in building trans political power, and in moving away from a medicalized gaze on the trans body/identity, and toward a political gaze from trans experience onto oppressive institutions.

Three Essays on Art, Academia, and Economics

By Jessica Lawless

Just Turn Around Now

When I was a kid I was obsessed with revenge stories. My favorite was *The Girl Most Likely to . . .* , an obscure made-for-TV movie from the 1970s starring Stockard Channing. Channing is the "ugly girl" who gets into a car accident, has plastic surgery, becomes "beautiful," and, one by one, picks off the people who made her life miserable. This gave me hope. As a shy, chubby, not very athletic or popular frizzy-haired girl, revenge meant liberation from my lonely outsider status. I've gotten over the need to avenge my childhood years—for the most part. What I find curious is that I continue to buy into the idea that "success is the best revenge." That there is some fantasy I'm still chasing.

Recently, walking down a corridor of a building on the college campus where I teach, I was reminded of another old fantasy. A decade earlier I had been walking down the corridor of the History of Consciousness department at UC Santa Cruz. I walked by

Originally published in *make/shift* no. 6 (fall/winter 2009/2010)

Donna Haraway's office and my heart started racing like I was a teenager in love. I walked by Angela Davis's office expecting angels to start singing. My palms were sweating. I expected a security guard to appear and escort me from the building. The irony was that I lived in Seattle, the heyday of the grunge-music scene. I couldn't spit without hitting an actual rock star. But that empty corridor on a secluded college campus in a small hippie town was where *my* rock stars hung out. Behind the one open door was James Clifford, the historian who flipped anthropology on its ass and who I was meeting to learn more about this graduate program. (For those of you keeping track, this was an informational visit; I hadn't even filled out an application yet.) I had a fantasy of hanging out with these folks, reading, talking politics, taking down institutional oppressions. I fantasized about becoming Dr. Lawless, a superhero, the avenging academic, the girl most likely to save the world from intersectional isms.

However, as I was standing there, a different story emerged. The banality of the corridor struck me like a physical blow. Though there were posters on the walls announcing great events, great speakers, great films, great greatness that was happening on the campus, almost every door in the hallway was shut. Through the ones that were open, someone was sitting alone at a computer. Where was the activity, the action, the knowledge being generated? Community, political debate, and artistic collaborations were more evident in the way-too-cool Seattle bars and music scene I was desperately bored with. Too many drunken nights, bad relationships, and painful fights over organizing goals with my sister collective members in the self-defense organization I'd been a part of for the past five years had led to fantasizing about graduate school as my ticket out. So I wasn't willing to see the intense solitude and loneliness permeating the university corridor. At the time I chalked up the discomfort to my usual sense of outsider status. I was looking for the next big thing in my life, and I had decided Dr. Lawless was it.

This fantasy didn't appear out of nowhere. A year earlier I was at the annual conference of the Washington State Coalition Against Domestic Violence. I was the keynote speaker at the Women of Color Caucus's breakfast. My friend Tracy had invited me to speak about the self-defense program she and I and another friend had created for women in domestic-violence situations. One reason Tracy had asked me was because I had left a violent relationship and ended up in a shelter a few years earlier. That happened the same year my friend Mia was raped and murdered. These were the facts of my life at the time, and it was hard to imagine a time when they wouldn't be. So I was in great awe when Beth Richie gave the opening keynote of the conference and giddily said she is also known as Dr. Richie or Professor Richie, names she never could have imagined being called several years earlier when she was in a violent relationship.[1]

That was truly a revelatory moment. Formerly battered woman does more than survive. As I listened to Beth Richie's talk, the fantasy of Dr. Lawless began. Being a survivor has never been far enough away from being a victim for me. I wanted more. Becoming Professor Lawless would be my best revenge against ex-lovers, ex-friends, family members I wish I could break up with, and the entirety of grades K through 12.

Several years later, when I was living in Pomona, California, and working on my MA in cultural studies, I didn't fully understand the intense loneliness of the academic corridor I had visited at Santa Cruz. I wish I had. Or at least that I had given more consideration to the

---

1. This isn't true. I apologize, Dr. Richie and *make/shift* readers, for not checking my memory until recently, and for stating that Dr. Richie was in an abusive relationship. In 2017, while editing this story for a longer project on the topic of higher ed becoming a Ponzi scheme in the post-recession economy, I asked a friend to put me in touch with Beth Richie. Dr. Richie graciously let me know that my memory is for shit. She did not tell the story I thought she told; she makes clear in her work that she has never been in a violent relationship with an intimate partner. I'm sorry I put out false information about a person I admire who approaches her own work with clarity and integrity. I'm embarrassed of my buy-in to the American dream despite knowing better. Part of the knowing better was the nagging question in my mind about the fact that Beth Richie has been out and with a female partner for as long as I've known of her work, while the story in my mind involved an abusive cis man. I also couldn't square the date she completed her PhD with the date of the conference I attended. I was so committed to my own myth-making that I ignored the raging red flags. My memory and creativity formed a narrative to serve my unexpected acceptance of the idea that education would ensure an even playing field where I could "pull myself up" into middle-class stability. I'm fascinated with my buy-in to the Horatio Alger bullshit I've been challenging in art, writing, and activism for years. At the same time, this memory being for shit is different from the idea of "false memory," or misremembering traumatic events. I am purposefully using creative license to narrativize my experiences. It makes perfect sense that my origin story about becoming a professor is not true. What I was going for—economic and emotional stability—was never going to be found in academia. The more compelling story is how I moved through that buy-in mind-set to find new concepts of stability and security as an aging, queer, anti-capitalist feminist.

fact that as soon as I finished the GRE I went to a bar. Conclusion: academics make me feel profoundly alone and in need of a drink. Two years of grad school was enough. I would become Dr. Lawless by checking the appropriate box on forms that offered a "title" section. Fuck the PhD.

Timing being everything, I finished my MA in September 2001. My thesis on the renewed interest in anarchism via the anti–corporate globalization movements and the institutional mechanisms of racial profiling did not make me particularly marketable amid the rabid patriotism of the post-9/11 era. After several months of unemployment and then working for the same wage I had earned before I had a master's degree—except for fewer hours and no health care—I revived the fantasy of Dr. Lawless. Like many others do in bad economies, I decided to go back to school.

Except I was rejected by every PhD program I applied to. My best friend cheered me up by pointing out that I had been working against institutions most of my life and shouldn't be surprised if they don't throw open the doors every time I knock. I let go of Dr. Lawless once again, but not Professor Lawless. The following year, I was accepted into an MFA program, which really made more sense, since my cultural studies thesis was a video and not a paper.

Eight years after hearing Beth Richie speak, I had two graduate degrees, $85,000 in student loans, and the honor of being called Professor Lawless at several part-time, adjunct-faculty teaching positions in various Southern California colleges. Academia had become my home. But it was a rental property I couldn't afford. Adjunct professors are contracted semester to semester. We are lucky if this includes an office to meet with students. After subtracting expenditures for preparation, travel, and supplies, our salaries can be as low as ten dollars an hour. There is no health care; these positions almost never become full-time. We are always, always looking for work, trying to secure the next contract while also looking for a tenure-track (permanent) job. At the same time, we must prove our value to our field by exhibiting, publishing, and presenting—all paid for out of our pockets. Classroom teaching is almost an aside, though negative evaluations from students can keep us from being rehired. We are contingent to the universities, not paid enough to get our student loans out of forbearance, and not given health care. My new home, which had once been a fantasy, turned into a bad dream, reminiscent of when I was homeless a decade earlier. Well, sort of.

I was homeless in Seattle after I left a violent relationship. I qualified for a thirty-day stay in a confidential domestic-violence shelter the night Bryan grabbed the knives from the kitchen drawer, smashed the thirty-inch TV in the street, chased after me in his truck as I left the house on foot, and shot off his gun (the one he had for "the revolution"). After staying in the shelter, I couch surfed until I was able to get back on my feet and off welfare.

Being an adjunct professor is not really like my relationship with Bryan or its aftermath. There are distinct differences between then and now in terms of my socioeconomic status—homeless welfare recipient versus university professor—and my quality of life—I have a loving partner with whom I share a West Hollywood apartment. However, the intense lack of security, self-doubt, isolation, and never knowing what's coming next has painful similarities to being in an abusive relationship.

My first year out of grad school, I had a one-year full-time position with a good salary and benefits. For the couple of years since, I've been doing the equivalent of couch surfing, temporarily setting up shop in other people's classrooms while they're on sabbatical advancing their careers. The nagging question about where I fit in remains. Once it was connected to a peer group; now it is connected to a paycheck. It has always been connected to a fantasy about having something more.

And that's the problem. Having more is a terribly limited goal tangled up in the American dream, a belief that hard work pays off equally and fairly. What happens if you work hard and you don't reach your goal? What happens if you work hard for a home and then lose it? What if that home isn't safe or your basic needs aren't met? What happens if you work hard and all you find is deep loneliness? Success isn't the best revenge if all you're doing is working.

Of course, having more is no longer a reality for most of us. My dream of being a tenured university professor crashed this past winter as the U.S. economy crashed. In response to the thick application packets I sent out, I received letters that read,

Dear Ms. Lawless,

> Unfortunately the [fill in the blank] state budget deficit
> was greater than anticipated, and the search for the posi-
> tion in [fill in the blank] has been cancelled.

Having my career end before it takes off sucks. Yet, like when Bryan
shot off the gun, this is my exit from a situation I am happy to leave. The
truth is, I did go from being a homeless woman to being a university
professor. Now I am going to go from being a university professor to
who knows what. What I do know is that it's going to be so much more
than just surviving.

That's How the Light Gets In

In June 2009 I was sitting in my apartment in Los Angeles writing about
falling out of a stalled career in academia into the unknown of our crap
economy. A year later, writing from my sweet adobe house in Santa
Fe, New Mexico, I am very aware that the changes I've made are about
much more than geography.

In L.A. the phrase "just turn around now" floated through my head
like a command. It's a line from the Gloria Gaynor song (and the gay
anthem) "I Will Survive." I've been dancing around survival my whole
life. Taking stock of my situation last summer, I was reminded that surviving is not enough. Really embracing life means believing I deserve
more than simply surviving (though it is never simple!). Believing is
the challenge. It takes a leap of faith—a daunting proposition since I
don't subscribe to any organized belief systems. So I learned to just turn
around. To look in the cracks and crevices, shifting my viewpoint until
the focus is slightly askew. To queer things up, if
you will. Or, to quote another anthem, "Anthem"
by Leonard Cohen, "There is a crack in everything, that's how the light gets in."

Originally published
in *make/shift* no. 8
fall/winter 2010/2011)

My last couple of years in L.A. I felt stuck, so beat down that change seemed impossible. I started to believe, like a needle stuck in the groove of a record, that there was something wrong with me, personally. What was actually wrong was that I was thinking of myself as an individual, forgetting that I was connected to various systems with deep systemic problems. The state of California and the state of higher ed in California were bankrupt and corrupt. The shifting grounds were too unstable to find my footing. While there were movements building around this, the lack of stability in my income and the lack of health-care benefits as an adjunct professor meant my involvement in those movements was not sustainable. Movement, for me, meant moving out of the state.

Movement also meant moving out of a state of depression. For several years my partner and I were taking turns being unemployed or underemployed. When we were employed, V was working seven days a week while I put in a second forty hours a week on tenure-track job applications that never panned out. We didn't have material things to lose, but we were hit hard by the crashing economy. Opportunity was shutting down all around us. Merely living hand-to-mouth was becoming a luxury.

The depression began to lift when we stopped correlating employment with success and unemployment with personal failure. By shifting our perspective we realized what we already knew: capitalism is a sick, insidious system that makes it difficult to see one's own complicity with it. For us, movement needed to be about love, not earning more money. We needed to make a move toward happiness rather than career opportunism. We chose northern New Mexico for its absolute and stunning beauty and Santa Fe for its art-centric atmosphere.

Surrounded by beauty and with a renewed relationship to creativity, we found that love easily became a more central location in our lives. We began to see ourselves as family. This is no small feat since we don't believe in marriage as the great equalizer, and we left California while the state was in a tizzy over the passage of Prop 8, the "California Marriage Protection Act," which overturned a previous ruling in favor of same-sex marriage. We were living in West Hollywood, one of the country's gay capitals, where marriage had become the defining factor of family rather than the normalizing, assimilationist force that it is.

Our "community" didn't have room for our queer, gender-nonconforming, anticapitalist relationship. Here, in our new location, we've met a lot of straight couples who have been together for decades without getting married or having kids. Oddly, in this small, relatively rural community, I feel less of an outsider than I did in West Hollywood as a queer woman in my forties who has a genderqueer partner, has never been married, is not planning on getting married, and has happily chosen not to have kids.

Finding our own way to define ourselves as family means we've recognized ways in which we are a conduit between our families of origin. For example, we financially help V's family members, who also live hand-to-mouth, while my father, whose class identity as an immigrant has spanned working class to upper middle class, has helped us out at crucial moments. Besides our other contributions, when we receive money from my dad, we always pass some of it on to V's family. This is a fundamental part of our shared budget.

Being a conduit between our families of origin also means that V, for the first time in his life, has a parental figure who can provide a safety net. I finally have family members who recognize me as a grown person able to take care of myself and others, while my father is still wondering when I am going to "make it" in my career. Through this, V and I now have identities affected by each other's rather than rooted solely in our families of origin. Clearly we retain our individual histories, but together we have a combined class identity different from the ones we grew up in.

Away from the normalizing forces of the mainstream gay community, academia, and the Los Angeles art market, and seeing myself in a new way in relation to family, I've become free from the single-minded focus on career I had after earning my MFA. I expected my graduate degrees would mean entrée into the middle classes, and, when that didn't occur, I felt like I had failed. Now, I find myself wondering why I expected something different from what I have, and why I get stuck thinking I need more.

It's a hard story to change. It's going up against the myth of the American dream, assimilation, and the idea that education guarantees movement. It's going up against the story of my dad's family—a family that was not seen as white when they immigrated (neither here nor in their country of origin), yet now has the trappings and privileges of whiteness. As a second-generation U.S. citizen, is it my job to continue the myth of that dream, or is it my job to have the strength to change my family story? In my move toward love, I am finding the strength to be a catalyst for changing these family histories.

It is no coincidence that these connections emerged as I made my way through the California higher-ed diaspora. I had moved there to attend graduate school and change my status from "formerly homeless woman due to domestic violence" to "professor." I put a lot of cachet on that, and when it didn't happen, I felt lost. But by changing my story from one of individual failure to one of systemic failure, I am also changing the family stories I was directly and indirectly asked to uphold. I am putting an end to the cover-up.

In some cases the cover-up was quite literal—like the hole my high-school boyfriend put in a wall in my mother's home during a fight in which he broke my arm. My stepdad simply covered the hole with a pretty picture. The perfect metaphor. If everything looks okay, then it must be. That's our unspoken agreement, our covenant of silence. I took our covenant forward for a long time. Now, I am turning back to look through the cracks in that old drywall. Staring me right in the face is my grandmother Ilonka.

I can count on one hand the number of times I met her. I was told she was too difficult to be around. There is a story that she is to blame for her brother's suicide. My dad's childhood memories include his mother, Ilonka, sitting at the kitchen table, sobbing for hours, and that she was in and out of psych wards. He remembers not being able to sleep because his parents were fighting so loudly. He has insomnia to this day.

These stories don't reveal the fact that Ilonka was brought to the United States against her will, by her cousin, my grandfather. He was the one who forged a path for the family to escape anti-Semitism in Hungary, a needed role. But he wanted a Hungarian wife and Hungarian children. My grandmother became the family's sacrificial lamb. She probably sat at the table crying because she was forced to leave her Sephardic, Romani, Hungarian roots to live a life she didn't choose. One of her acts of resistance was to never learn English very well.

Of course, she may have sat at the table crying because so much of the family was killed in the Holocaust/Porrajmos[2] while she and my grandfather were on the fast road to assimilation. Maybe she knew something important was being left behind. Maybe she felt shame for her complicity in wiping out her culture for future generations. As a member of those future generations, this makes more sense to me than blaming her for all of the family's unhappiness. It also makes sense to me, a girl child a generation removed, that my story is not the same as my father's. I didn't pull myself up out of violence into the middle classes never to look back again.

My story is about a family who cut itself off from its own history to escape war, a family whose assimilation into whiteness meant a loss of culture and ethnicity. It's a story of diaspora and forced immigration. One of the most violent acts in this story was cutting me off from my grandmother. The message was, there is something so wrong with a part of who you are that you have to leave it behind. But I see the cracks in the story. I see I'm not the only woman in the family who struggled to live outside the framework of violence. I see it all because I simply turned around.

Educate then Agitate:
Adjunct Faculty Are Standing Up and Fighting Back

Snapshot: Broken bones, black eyes, alcohol, heroin, food stamps, general assistance, domestic-violence shelter, homelessness, couch surfing, sexual assault, friends dying from overdoses and illnesses, a friend raped and murdered, a college degree earned and forgotten.

Snapshot: Forty years old and on another side of my own history, two graduate degrees and $90,000 of student debt yet hopeful for something new.

Originally published in *make/shift* no. 18 (winter/spring 2015/2016)

2. *Porrajmos* is the Romani word for the Holocaust.

Snapshot: Hope fading, a college professor hustling for teaching gigs, editing gay porn, working as a home health-care aide, working in non-profits, searching and searching for a tenure-track job, an economic collapse, bankruptcy, contracting at nonprofits, searching and searching for any job, unemployment checks in the summers, food stamps, state-funded dental and health care, a move to a less expensive state.

Snapshot: Teaching at a community college and never shutting up about the inequitable system creating the adjunct crisis, being elected to Faculty Senate, asking the new college president (a Latina known for her innovative policies to increase Latin@ student enrollment) what she's going to do to create better working conditions for the three hundred adjunct faculty and getting the response, "It isn't going to be the first thing on the docket, and adjuncts just don't make much money anywhere so I suggest you marry well."

Snapshot: Depression, anxiety, isolation, and an intense sense of failure tinged with embarrassed amusement when telling a friend who routinely exposes the assimilationist scam of "marriage equality" that my immediate response to the college president—"not all of us can legally get married"—was met with a round of applause while I desperately wanted to rescind my statement and break down the clusterfuck of issues at hand.

Snapshot: More regularly writing and publishing my story while participating in adjunct activist e-mail lists and Facebook pages, organizing a simple event for Campus Equity Week, learning from a New Faculty Majority organizer that this small action held great significance for the movement because it put my state on the map, having a colleague tweet a photo of us at our event that went viral and was picked up by *Al Jazeera* for a piece on higher education in the United States, catching my breath in fear for my job while in the same moment realizing that being public is the best job security I could have.

Snapshot: Attending a town-hall meeting on labor and justice, nervously taking the mic at the urging of the friend sitting to my right, after the friend sitting to my left demanded a trans*-inclusive curriculum in public schools, and describing our precarious working conditions at the community college in front of two of the college's vice presidents, getting loud applause and a card from a labor lawyer in case there are any issues with my bosses as well as an invitation to speak at the next Community Labor Council meeting, realizing that no matter how many committees or task forces are established colleges are not going to change adjunct faculty working conditions—change is going to come from working with the labor movement.

Snapshot: A decade after being hired for my first temporary teaching job and a decade into my post-graduate-degree job search, being hired by Service Employees International Union (SEIU) on the recently launched higher-ed campaign unionizing adjunct faculty, quitting my current teaching job midsemester, moving back to the state I left during the economic collapse, leaving my partner and kitties until they can join me three months later, becoming part of an organizing team that won five union elections in less than a year.

Snapshot: Being in a room filled with six hundred union members from every work sector imaginable and listening to everyone break into loud applause as my friend Jessica Beard, another adjunct professor, walks onto the stage and introduces herself, getting tears in my eyes because I am no longer alone.

I am still trying to understand the whirlwind of changes in my life since I left academia and became a union organizer. I had invested years of intellectual and emotional labor, and my sense of self, in being a professor and looking for a full-time academic job. The intensity and competitiveness of academia messed with my head and confused many of my long-held personal values.

Before I earned my graduate degrees I existed on the margins, living, loving, and organizing, content in my location. Getting my degrees created a bizarre belief in some Horatio Alger bullshit. I got stuck on the singular narrative of "Domestic-violence survivor and former addict becomes professor." Of course, moving through cultural and class statuses by sheer determination and rugged individualism isn't feasible for most people. To get old-school, the imperialist white-supremacist capitalist heterosexist patriarchy is real. It's painfully lonely to believe one is capable of existing outside of this. It's a different pain than the weight of systemic oppression because the trap of individualism prevents people from seeing how to fight what truly needs to be fought.

What broke me out of nearly debilitating depression were several moments when I recognized that I was standing in the center of a growing movement. I was fighting back with my friends and colleagues, all of whom have equally thick stories about the financial, emotional, and physical consequences of no job security, no employer-provided health care, no living wage, no regular channels of participation in campus governance or community, and unfathomable debt.

There are over one million adjunct professors in the United States. That's a lot of people with a brick ceiling blocking their career paths. It's also a lot of people organizing.

Obviously with so many people come differences in goals, tactics, strategies, and values. Most of those in the movement leadership are straight, cisgender, middle-aged white men. Those of us who do not fall into all of those categories are people with cultural capital despite the lack of economic and other privileges. Or we are union staff. At times, what we are doing *feels* radical in its historicity, yet it is ultimately a re-form movement. I agree with the current goals—it's the best option we have at this point—but I wonder if a more radical movement is possible. Specifically, I wonder if we can organize from an intersectional feminist framework approaching equity with radical inclusivity. I wonder this especially as the Black Lives Matter movement is beautifully modeling ways to address these very questions.

This is not a random or irrelevant query. Sixty percent of adjunct professors are female.[3] Ten percent of *all* college professors are under-represented racial and ethnic groups, and 73 percent of that 10 percent are contingent faculty. This movement has to address race and gender. I invited Irina Contreras to have a drink one afternoon and chew on this problem together with me. Irina is a friend and co-conspirator of many

3. The research uses the terms "women" and "men." Genderqueer, trans, gender-non-conforming, and non-binary genders are not included. I am using the term "female" with the assumption that within that 60 percent of people marked "woman," there are people who do not identify that way.

years who was finishing up her MFA at California College of the Arts (CCA) in the Bay Area when I was assigned to organize the contingent[4] faculty there. Having been an adjunct before, and very aware that she had been educated mostly by adjunct faculty, Irina has been active in the CCA unionization effort.

Irina noted that the creation of a faceless precarious workforce is not new. Adjunct professors are just the next wave in the rolling tide and, as she pointed out, not the only academic workers caught in the undertow. Janitorial staff, food-service workers, graduate-student teaching assistants, administrative support staff, and undergraduate work-study students are all struggling. Joining forces with these different stakeholders is an obvious way to grow the movement and break down the hierarchical nature of the university. Irina also pointed to the relationship between policing college campuses and gentrification. At CCA this plays out in a fear of houseless Black men who set up encampments near the campus. Administrative policy assumes students and faculty must be protected from this imagined "bogeyman." The school creates a system where Black security guards are hired to keep Black folks off campus. The school-to-prison pipeline and Proposition 209 (a 1996 law that banned affirmative action in hiring and admissions in California's public institutions) ensure a dearth of Black students on campus, so CCA's systemic policing is not suspect to most.

Stephanie Young, a poet and professor at Mills College in Oakland, California, who has been central to creating their union, told me in a conversation we had in her backyard one afternoon that she is not convinced it is possible for the adjunct movement to organize from an intersectional feminist framework. Stephanie did consider one way that intersectionality could be possible: through alliances with students around the issues we share—student debt, questioning the necessity for formal education, housing costs, gentrification, and the racial-justice movements actively using queer feminist organizing.

---

4. There are a lot of different terms for adjunct faculty. Part of this is institutional bureaucracy, and part of it is movement debates à la 1990s identity politics. I use "adjunct" and "contingent" interchangeably and generally follow each term by "faculty" unless I am making a point of reclaiming the term "adjunct" as a positive location in the university rather than a mark of failure.

Stephanie further explained that if contingent faculty were aligned with students rather than with university administration, this would destabilize the locus of power and allow the movement to make concrete structural changes instead of simply fighting to "get our piece of the pie."[5]

The adjunctification of the university began in the 1970s and 1980s, exactly as women, people of color, and queer and trans* folks entered academia in measurable numbers. Tenure was destroyed because of institutionalized misogyny, racism, cissexism, and homophobia deployed through neoliberal economic policies. Yet we still hold on to the cultural mythology that education is the great equalizer. It's true that students of color earn higher wages with a college degree. On the other hand, Stephanie brought up the troubling idea that many of the women of color she teaches will enter the workforce with such massive debt that they would potentially be in a better position not taking out tens of thousands of dollars of student loans.

A student I've worked closely with over the past year, Lukaza Branfman-Verissimo, recently graduated from CCA. Active in the Students of Color Coalition, Lukaza was part of the union organizing on campus and fearlessly spoke up to the administration in support of her professors. During our communications about the possibility of an intersectional feminist adjunct movement, Lukaza echoed Irina: the history of U.S. labor is largely the history of Black labor. Lukaza highlighted the clear and inherent links between the struggles for racial justice and economic justice during a Black Brunch–style intervention at an event we organized. She wrote:

> On this day in which we consider the power and strength that we gain from coming together to form unions, we also honor those who have come before us. Those union organizers who have fought for workers' rights and died for us to have a living wage, an eight-hour work day, health insurance, social security, family and maternity leave.

5. These ideas are actually from several conversations with Stephanie in real life, on Facebook, and at panel discussions. She and I both think and write about similar concerns in higher ed, and our conversations bleed into each other.

These people stood up to a system that used brutal force to try to stop them from empowering working people. And, as we honor this legacy of organizers in the United States, we also honor those thousands of people of color who continue to be killed at the hands of police in the streets of our country today. Those that hold the power in this country have a vested interest in our not coming together, not drawing the connection between the people's struggles for survival past and present. But we refuse that amnesia. So, we place the memory of all these people side by side. Let their names be called out and heard.

Snapshot: Standing in an art gallery in San Francisco's Mission District, a space that is often predominantly white but is not today because we organized this event with a consciousness about race and gender, surrounded by union members, adjunct faculty, artists, students, low-wage workers fighting for $15 and a union, Black Lives Matter activists, Critical Resistance organizers, Google bus/gentrification resisters, student-debt strikers, labor archivists and historians, a labor choir, legendary Bay Area artists, first-time spoken-word performers, my coworkers, my best friend, my partner, I confidently take the mic to a roomful of applause and say, "Thank you for being here."

Debt

By Javon Johnson

I am a full-time university professor and
my job is exactly as sexy as it sounds.
On most days I read
an ungodly amount. And,
when I am not doing that, I'm teaching
and when I am not doing that
I am either grading,
prepping classes,
in committee meetings,
or doing service work. And,
when I am not doing that
I'm advising and mentoring students,
serving the community in which I live,
conducting my own research, while
managing a full-time performance career,
in other words, I put in work.

I love my job though.
On most days teaching is a lot
like one of those complicated math problems
where if Jonny had 7 candy bars and
a train left Kansas at 3 p.m.
going 90 miles an hour,
how many basketballs

Originally published
in *make/shift* no. 18
(winter/spring 2015/2016)

can he cook on the roof
before the kids start smiling?
It is confusing but
I love how we come together
and almost always figure it out.

I had this one student,
who's as Brown as the border
that crossed her.
Asked me if I think
her white colleagues understand
that her family had been trying
to get her into college for generations?
Wondered if they understood
the weight of that? If they knew
she picked this university
the same way
her grandfather picked fruit:
slow and painful,
but what else was she gonna do?

We spoke about why so many of
her colleagues seemed angrier
with "illegal immigration"
than with illegal banking
practices. Fact:
It would cost this government
63 billion to pay for everyone's tuition
at public colleges and universities,
yet they spend 69 billion
to subsidize the costs,
and another 107 billion on student loans.

When tuition is steadily rising and
the starting salaries
are dropping for recent graduates,
degrees are no different
than your designer bag,

a cheap fashion statement
not even worth the trip to the mall.
No one ever tells you that
you have to drown in debt
in hopes of making it
to the shore; that
the loan system is a lot
like Alcatraz, like Rikers Island,
like getting fucked while
the guards don't even have the decency
to pretend to look the other way.
The difference between prisoners
and student debtors
is that students are taught to think
they are on the outside of the bars.

What kind of world do we live in
where it's okay to bail out banks
who are "too big to fail"
even though they bank on
the failure of students?
What world do we live in
where as a college professor
I too struggle to pay back student loans?
It's like I learned nothing
from Biggie, like I'm getting high
on my own supply.
Like I'm selling crack
to pay down my crack debt.
But I am the American Dream,
all shiny and bright lights. Beautiful,
like pulled-up bootstraps.

Some days I feel like a wolf
in sheep's clothing, like
a shepherd leading his flock to slaughter.
I teach classes on performance, structural

racism and gender inequality in a system
that is more willing to punish students
for plagiarism than for sexual assault.
What are we teaching our students
when we tell them that the thoughts
of dead white men
are far more valuable than their own
living bodies? Students have become nothing
more than Black Friday customers
whose pockets have been picked
clean long before they walked in
the store. The university
does not have time to worry
about whose body gets trampled
in the stampede of it all.

But our Black and Brown bodies being
here is a revolutionary act.
We force them to peel back the curtains
to a well-manicured show;
to deal with the borders,
the rape, the prison system, and
the racism it's all built on.
We watch them squirm
when we open our mouths
because they know we are not satisfied
with just getting into the tower,
we want to claw it down.
And, they should be uncomfortable with that;
it ain't called growing pains for nothing.

So, if Jonny boarded a train
from Kansas with more than
170,000 in debt leaving at 3 p.m.,
how long will it take for us to realize
that cooking basketballs on a roof
makes so much more sense than this?

Dear Nomy

Excerpts from the ongoing
advice column by Nomy Lamm

Q: I recently got a job wherein for the first time I have a 401(k) option. I'm torn between putting away a few hundred dollars a month for my retirement (which is decades off) and donating that money to a progressive nonprofit or someplace else where it may be more needed. What do you think?

A: Having money to save or give away is a privilege, and it's always good to think about what effect you want to have on the world. If I had been asked this question five years ago, I would have said that the system won't exist anymore by the time you're of retirement age, that there are a lot of projects that need your money, and that the universe will provide if you live how you want the world to be. Put your money toward building a future that can support you when all this other shit topples.

That was before I had to file five years' worth of taxes all at once. Idealism can lead to harsh awakenings. Who knows if the world will take care of you if you don't plan to take care of yourself? The world-weary thing to do would be to take full advantage and save that shit. You never know what your life will be like in thirty years.

Both things are true, so why not split it up? Half goes into your retirement fund, half goes to organizations and projects that need it. You might want to prioritize funding youth projects, since they'll be running things when you and I are old. (Might I suggest the Young Women's Empowerment Project? Check it out at www.youarepriceless.org.)

Q: A few months ago, I lost my cushy grant-writing job, and I'm close to broke. Last week, I was offered some freelance work with a company whose business I have ethical/political issues with. The job involves writing ad copy for an agency that works with some gigantic multinationals that are definitely part of an overall system I spend much of my time and energy resisting. In fact, I've been boycotting one of the client companies for years. The ads I'd be working on aren't for these particular notorious companies, but they're for pretty big corporations. So, I don't know—do I take the freelance gig to get some of their cash into my fast-draining checking account, or hold out for something more in line with my values?

A: It seems like your answer boils down to two things: (1) whether or not you *can* do this job, and (2) whether or not you *have to* do this job. When you imagine yourself sitting down to write ad copy for this company, does it feel possible to do a good job for them? Would it be a simple task, or would it mean pushing yourself in ways that make you feel icky and stolen from?

Consistency is important if you want your actions to have meaning in the world. But if you really do need the money, and this is your only option, then do it. No shame in survival. What matters is your own internal sense of balance. Do what you need to, and don't glorify your decision.

I almost ended with a snide comment about how we're all cockroaches—as important as our lives feel, we're also an infestation, and our little choices don't really change that much. When I think about ethical debates around work and consumption, I think about class and privilege, access to options. Most people do shit for money that we don't want to do or don't agree with. Our ways of resisting and transforming are unique to our lives and communities. But I think we all dream of being able to live in ways that feel ethically and energetically whole, so if that is something that's within your reach, by all means, hold out for it.

Trashing Neoliberalism

By Yasmin Nair

Trashing the Neoliberal City by AREA is a pamphlet/free PDF, a record of conceptual performances against the neoliberalization of a city ruled by the free-market economy and privatization (full disclosure: I helped fund another AREA project). The resulting demolition of public life becomes a justification for further privatization. As Pauline Lipman, a professor of education at DePaul University, puts it, "Chicago . . . officials . . . fail to educate students and then use that failure as a reason to privatize schools."

Trashing is a contradiction: a textual archive of transient acts whose effectiveness depends on their ephemerality. But without a record, such moments of resistance can easily be forgotten. *Trashing* tells us that in late 2004, the Chicago Housing Authority (CHA) put up a series of slickly executed posters around the theme "This is CHAnge." These extolled the virtues of Chicago's public-housing system and ignored the reality: the displacement of Chicagoans by voracious urban development. So, a group of anonymous artists, subversively named CHAos, replaced the CHA posters on May 27, 2005,

Originally published in *make/shift* no. 3 (spring/summer 2008)

with equally slick replicas whose words questioned the city's motives: "Do developers deserve a tax break more than you do?"

Not all the projects seem designed to raise critical awareness within communities. One article describes the rise of the Podmajersky family, which has, since the 1960s, fashioned a real-estate empire out of the mostly Latina/o and blue-collar Pilsen neighborhood, aggressively branding it as the "Chicago Arts District." The family offers cheap rents to artists, described by the anonymous writers of the article as "primarily young and white cultural producers." In 2004, a group named Ultramar Baymount plastered the area with fake family crescents of the "Principality of Podmajersky." We're told: "On the project's website a lively debate emerged about real-estate development and gentrification in the neighborhood." To what end? Much of this online discussion reflects a diffuse critique of gentrification but is dissociated from the concerns of nonartist residents.

Trashing's major flaw is that its understanding of neoliberalism, the problem du jour for the Left, is oddly ahistorical. The economic shifts brought about by neoliberalism—like the state-sponsored backlash against labor unions—began in the 1970s, and they had profound effects on areas like Pilsen. Artists have traditionally been pitted against working-class residents in poorer neighborhoods—and the Podmajerskys have been buying land in Pilsen since the 1960s. In failing to account for how and why Pilsen is symptomatic of neoliberalism and not just age-old gentrification, *Trashing* simply appropriates a cool term and leaves us without a historical understanding of the phenomenon or the means with which to dismantle it.

The editors emphasize that *Trashing* records "a unique period of cultural activism . . . from 2000–2005." Presumably, something accounts for said uniqueness, but we're left clueless as to what that might be. The aftermath of 9/11 brought about drastic changes in urban space with new surveillance technologies, antiterrorism laws, and the policing of un-American bodies. *Trashing* ignores these. The pamphlet is named for a spring 2001 conceptual work by the Department of Space and Land Reclamation, when artists rolled a giant pile of trash down Michigan Avenue. Would this be possible today? If so, what if the practitioners did not look like relatively privileged artsy types whose work could be assimilated into Chicago's carefully cultivated image as a haven for public art? *Trashing* wants to situate itself within a critique of neoliberalism, but it ends up dehistoricizing and depoliticizing the conditions of production surrounding the projects under discussion.

A sociopolitical archive that highlights and relentlessly challenges its own conditions of production, *The Laurence Rassel Show* is a two-CD collection, most of it available for free download. A collaborative effort between the Brussels-based cyberfeminist Laurence Rassel and trans activist and musician Terre Thaemlitz, *LRS* is a meditation on, among other topics, gender and authorship, the literal and metaphorical murder of female writers, copyright laws, and the sharing and reclamation of public common ground. It consists of "readings" by authors such as Michel Foucault (on the death of the author) and Joan Smith (on the link between the ownership of land and the ownership of women), as well as an intense conversation between Thaemlitz and Rassel about the making of the production. All of this is linked by excerpts from *Murder, She Wrote*, featuring the distinctive voice of Angela Lansbury as the female sleuth Jessica Fletcher.

This is a brilliant, beautiful, and extraordinarily textured ambient show and aural drama whose effects are different with each listening. Yet, the overall aesthetics don't distract from the very precise historical points made. Over the course of a little over two hours, we're led, in a nonlinear fashion, through the development of a labyrinthine network of laws made for the "common good" that have, since at least the eighteenth century, produced an increasingly globalized and direct link between the growth of capitalism and the production of bodies as purveyors of privatization. A discussion between Thaemlitz and Rassel sheds light on why the radio show was supposedly cancelled. But this is a highly sophisticated piece, and truth itself is always in doubt. It really doesn't matter whether the show was cancelled, or even if this is a show. Listening to it, I'm reminded of the importance of transience and the power of insurgent and sometimes fictive acts like those of CHAos, acts that appear under cover or in the quiet of night, make their point, and disappear. Disappearance is part of the point.

Community Reparations Now!

Roan Boucher and Tiny aka Lisa Gray-Garcia Talk Revolutionary Giving, Class, Privilege, and More

Tiny aka Lisa Gray-Garcia is the cofounder (with her late mama, Dee) of *POOR Magazine*, a grassroots arts and media-justice organization in San Francisco. Tiny and Dee were houseless for much of Tiny's childhood, evading various systems that threatened to institutionalize, exploit, and incarcerate them. They survived and fought back by remaining fiercely dedicated to each other, creating independent microbusinesses to make ends meet, becoming underground avant-garde art celebrities, and creating *POOR Magazine* to make silenced voices of poor and indigenous people heard through media and art. Tiny tells their story in her 2006 memoir, *Criminal of Poverty: Growing up Homeless in America* (City Lights).

Tiny has been a friend and mentor to me since 2007, when I invited her and four others from POOR to present at Making Money Make Change (MMMC), a yearly social-justice conference I helped organize for young people with wealth. My story, in brief, is that I was raised in a newly wealthy

Originally published in *make/shift* no. 7 (spring/summer 2010)

family, developed anticapitalist politics while hitchhiking around the country in my teens, and began organizing other young rich kids with secret trust funds to give away their inheritances to revolutionary organizing and fight for social justice.

I was inspired by POOR's work and vision. A poor-people-led organization with no paid staff and next to no traditional funding, POOR has a huge scope. Started as a print magazine, POOR now publishes content weekly at www.poormagazine.org. POOR's members are educators, cultural workers, trainers, poets, journalists, performers, and media producers. In part because they refuse to yield to the demands of traditional funders and corporate media, POOR maintains a holistic and transformative vision. Their work exceeds typical definitions of media justice to encompass a wide range of activism and organizing for poor people's rights, as well as a commitment to community building, eldership, ritual and spirituality, and working for the global reclamation of poor people's stolen land and resources.

My relationship with Tiny has thrived on recognizing the tensions and differences between our identities, in regards to class as well as race and gender. (I'm a white trans person and Tiny is a mixed-race, nontrans woman.) We've built trust by talking candidly about what it means to be rooted in our individual histories, communities, and relationships to systemic power while working for a shared vision of economic justice.

Since MMMC, we've had many conversations about reparations, funding revolutionary work beyond the nonprofit industrial complex, and how privileged radicals can leverage resources and power in support of movements led by poor people. In 2009, we collaborated with other members and allies of POOR to create Revolutionary Giving, a weekend-long strategy session held at POOR's offices that focused on building movement dialogue around funding, reparations, and economic justice; about twenty fundraisers, activists, donors, students, and members of POOR participated.

The following offers a glimpse of our ongoing dialogue.

—Roan Boucher

Roan: An important thing that defined the Revolutionary Giving session was that poor people were framing the conversation, not funders—so we were able to talk about the role that structural violence and histories of oppression play in funding dynamics. Those conversations don't usually happen because of how much is at stake—there's often a silent imperative not to alienate donors by talking about oppression in a way that implicates them. POOR reframes the dynamic so that funders are responsible to grassroots organizers instead of the other way around.

Tiny: The way POOR thinks about funding is completely informed by our beliefs about poverty scholarship. It's crucial to look at whose knowledge is considered valuable. Who knows how to best meet the needs of poor people and other marginalized communities—a wealthy funder with a master's, or an *indigena* elder who's been in poverty their whole life? Revolutionary giving is about recognizing that having wealth doesn't qualify you to direct movements. And it doesn't entitle you to keep that wealth—that's what community reparations is about.

Roan: Can you talk more about community reparations?

Tiny: Community reparations means that decisions about how to help people in struggle are made by people in struggle—and that people with resources hear that knowledge and take action accordingly.

Reparations is about repairing a wrong—if you know your money comes from wrong-ass places, if you have an understanding of histories of oppression and stolen resources, then there should be no question that you'll direct that money back towards the communities or movements that were harmed in the creation of that wealth.

One beautiful example is that one of the solidarity-board members at POOR is launching an effort to get land for [our] Homefulness [project]—because that's where her reparations need to go, because her family made money on real-estate development and speculation.

Community reparations is a spectrum; it's a way of life. It's about not devaluing or criminalizing the choices poor people make, the things we do to survive. The way that we've managed to do so much of what we've done at POOR is through what I call "underground economic strategies"—i.e., beg, borrow, and steal. And that's essentially how all us poor folks ever do anything—we use economic strategies that are criminalized. When poor people figure out how to do something outside of the norm, it's criminalized—whereas if Dick Cheney figures out how to do something outside of a norm, it's called a corporation.

So another level of community reparations would be giving money to underground economic strategists panhandling on the street, without tripping about what they're going to do with the money. A CEO of Chevron doesn't get questions about what they're doing with their money—why should a panhandler?

Roan: It's a powerful model to apply to philanthropy because it shifts the focus away from outcomes—receiving grants is usually dependent on having the right language, the best application, the right kind of reporting—doing what funders want, basically.

Tiny: Exactly. At POOR, we refuse to talk in outcomes—how many poor people did you teach in 2009, how much did they learn, how many jobs did they get, how long did they stay in their housing, and all that crap.

Not only is that shit disrespectful, but it wastes a lot of time, a lot of energy, a lot of fucking trees, and a lot of people's work that could be spent on actual solutions.

Roan: It feels like community reparations is more challenging to implement the larger the scale becomes—like the more privilege/power/resources people have, the more desperately we try to hold onto it.

And you can go to a session like Revolutionary Giving and be inspired by concepts like community reparations, but if you have certain kinds of privilege it's easy to retreat back into a community that's detached from people in struggle.

Tiny: That's why we have deeper conversations about interdependence. How do you teach people to be connected to their fellow humans? How do you teach people to be not just in relation to each other—like, say, hello to the panhandler or whatever—but to actually have a responsibility to caregiving?

The teaching of that is rooted in figuring out your relationship to the planet, to your fellow beings. And not just a cute fuzzy cat, but the mama with six kids who has no money. It requires a very intense level of nonselfishness . . . really feeling like you are responsible for your fellow human being.

There are so many people who have nothing who live that way. That's a mindfuck for a lot of people raised in capitalism, that there are many people whose primary, most deeply held value is taking care of their family and community. That is the final, and probably the deepest, strain of community reparations.

Roan: That's what inspires me most when I organize other privileged folks—seeing people act not from a sense of guilt or charity or even a tight political analysis, but from a feeling of being bound up with other people on the planet. The bigger goal is moving people toward community and interdependence—and understanding how that can be a form of wealth that offers more safety and security than individual power and resources. Getting to that place feels like a spiritual process in some ways.

Tiny: Exactly. At POOR, we root what we do in spirituality and love and ancestor worship. It's not religious—it's an understanding that everyone comes with different relationships to the earth and our spirits and our beings and our gods and our folks, and the bigger understanding that we're all really invested in the care of each other.

Roan: At the Revolutionary Giving session, we talked about the idea of living with/caring for families of origin. You posed it as a challenge to privileged people: "Would you be willing to move back home as part of your commitment to revolutionary giving?" It was pretty challenging and provocative for people. Could you talk more about what this idea means to you?

Tiny: There are a few different threads to this. The first one is the concrete level: the tangible results of collective living—resource sharing, reducing consumption, and so on—are in themselves radical acts that challenge capitalism.

But the other thread, the deeper one, is about redesigning ways that people are in relationship with each other. At POOR, we believe that if we aim to transform the world and to caretake communities and movements, caretaking has to start with our roots—our family, if that's possible. Instead of behaving like a twenty-first-century missionary activist, only taking action in communities that you aren't a part of or that are more oppressed than you, you also need to care for your own people. There's a separation that results from a certain kind of activism; increasingly, the nonprofit industrial complex creates compartmentalization between our personal lives and our movement work. But justice in the world and justice in our families—we don't see these things as separate. So to us, if you talk about community reparations, you need to also talk about how are you caregiving for the elders in your family.

Often it's easier to say, "My family are Republicans, my family are capitalists, they told me to get out at eighteen, they have an attitude, my mom is a nightmare, my mom's *crazy*."

So fucking what. I caregave for a mom who had a horrible life, and from a western, Eurocentric perspective she *was* considered crazy. She was extremely not user-friendly and not easy to deal with. And it's in my deep structure as a person of color, as an indigenous person, that that doesn't matter. It's not an excuse or a reason to abandon her or to warehouse her.

Now, I know that this gets really touchy with folks. Especially folks who've had a lot of years of therapy. No, seriously—I want to call that out. In dominant culture, the support is not given for staying and caregiving. The support is given to leave, cut ties, and become independent. That's really embedded in western psychotherapy, in Freudian and Jungian theory. And let's be real about white folks—that's a lot of where their knowledge comes from, especially folks with privilege.

Roan: I agree, and one of the things that inspires me about POOR is this commitment to approaching the work holistically, with so much respect and connection to elders, youth, ancestors, and community. I think it's also important to talk about ways of building community outside of family of origin, which I see happening in healing ways within queer communities, and also within the incredibly diverse community that POOR is creating. I have a very close relationship with my family and feel grateful for that, but so many people have families that are abusive, or rejected them for being queer or different. What do these ideas mean in those contexts?

Tiny: That's absolutely real—I don't want to invalidate that. I pose it as a challenge partly for shock value, to make people think. In some ways it's just a metaphor. Most people in the U.S. have been taught to relate to their families in this detached, capitalist paradigm that's about individualism. How do you get people to think deeply about that in, like, two seconds? I pose it as a challenge because I want people to rethink this paradigm that pathologizes staying with and caretaking for family of origin—but the specific action people take is completely related to their particular situation.

Roan: As a poor people's organization, how did POOR start teaching and training people with privilege, and how do you see that being connected to your work?

Tiny: Before there was a *POOR Magazine*, my mom and I made conceptual art—similar to stuff that Linda Montano or Yoko Ono were making. We started making art while living through houselessness.

The art world itself is privileged—in terms of who's considered an artist and, most importantly, who's supported in art making. We got to know lots of privileged trust-funder artists. There were a lot of folks who, although they appreciated the art that we were doing, saw no problem in the fact that we were never able to work in a gallery, never got grants, were never supported in the art that we were doing beyond this fetishized, marginalized "outsider art" reality.

But we met some really great cats as well. Evri Kwong is a Tibetan American artist who did the cover art for two of our magazines, just an amazingly beautiful guy in so many ways. We had an art auction when we were launching *POOR* and had no money, and Evri kicked down a $2,000 painting. And because he was a known artist, it sold. And that's how *POOR Magazine* was finally published—through that relationship between folks with privilege and folks without it.

As POOR developed into an organization, suddenly people who weren't poor wanted to help us—which raised questions about our vision and about poor-people leadership. A lot of the worst destructions in herstory have happened because of the idea of help; "help" is the root of colonization, the root of missionary work, right?

It was very important for help not to become missionary or hierarchical or—the worst thing of all—default leadership. This is a big risk in media production because you need a particular skill set that often comes from having resources or formal education. When you talk in terms of media production, the "help" often becomes the leadership if you're not being overt about what is valued as knowledge and what isn't.

We had to create relationships with folks who had media-production skills because we needed to learn those skills. But in order to remain poor-people-led, we had to flip the notion of education, to redefine scholarship. The folks with formal education who were trying to help would need to be educated by the poverty scholars. The education that they already held from formal institutions of learning would need to be reframed as only *one* form of education, not *the* form of education.

We formed the Race, Poverty, and Media Justice Institute (RPMJ)—a project of POOR that creates seminars and trainings—to provide a forum for our poverty scholars to teach, and to have our knowledge honored and respected rather than colonized, stolen, borrowed from, and co-opted.

Roan: Could you describe what you mean by poverty scholarship?

Tiny: Poverty scholarship means valuing lived experience over formal education. It means that the people who are best equipped to report and teach about poverty, racism, police violence, etcetera, are the people who experience it. In most media production and academic work, there's a voyeuristic aspect—to us, the primary source has to be someone who's dealt with the issue firsthand. In other words, the person who's usually the subject of media has to be the author, the broadcaster, the producer.

Roan: Will you talk about Homefulness, as a concrete example of the ways that POOR is working with the ideas of interdependence and community reparations?

Tiny: Homefulness is a project that we're working towards, rooted in the landlessness (we don't use "homelessness" anymore) of so many of our people. It's a sweat-equity cohousing model, meaning that people [will] work in the community in exchange for living there. It includes gardens, microbusinesses, community spaces—it could be small, it could be large, but the idea is about moving off the grid of social-service management of poor people's lives. It's about creating healing and equity for landless, urban, *indigena* families. As a permanent solution to landlessness.

On Not Being Virginia Woolf

By Jennifer New

1.

I say to my husband, "I'm worried about my writing." He doesn't miss a beat: "What writing?" It's half question, half statement. That is all. Indeed. *What* writing?

2.

It's late. My husband and I are standing in the kitchen, which is lit only by a small bulb above the stove. I can tell he's tired, but I'm hungry for conversation after being with two semiverbal people all day. I ask questions and drop provocative lines until I entice him into talking about child rearing via his two chief weaknesses: travel and art.

"If you need to be polite in order to raise a polite child," Andrew philosophizes, "then it stands to reason that to have adventurous children, you need to be adventurous yourself. To have creative children, they need to see you creating. So we've got to get 'em out of here; get them messy with paint. And keep feeding them stuff they *think* they don't like. Because they will."

Originally published in *make/shift* no. 1 (spring/summer 2007)

He moves away from the counter and opens the fridge. The liberated light leaps across the kitchen walls before he grabs another bottle of Rolling Rock and closes the door. "Bottom line: our kids need to see us creating our own stuff."

I groan. It seems easy for my husband to say this. His creative life is his play; he doesn't make a living from it. His music and photography practices are interactive, the kids his eager collaborators. Bella already has her own camera, a hand-me-down held together with duct tape. But she can't yet write; the alphabet is barely coming into focus.

I, on the other hand, write out of my children's sight, beyond the reach of their tiny hands that hunt and peck at the keyboard until screens I've never seen before pop up and freak me out. *But where did Mama's article go?* I write in our attic or in coffee shops. My writing must seem to them an imaginary act.

His face now completely lost in the dark, Andrew dreams aloud about taking the kids hiking in the Pacific Northwest, living in Kenya, building the mother of all tree houses. He's warmed to the subject, but I'm only half-listening. I am plotting tomorrow's dinner and totaling bills that need to be paid.

3.

When I was pregnant with my daughter, hugely pregnant, my husband and a friend hefted my desk out of what had been my study but would soon be my daughter's bedroom. It was a lovely desk: wide and sturdy with deep drawers and pullout writing wings on either side. Since I wrote my first book at it, the desk had taken on anthropomorphic qualities. It was imposing, weighty, and powerful. Behind it, I was too.

But down it went, my maternal desire for a proper nursery having won out. Virginia Woolf would have stuck by the desk. Babies can sleep in closets, right?

When Bella arrived, I was so smitten that I would have given her every inch of our house if she'd needed it. The only place for the desk to go was smack in the living room. Every time we had people for dinner, there was my desk sharing the space with coffee and dessert. It appears hunkered in the background of holiday and birthday photos, a functional object stripped of its magical aura. Its place was like mine: in the absolute center of our home. Not some Grecian pillar, beautifully sculpted and aligned, but plain and essential to the well-being of the rest of the structure; it was what you would call load-bearing.

When we moved to a larger house, I sold the desk. My writerly trappings went up to the attic, including a willowy Ikea table without any history. I was just where I'd longed to be: apart from the chaos of our house. Alone. So why did I feel like the madwoman in the attic?

4.

I cut the photo from the front page of the local paper in the midst of a cold snap. I described it to a lot of people, assuming that everyone would recognize its dead-on absurdity. Looking back, I doubt any of them did.

The woman's face fills the frame. She's pulled the hood of her fur-lined parka tight against the frigid January air. Large dark glasses reflect the glare of the sun. A hiss of breath escapes her lips. The caption, meant to elucidate, only provokes questions: "Between raising three young children, Judy Ferris takes time out to study Mandarin."

Why Mandarin? And is there such a thing as *between raising three young children?* There is no between, no space, no moment of reprieve when a sippy cup isn't being demanded, or a small, plastic doll not underfoot. And if such a reprieve existed, why wouldn't Ms. Ferris be in the bathtub breathing deeply, or on the next plane to Aruba? There is also, of course, the unmentioned visual text: the hood and sunglasses suggest a disguise. Or perhaps they are protection against the bitter elements, as though enough layers might defend her from mothering.

It is, I believe, the most perfect commentary on motherhood I've seen.

5.

Bella sits in her high chair finishing dinner. I'm on the sofa nursing Tobey. Andrew paces the room talking on the phone. I'm listening to an animated conversation Bella is having with someone (and it does seem to be a *someone*, not just herself). After laughing at her own joke—*my, I'm witty!*—she turns to introduce us to her invisible friend. "Tobey," she begins (since his birth two months ago, he is always first). "Hannah," she continues, pointing toward our much-neglected brown lab sprawled at my feet. "Andrew!" she sings, excited to use my husband's name. We're not sure how or why she adopted this, but she uses his name frequently these days.

Then she stops. I'm staring right at her, smiling encouragingly. But nothing. I wave at her and feel a bit pathetic.

There's a long pause, during which Andrew rattles off a URL, the dog sighs, and Tobey gurgles. Finally. "Mama!"

6.

Walking into Megan's house, I breathe in the quiet air, which is more revitalizing than the cold lemonade she greets me with. Though I am here to talk with my friend, I suddenly find myself mute. Rather than chatting, I long to savor the library-like silence of the shady room. Would it be rude to ask Megan to leave me alone for a bit?

I find my way to a chair at her kitchen table and feel my spine lengthen, vertebra by vertebra. I think of how my back feels most nights at dinner: rounded and tensed like a cat's from crouching on the edge of my chair, ready to leap up for the random cries or requests that punctuate each meal.

It's been a while since my friend and I have seen each other, and when we finally get down to the business of reconnecting, we stagger a bit to find the path through the rocky terrain that can separate those with children from those without. I often don't talk about my kids with her. I never cared for hearing about other people's kids when I was among the nonparental. But also, I need a respite from them.

She talks about her teaching work, and I scan the room, struck again by its stillness. There is no clutter, though with its neat stacks of magazines and books the house is hardly antiseptic. The hushed rooms feel cleansing, a deep, cool pool that I could float in effortlessly. Most amazing of all are the floors, smooth and shiny with their lack of toast crumbs, dog hair, and strewn toys. I want to lie down on the wooden planks. A monk's bed of solitude and contemplation.

If I had these floors, I could write. It's not money or time, I see now, but clean floors that hold the secret to creative power.

7.

I need to get through the grocery shopping as quickly as possible, but with my cart still empty I can't resist the magazine rack. Just a moment to gaze at other people's neat, well-lit lives.

In a popular magazine that tells how to live a more simple existence, I read an essay by a successful writer about her woes balancing motherhood and craft. Her husband jets about on business and is rarely home. Her daughter is needy in the ways children are. Hiring babysitters is a never-ending, time-consuming balancing act. The writer feels unfocused, unable to get anything done well because her life is so fragmented.

Except for the deadbeat, jet-setting dad, I'm right there rooting for this woman. "Yeah," I say aloud right there between the Chinese-carryout table and the video-rental line, "Tell it like it is! Ain't that the truth?!"

But then I come to the denouement. "Dear reader," she tells us, "I fixed this stressful problem by hiring a live-in nanny. Now I can work as much as I need to *and* see my daughter whenever I want. Why didn't I think of this before?"

Indeed! And why didn't you mention that you can afford a live-in nanny a few paragraphs up? Why write this piece at all? Because it certainly doesn't strike me as a simple solution, and it's certainly not reflective of the Average Jane's options. I stuff the magazine back into the rack, not caring when I bend the cover.

I'm still muttering to myself with disgust as I schlep the contents of my cart onto the checkout counter and watch the bananas and paper towels roll by. *Nanny? My ass!*

8.

I go to yoga—stretch, breathe, relax—and think about my children. I swim, lap after lap, the smell of chlorine filling my nose and the luscious warmth of the summer sun on my back. I think about my children.

My husband and I go to a movie, a real floozy of Hollywood sentimentality, handkerchiefs all around. I'm crying too, but not about the lame horse. I'm crying about my children. What if *they* have to live through the next depression? What if one of them breaks a leg and never walks again? What if they routinely come to this stupid mall when they're teenagers? All of this makes me cry.

At night, I dream about my children. We're playing with clay. We're in the ocean. My daughter is combing my hair.

I write an article about a school in Alabama. It is work I was hired to do long before my son was born. It's a paycheck. And yet I love the *process*. I am trying to capture a high-school English teacher whose press-your-ear-to-the-phone, lilting accent belies the eloquent venom she is dispensing about the local school board that closed her tiny, rural school.

Sliding my finger over the laptop's mouse, I copy and paste chunks of text, trying a phrase here and then there. Every word, every comma can shift the meaning and tone. I love this about writing. It makes me feel like a tennis player. What happens when, *twhack*, I send the ball this way? The game immerses me.

I am not thinking about my children. I am writing.

Mamahood, Now

An installment of the column "Rockslinga" by Randa Jarrar

I don't know whether it's my almost-eleven-year-old son's hormones, my twenty-ninth year, or the relatively grown-up, settled nature of my life right now, but recently, I've been really into the fact that I am a mom and I have a son.

I went to a queer bookstore yesterday, and, surprisingly, I didn't buy porn: I bought *Raising a Son* . . . a parenting book (and, to be fair, a collection of Jeanette Winterson's stories).

Recently, my son had a fit after I told him we were going to a reading.

"Mom, I'm sick of it! I'm sick of all the art shows, readings, writers' conferences, and film festivals! That's enough!"

I laughed at this, of course. Which pissed him off more.

I grew up in a household that saw shopping as a cultural outing. I was stifled and hated every minute of my childhood. But now, my kid wants nothing but long afternoons in front of the TV, watching reruns of *High School Musical* or playing Guitar Hero.

Originally published in *make/shift* no. 3 (spring/summer 2008)

Sometimes I try to understand what it's like for him to be a writer's kid. Then, I think of all the talk out there that it's impossible to be an Artist (capital *A* intended) and a parent.

I have done all I can for the past eleven years to make sure I could do both. I lived cheaply. In 2001, in order to make it easier to write full-time *and* make sure my son was doing something fun, I moved into a trailer in a small Texas town. The trailer was on a huge property, and my son climbed trees and fed the koi in the pond on the patio. In the mornings, I dropped him off at a pre-K program that was only available to lower-income families. He loved it there. And so did I: his teacher was cool, I wrote six hours a day, and my rent was two hundred dollars a month. And every morning, after we ate food-stamps-bought cereal, I'd drop him off at pre-K and say, "Have a fun time, sweetie," and he'd say, "Write ten pages today, Mom!"

That's what I have a hard time explaining to people: it's easier being an artist and a mom when you give up all the bourgie shit that you think you need in order to be a good writer and a good mom. It's when I get down with grad school, or with freelancing, that I'm a better writer, because I have the time to be, and a better mom, for the same reason.

Things aren't always perfect in the Writer Mom household. My son, a budding musician, gives me grief on an every-other-day basis.

Here, I would like to share a scene from my life.

EXT. Corolla with single MOM in it pulls up to a "Learning Community" to pick up BOY. Boy appears carrying a glow-in-the-dark basketball and a lunch box empty of everything except for the fruit Mom packed. He gets into the car. Car instantly smells of goats. Mom goes to kiss Boy on forehead, but he pulls back.

BOY

What the hell???

MOM

Hi?

Boy presses eject button on CD player. Mom's Le Tigre CD is ejected and replaced with Boy's CD, which is titled, by Boy's hand, *Boy's Bitchen Tunes*. Parliament's "Tear the Roof Off the Sucka" comes on. Boy turns it up, leans back in chair, and puts Converse high-top on glove compartment, dirtying it further.

>   MOM
> Okay, you just did, like, five things wrong.

>   BOY (yells)
> What the hell are you talking about?

>   MOM
> That, first of all. You are yelling. Second, you were unkind about me greeting you. Third, you changed my music without asking. Fourth, you are just being totally rude to me. Fifth, you have your nasty little feet on the glove compartment.

>   BOY
> So???

>   MOM
> So, see how dirty it is?

>   BOY
> You can just get a napkin and clean it up.

>   MOM
> F-u-c-k you. You are going to put your foot down. You are going to clean it up.

Mom turns music off.

>   MOM
>   (continuing)

You are going to sit up straight and keep your mouth closed until we get home. Then, you are going to think about what you did wrong while you clean the car. Then, you will apologize. And then, I will think about driving you to your bass-guitar lesson.

BOY

Fine. When do I have therapy?

MOM

Tomorrow. Why?

BOY

I want to tell my therapist how much you piss me off.

MOM

Good. It's what he's there for.

BOY

Oh, yeah, I started a new novel today. It's about [I'm not allowed to tell readers. I have been sworn to secrecy.]. I wrote a page today.

MOM

Awesome! I haven't started a new novel yet. I can't decide what to write about. Too many ideas.

BOY

Don't worry, you'll figure it out. Just don't steal mine.

And this goes on until I feel like I've done an okay job, until I know that no one will accuse me of being a good artist and a bad parent, or a bad artist and a good parent . . . I'm not sure which is worse.

In the Kitchens of the Metropolis
An Interview with Silvia Federici

By Raia Small

In 1972, Silvia Federici participated in founding the Wages for Housework campaign of the International Feminist Collective, which formed chapters in Italy, the United Kingdom, and the United States to demand wages from their respective federal governments for the labor that women do in the home. Born and raised in Italy, she moved to New York in 1967 to study at the State University of New York at Buffalo. Federici has published *Caliban and the Witch: Women, the Body, and Primitive Accumulation* (2004) and *Revolution at Point Zero: Housework, Reproduction, and Feminist Struggle* (2012). As an activist, writer, and teacher, she has fought against women's exploitation, capital punishment, and neoliberal austerity. In January 2015, I spoke to her about the theoretical underpinnings and tactical strategy of the Wages for Housework campaign, how it challenged other movements on the Left, and the importance of making demands that give us more terrain from which to struggle.

Originally published in make/shift no. 17 (summer/fall 2015)

RS: What experiences made you want to join the women's movement?

SF: I'd been very aware throughout my adolescence of all the things I couldn't do because I was a woman. I grew up in Italy in the postwar period. Fascism had ended, but it had created an intensely patriarchal culture. Women were supposed to produce ten or twenty children for the fatherland. From very early on, I was in revolt against my place as a woman in society.

How did the Wages for Housework campaign develop?

In 1972, in Padua, Italy, there was a meeting between a group of feminists from Italy, including Mariarosa Dalla Costa, and some women from abroad, including Selma James and myself. At this time, the women's movement was forming and looking for a strategy. The demand of wages for housework was the logical development of the analysis that Mariarosa Dalla Costa had presented in her 1971 article, "Women and the Subversion of Community," which argued that women's unpaid domestic work is a central element of capital accumulation because it is the work that produces the workforce. From this analysis stemmed the conclusion that the material basis of sexual discrimination and the unequal sexual division of labor under capitalism is women's unpaid domestic work.

Wages for Housework was also inspired by struggles in England and the U.S. In 1972, the government in England announced that it would cut the Family Allowance, a source of welfare money that women had been receiving directly from the state, not through their husbands' paychecks, since the 1940s. The mobilization that formed to resist the cut was important for the formation of the Wages for Housework campaign, as it was clear that this money was a crucial source of autonomy for women. The struggle of mothers on welfare in the United States was also an important factor.

The other component of Wages for Housework was a critique of the New Left and the whole Marxist tradition that both Selma James and Mariarosa Dalla Costa came from. Selma James was married to C. L. R. James [an anticolonial activist, Marxist, and writer] and had lived in Trinidad in the late 1950s during the anticolonial struggle. She had realized that the wage worker is not the only subject of exploitation and revolutionary potential in the capitalist society. There's a whole other world: the colonial world. If you can see those connections—between the anticolonial struggle and the rise of the women's movement—then you can make the connection between the unwaged workers of the colonial world and the unwaged workers in the kitchens of the metropolis.

Did you discuss the strategy of fighting for a reform (wages) without intending to create a new, paid job under capitalism but to fight the system as a whole?

Not everyone understood that theoretical perspective, but certainly it was a strategy to change power relations. We rejected the idea that women could acquire autonomy from men only by taking a second job and doing double work. We thought that unless we changed the unwaged nature of our work, we wouldn't be able to change our lives significantly in any other respect. This was the center of the disease. Even to change the condition of waged work, to change the issue of services—childcare, eldercare—we had to question the nature of unwaged work. Reflecting on the unpaid labor of women was like a window onto the nature of capitalism. I saw that devaluing the reproduction of human life was a central pillar of capitalism, one of the main engines of the accumulation process. So not only was it an entry point to change the situation of women, but also to understand capitalism in a different way.

What was it about the early 1970s that made these movements possible?

It was the Black movement. The civil rights movement gave power to everybody. This was the second time in American history that in the wake of an antislavery movement—because the civil rights movement was also an anti–Jim Crow, anti-apartheid, antislavery movement—a women's movement began. The Seneca Falls Convention of 1848—the first feminist convention in the U.S.—came at the peak of the abolitionist movement, and it was organized by women who had been involved in the antislavery campaign but found themselves marginalized within it and saw the need to start their own struggle. The same thing happened in the 1970s: it was the civil rights movement that gave women the power to rebel. Women were making connections between these different types of slavery and between racism and sexism. The welfare movement was very much the product of the civil rights movement. Even though Black women were a minority among welfare recipients, they were at the forefront because they were from communities in struggle.

Was Wages for Housework imperative to your life as a single woman without children?

Yes, because I saw Wages for Housework not as payment for specific tasks, but as a broad movement and as a strategy to establish the value of women's work. It was such a revelatory power even just to name "wages for housework." It said, these homes are the factories in which we work. It was a question of denaturalizing housework and showing the social, historical character of the work. For example, if you had wages, men could also do that work. We wanted to disconnect it from femininity because the naturalization was a big impediment to struggling against it.

Were you inspired by the Welfare Mothers Movement in the United States? Did you see your campaign as an extension of that struggle?

We were definitely inspired by the Welfare Mothers Movement. They would say things like, "If the government doesn't think that housework is work because the children are our own, then we'll swap children!" However, Wages for Housework was not an extension of the welfare rights movement because we had a broader critique of capitalist society and the capitalist organization of work. It started from the perspective of housework, from which we examined and fought against the whole of capitalism.

Did Wages for Housework form alliances with welfare mothers?

We made some connections with women on welfare in 1975–1976. Nationwide, welfare benefits—particularly Aid to Families with

Dependent Children—had been under attack since 1973. But starting in 1976 in NYC, benefits were substantially reduced while eligibility criteria were also reviewed. Moving expenses and security deposits on new apartments were cut. Also, women were pressured to reveal the name of their children's father or have their checks terminated. Women didn't want to reveal the father because sometimes they didn't know, and other times they didn't want anything to do with him and didn't want him to have rights over their children. In response, we organized a conference and a rally, and for these occasions we distributed flyers and a journal on welfare.

How successful do you feel these campaigns were from today's vantage point?

We were not successful. Welfare has been practically eliminated and we did not win wages for housework. But we raised consciousness about the fact that housework is real work and it benefits all employers. I think it broadened the women's movement beyond the whole equality and right-to-work perspectives. We raised the whole issue of exploitation in the home, in connection with welfare, at a crucial time, when the state was criminalizing welfare women, mostly Black women, and portraying them as cheaters and frauds. In the late 1970s in New York, they introduced security guards in welfare offices because women were crying and protesting when they were denied and the cuts were coming down.

Did Wages for Housework clash with mainstream, second-wave feminism?

Wages for Housework did clash with mainstream feminism, and also with the Left. The Left was very hostile to us. At the time, men were very critical of the women's movement as a whole, accusing it of being divisive. On the Left, they criticized us as economistic, and as a movement that institutionalized women in the home. We had to counter that we had been institutionalized already precisely because of the lack of money. What was most concerning for us was that many feminists thought that the only place women could have power was in the waged workplace. They thought that in the community, there was no power. For us, this was striking because the Black movement was not based in factories, it was based in communities. To imagine that we cannot have any power to fight against capitalism unless we work outside the home and join a union is to accept the bourgeois ideology that the home is not a place of work but a place of personal relations. Some feminists also rejected our analysis because they thought that the home was the only place free from the reach of capitalist relations. They placed capitalism outside the home and saw the latter as a safe haven for the working class.

Like Marx, in your writing you stress the primacy of social relations. Wages mask an underlying relation of exploitation. Can you explain what made Wages for Housework a transformative demand that would disrupt existing social relations between women and men and between women and the state?

I think it was transformative because in the whole leftist, Marxist, anarchist tradition, there was nothing about housework. It was invisible. Even just being able to say "this is work" helped make it possible to fight against it. We thought that Wages for Housework would not be an endpoint, but would contribute to changing social relations in ways favorable to us and our struggle. We believed it would change the relation between women, capital, and the state by putting an end to men's mediating role. This was not an ordinary wage struggle because it changed the relation between women and men and women and the state by exposing the value of our labor and the immense wealth capital has accumulated out of our unpaid labor. The goal was to get wages for housework in order to raise the level of our struggle, not to end it.

Toward New Visions of Sex and Culture Entirely

By Conner Habib

"Sex work is work!" is the rallying cry at the heart of four recent books, all part of the growing public discussion about how to think about sex work today.

As far as slogans go, "Sex work is work" isn't a bad one: the implication is that services involving sex (prostitution most obviously, but also porn, erotic dancing, and so forth) are not—in economic terms, at least—worthy of being singled out as invalid and subsequently legislated against or made illegal. If we legitimize sex work as labor, say many sex workers and advocates, including the authors of these four titles, we'll take great strides toward protecting sex workers and improving quality of life.

As a sex worker myself (a porn actor for nearly seven years), I have experienced, have been touched by, or at least recognize the pitfalls that sex workers face. Sex workers are targeted by law enforcement, discriminated against by employers in other jobs, used as pawns by overzealous politicians and "rescue" organizations, socially stigmatized,

Originally published in *make/shift* no. 16 (winter/spring 2014/2015)

and face prejudice in personal relationships. On top of these problems, many sex workers—particularly "outdoor" or "street-walking" prostitutes (as opposed to "indoor" prostitutes who can screen their clientele, often simply referred to as "escorts")—face physical violence. The violence might, yes, be from pimps and johns, but it also comes from the police who are meant to protect sex workers, and who sometimes feel at liberty to abuse, harass, and sexually assault a marginalized and criminalized population.

But the slogan and sentiment contain their own issues. First, sex work isn't *merely* work, and focusing on labor can come at the expense of ignoring sex and doing nothing to end sexual stigma itself. *Playing the Whore: The Work of Sex Work*, by Melissa Gira Grant, navigates this tension, largely successfully. By portraying the demonization of whores, Grant exposes the demonizers—police, legislators, anti–sex work activists—and reveals their baseless attitudes and oppressive actions. Misogyny pulses through this bigotry and is a main target of Grant's critique, particularly as it relates to women's sexual desire. "Forget embracing your desires, girls," she writes mockingly, "just swap your bikini for a sweater and the psychic wounds of patriarchy will be healed."

Playing the Whore is a spirited and readable critique. Still, I found myself longing for more exploration of the sex of sex work. Some of what Grant leaves out of *Playing the Whore* appears in *For Love or Money*, the shortest but most satisfying of the four titles reviewed here. Here, Grant and journalist Sarah Jaffe engage in illuminating and bold dialogue. Often, they move toward new visions of and approaches to sex and culture entirely, and it's thrilling.

> What if instead of fighting to make cities places where sexual violence was unwelcome, we looked at . . . how to care for a place so that it was good for sex? I'm beyond reluctant to frame the danger I face taking up space in my life as primarily a sexual danger. As if that's somehow always the worst. The most unrecoverable. Can we understand that eviction is also traumatic? That arrest is traumatic? . . . Where do the targeted parts of our bodies begin and end?

The chapbook circles around pleasure and is itself pleasurable to read.

If Grant's book and her conversation with Jaffe are a critique and a vision, then *Sex Workers Unite: A History of the Movement from Stonewall to Slut Walk*, by Melinda Chateauvert, is a polemic well dressed as a history lesson. A tour through key events and figures in the evolving sex workers' rights movement, the book is an attack against unthinking attitudes toward sex work. Indeed, its first sentence, "Sex workers are fighters," is a call to battle. The anger is justifiable, and the justification is found in these pages. Chateauvert gives plenty of space to expressing the exclusion sex workers have experienced in other human rights battles, even as they were a driving force in them (most notably the lesbian and gay rights movement, which often works to disenfranchise the sexually open and happily promiscuous). She also exposes the policies that have worked against sex workers' safety. Thankfully, though the book is about on-the-ground activism, Chateauvert doesn't shy from thinking about cultural structures and systems.

There's a curious problem of audience here, however. On the one hand, many of the people who will find themselves enlivened by Chateauvert's anger will be familiar with many of these chapters in history. On the other, readers unfamiliar with this history may need a more welcoming introduction to *why* sex workers aren't simply victims of patriarchy.

I wanted *Sex Workers Unite* to take a decisive step in one direction or another—into the even more relentless and free voice that Chateauvert has in interviews, or toward a more understanding tone for new and unfamiliar readers. As it stands, the book is still a mine of valuable information and a touchstone of strength for activists. Most importantly, perhaps, *Sex Workers Unite* shows readers that the sex workers' rights movement is, truly, a movement.

Negotiating Sex Work: Unintended Consequences of Policy and Activism, edited by Carisa R. Showden and Samantha Majic, doesn't suffer from an audience problem—it's by academics for academics.

Academia does not legitimize sex work; sex work legitimizes academic study. This is something many of the authors and particularly the editors of *Negotiating Sex Work* seem to struggle with when they're not forgetting it entirely. There are chapters that try to reclaim or at least detail the relevance of academic work in sex-worker communities—some successfully ("Participant-Driven Action Research [PDAR] with Sex Workers in Vancouver" by Raven Bowen and Tamara O'Doherty), others not so successfully.

It's a nice effort, and the gesture toward creating understanding between researchers and sex workers should be applauded. But to be frank, as a sex worker, I'm not sure what the book is meant to *do*. This would be fine—books don't have to serve a *function* to be worthwhile—except for the book's certainty that it is *doing work*. *Negotiating Sex Work* is framed in the introduction as an "intervention." Though it's not really clear how it would be an intervention for anyone, since the academics already studying sex-work communities, and that compose the audience for this book, are unlikely to need this intervention. *Negotiating Sex Work*, then, is worth a read mostly for data reference. Sometimes the analysis elevates a chapter to a thoughtful and fuller perspective ("The Contested Citizenship of Sex Workers: The Case of the Netherlands"). For general audiences, there's not much of a way in, and sex workers reading the volume may feel a familiar sinking feeling of an unintended consequence: someone trying to validate and rescue them—even though these writers are genuine allies.

The titles, all published within the same year, signal a new complexity in how our culture thinks about sex workers, a more human analysis. Whatever sorts of audiences these books seek, their presence lends to a revitalized examination of the subject. "Sex work is work," however incomplete it is as a battle cry, moves us past the old reductive and damaging whimper of "save the sex workers from themselves."

Looking for Reproductive Justice
An Interview with Loretta J. Ross

By Celina R. De León

She ran a rape crisis center in 1979. She coordinated the first national conference of U.S. women of color on reproductive rights in 1987, and the first conference on these issues for African American women in 1990. And in 2004, Loretta J. Ross codirected the largest protest march in U.S. history—the March for Women's Lives.

Ross, thankfully, does not stop. She is currently the national coordinator of the SisterSong Women of Color Reproductive Health Collective. Founded in 1997 in Atlanta, SisterSong is made up of almost eighty women-of-color and allied organizations and more than four hundred individuals working on reproductive-justice issues. Their second national conference, "Let's Talk about Sex," will happen in Chicago this summer.

Make/shift staff writer Celina R. De León spoke with Ross about the conference and the reproductive-justice front lines.

Originally published in *make/shift* no. 1 (spring/summer 2007)

CDL: What are your thoughts on the role of women of color in the history of reproductive rights activism in the United States?

LR: I don't think women of color are respected for their contributions to the reproductive rights movement. And that lack of respect is demonstrated by the mainstream as well as by women of color. I cringe every time I hear the words "white women's movement." It fails to nuance the fact that there were women of color who were involved with it in the beginning. NOW's statement of purpose was [co]written by a Black woman!

We've always been there. But the media said the purpose of the women's movement was to burn bras and be only white women. That's the history that everybody learns. We really didn't care about the titties bouncing [*laughs*]. If you want to take off your bra, fine, all of us do that at the end of the day. But that's not the cause of the movement [*laughs*]. Some people at a Miss America contest threw their bras off to signify their liberation, and the media made it seem like that was all we wanted.

I would argue that African American women here as slaves practiced feminism that predated the women's movement. Even though we did not have an ideology to claim, or a life-safe language to use, we had slave women refusing to have children to support a slave economy by practicing birth control, abortion, and infanticide. I think by any modern interpretation, we would call that a feminist act.

We make it seem that white supremacy only happens on the Right, instead of seeing how leftists and progressives are somewhat vulnerable, particularly when they objectify or neglect history's role and the conditions of people of color.

You were one of the first Black women to win a suit against A. H. Robins, manufacturer of the Dalkon Shield, which sterilized you at age twenty-three. Can you talk more about this?

I had been implanted with the Dalkon Shield when I was a student at Howard University in '71 or '72. I was already a teen mother, and I had already undergone an abortion, so I was really trying to do contraceptives effectively. But even as my Dalkon Shield was implanted in me, there was research A. H. Robins was suppressing that showed it was dangerous and was leading to sterilization. The bottom of the Dalkon Shield had a string attached to it; [the Shield] was a little triangle of plastic. The purpose of that string was so the physician could pull at the string to remove [the Shield]. But that string served like a candlewick, and it wicked bacteria up into a woman's uterus and reproductive system. It was like a string on a tampon, except you don't leave a tampon in for five years! [*laughs*]

The doctor, instead of removing the Dalkon Shield, kept accusing me of having a nonspecific venereal disease he couldn't detect. So, for six weeks after being admitted to the hospital with acute pelvic inflammatory disease, he kept treating it as a venereal disease. It was not until my tubes ruptured, I went into a coma, and they did a hysterectomy, that he said, "Oops, maybe it was this Dalkon Shield."

Any doctor, with all the research and chatter by the AMA [American Medical Association], knew that there were problems developing with the Dalkon Shield. That was the basis of my lawsuit. They settled out of court, trying to prevent the news of the Dalkon Shield from making headlines. It didn't help because three years later, [several hundred thousand] women were [harmed] by this device *in the U.S.* before they withdrew it from the U.S. market.[1] A. H. Robins declared bankruptcy, and another company bought them out. They're prohibited from distributing the Dalkon Shield here, but I talked to women in South Africa as recently as 1998 who said they are using it.[2]

---

1. Various sources indicate that two hundred thousand to three hundred thousand women were harmed by the Shield, with injuries and damage including pelvic infections, pain, premature births, spontaneous abortions, numerous sterilizations, and several deaths. It is difficult to track down solid information on the number of U.S. women sterilized by the device, but Ross's unedited answer here—"700,000 women were sterilized"—gives a sense of the possible extent of the problem as perceived by reproductive-justice activists.

2. In a 1979 article for *Mother Jones*, Barbara Ehrenreich reported on the distribution (or "dumping") of the Dalkon Shield in so-called Third World countries after damaging information about the device's dangerousness began to surface in the United States.

Do you think many Americans are aware of the sterilizations that have occurred and resulted from the experimental use of birth control on certain groups of women?

I don't think so. Most Americans are amazingly oblivious when it comes to human rights violations in our country. I think they are becoming more aware because of the number of states that are now apologizing for these eugenical policies.[3]

Sterilization abuse is still taking place, and it's taking place more underground. We are still getting a lot of anecdotal stories of women, particularly poor, immigrant women, showing up in hospitals to deliver their babies, poorly speaking English, and the doctor asks them, "Do you want me to do your tubes now while we're down there?" We've gotten stories of people being told that these operations are reversible. So, they innocently accept sterilization and find out it is *not* reversible. [And then there are] judges that sentence people to sterilization or Norplant.

One of the most interesting things SisterSong has done is join an amicus brief on behalf of a white man. The Wisconsin Supreme Court decided [in 2001–2002] that this guy was not paying child support for the children he already had, so part of his sentence was to not have any more children. We took on the position that it is not the role of the court to decide who shall and who shall not procreate. Not only are you violating his human rights, but what punishment are you going to give to his wife or girlfriend if she gets pregnant? You're going to punish an even more innocent person to enact your social policy?

Can you talk about how SisterSong aims to discuss reproductive health and sexual rights from the perspectives of women of color?

As women of color, we are part of the pro-choice movement because we support the right of a woman to terminate a pregnancy or to prevent a

---

3. For much of the twentieth century, numerous U.S. states actively practiced sterilization to keep so-called undesirables from reproducing. In 2003, North Carolina was one of the first states to formally apologize for practices that sterilized many poor African American women and women on welfare. States such as California, Virginia, and Oregon have also apologized, and North Carolina lawmakers are debating possible reparations, but no state has yet authorized statewide reparations to forcibly sterilized women.

pregnancy by any means she chooses that is safe and legal. But as women of color, we come from communities that are often subjected to population control. So, while we fight for the right for a woman to terminate a pregnancy or prevent one, we also fight for the right for women to have the children they desire under the circumstances they choose.

The second aspect is to fight for the right to *have* children. Some women prefer to have out-of-hospital, midwife-assisted births. Some prefer to have hospital-assisted births. All women prefer to not have an unnecessary C-section. Doctors are increasingly using C-section births so they can go to their golf game. It has nothing to do with whether the pregnancy is complicated or not. We fight for the right to have children under the conditions that we want.

There's a third aspect to our struggle that also separates us from the mainstream pro-choice movement, and that's the right to parent the children we already have. Children of color are more subjected to removal from parental custody by our criminal-justice system and our foster-care system. Many Native Americans are still healing from the trauma of their forced removals to boarding schools. The whole question of interracial adoption is problematic. Instead of creating a market for the adoption of babies, why aren't we addressing the economic conditions that force parents to give up their children? For SisterSong, it's a three-way struggle: not to have a child, to have a child, to parent a child.

Do you think mainstream pro-choice organizers incorporate these perspectives?

One of the things we are concerned with, and have been since our founding in 1997, is the isolation of abortion and reproductive-health issues from all other social-justice issues. When you think about it, you don't have to wait long after taking that pregnancy test before your mind asks: Do I have health care? Will I get fired if I tell my boss I'm pregnant? Will I get beaten if I tell my partner I'm pregnant? Do I have a bedroom to put this child in? All of this is going through your mind and you just missed a cycle! When you isolate abortion from all these other issues, which we call human rights issues, you're really doing a disservice to the very complex thinking process women use when deciding whether or not to continue a pregnancy.

Quite often, women are forced to terminate pregnancies they would have rather kept if all those other things had been in place. "Pro-choice" is actually a great term when you have choices. When we say this, a lot of people think we're somehow not standing up for abortion rights or somehow supporting the anti-abortion side. We have pro-abortion *and* anti-abortion people in the same organization. The white movement is so divided on that issue. They don't realize that women of color have long recognized that we have a lot more in common than what divides us.

Our analysis is reproductive justice—reproductive rights married to social justice because you have to address how women are denied full achievement of their human rights. No woman can make an individual decision about what to do with her body if she is embedded in a context where her human rights are being denied! You can't make an individual determination, like the privacy framework that the abortion rights movement mostly uses, outside of the context of what's happening to your community. We've all thought that privacy in and of itself was a very weak defense for abortion rights, especially when you live in communities that are heavily monitored, heavily policed. As an African American, I have always felt that we should have been fighting for abortion rights as a form of involuntary slavery. Having one person's body subordinated to another person's body, that's called slavery. I don't care if the body is in your belly.

Can you talk more about the term "reproductive justice"?

We coined "reproductive justice" in 1994. Since 1997, different aspects of SisterSong, like Asian Communities for Reproductive Justice, New Voices for Reproductive Justice Pittsburgh, and others, have gone and added a rich analysis so that we make a distinction between three aspects of reproductive justice.

The first aspect is the reproductive-health wing. These are the people who are heavily preoccupied with providing services, which are absolutely vital. You have to have somewhere to go to get your Pap smears, abortion services, STD treatment, etcetera. We hear a lot of talk of health-care disparities, [different] races of people having different health-care outcomes. A reproductive-health approach would call that a health disparity, while a human rights approach would call that the impact of white supremacy on health care [*laughs*]. These are not outcomes that just happen. They are constructed and implemented by a system that advantages some and disadvantages others. But if you're a health-care provider, you're not working on the system, you're just working on the client.

The second aspect is the reproductive rights framework, keeping abortion safe, legal, and accessible. It is an effective framework when you understand that keeping that kind of access legal is very important. But the problem is that if you're already marginalized by the system, it's very hard for you to believe that the system is going to work for you. The main strategy of the reproductive rights framework is call your legislator, see your congressperson, march on Washington [*laughs*]. It's all about trying to put pressure on the political system to be responsive to your needs. But you first have to believe in the advocacy of the system, and that it will work. Secondly, that you have power in it to make it work. Now, most of us are not totally convinced that we can even get our votes counted. I don't want to say that we don't need a rights framework. But we cannot see it as a one-size-fits-all framework because it's not.

SisterSong's response to that is reproductive justice. We feel it is very necessary for people to include work against other issues like poverty or for immigrants' and workers' rights. When you look at the March for Women's Lives that took place in 2004, we had gotten the march people to change the name of the march from the "March for Freedom of Choice" to the "March for Women's Lives" using the reproductive-justice framework. Yet every media story in the mainstream media, no matter how we presented it, called it an abortion march. We had people there for immigrants' rights, people opposed to the war in Iraq, people opposed to the debt crisis. It was the biggest protest in U.S. history because it was the most diverse. Did the media pick up on that one? No! It was an abortion rights march.

We understand that we're offering a complicated, intersectional analysis for a shallow, one-dimensional world [*laughs*]. Our lives are complicated. I don't care how passionately you care about one issue, nobody walks through life as a single-issue person. You care about the environment, but you don't care about whether or not you get hit by a car? Whether you get raped on your way home? Nobody lives that kind of life. Yet they expect us to organize as if we were dealing with cardboard people.

How do you feel about feminism? Do you call yourself a feminist?

When I think of the phrase "coming out" as applied to me, it applies to me becoming a feminist. I was engaged in the women's movement for almost a decade before I would use the f-word for myself. I would walk around, like many of us, and say, "I'm not a feminist, but. . . . " I ran a rape-crisis center and would not use the f-word to describe myself. For me, at the time, feminism represented a highly stigmatized white women's movement. But I hadn't done my research.

It was 1985 when I embraced the f-word for myself and called myself a feminist. That was because I had enough history in the movement and understanding to really claim and redefine feminism for myself. I also have to add that it was when bell hooks wrote *Ain't I a Woman* in 1981; she added theory to our practice [*laughs*]. We didn't have anything that coalesced anything that we were thinking at the time, except for the word "feminism." There was the Combahee River Collective's "Statement of 1977," but that didn't get broadly distributed. And then it still took four years [for me to accept feminism].

When I came out to my family as a feminist, I think my mother would have really preferred that I came out as a lesbian [*laughs*]. My mom was a member of the National Council of Negro Women, with Mary McLeod Bethune, and she didn't associate herself as a feminist.

One of the stated goals of SisterSong is to "create a pro-sex space for the pro-choice movement." What do you mean by "pro-sex," and why do you think the pro-choice movement isn't being pro-sex?

That's our conference, "Let's Talk about Sex." The young members of SisterSong kept saying, "Everybody is telling us what *not to do*; no one is telling us what *to do*." As if the human right to a positive sexuality doesn't exist for you until you're eighteen and over [*laughs*]. They join us in not believing that "just say no" works. In fact, young children exposed to abstinence-only education are engaging in more sexually dangerous behaviors than the kids who actually get comprehensive sex education. They have oral and anal sex without protection because they don't think it's dangerous.

Our young people need people to stand up and say that all people, but young people in particular, have the right to a positive, nonprocreative, healthy sexuality. Hillary Clinton is the woman that most angers me because her whole approach is [that] abortion should be safe, legal, and never.[4] And a lot of advocates say, "Well, if they just get the right amount of sex education, if we just provide enough contraceptive access, then we can prevent the tragedy of abortion." Frankly, some of us don't like you describing abortion as a *tragedy* because it stigmatizes everyone who has one, like they're either stupid because they didn't get the right education, or they failed to use the contraceptive right. Frankly, I don't think the right wing needs any help stigmatizing abortion; they're doing pretty good by themselves.

We're going to focus on the human right to have fun, and on how to have safe fun.

---

4. Clinton's official stance at the time this article was originally published was that abortion should be "safe, legal, and rare."

Misdiagnosis

Reproductive Health and Our Environment

By Mariana Ruiz Firmat

1.

It is winter in New York City. I wake up sweating in the middle of the night, and I can't sleep because I'm too hot. The night sweats wake me several more times before my alarm finally goes off at 6:30 a.m. In the morning I'm anxious; this shouldn't be happening so frequently.

The winter advances from the isolated weather of January into the endless darkness of February and March. It's been three months since I stopped taking birth-control pills to regulate my fickle cycle, and my period has not returned. In the middle of the day, a flash of heat spreads over me, starting at the back of my neck, crawling over the back of my head, and ending on the other side of my body, between my rib cage and stomach. A cold chill immediately follows. I add this to a growing list of concerns to share with my doctor.

Nothing can prepare you for being told in your twenties that your reproductive system is similar to that of a fifty-year-old woman, your ovaries have shrunk to the size

Originally published in *make/shift* no. 3 (spring/summer 2008)

of raisins, and you most likely will never have another menstrual cycle. I was twenty-eight when a gynecologist told me that I had something called premature ovarian failure (POF), a reproductive disorder affecting 1 percent of women in the United States. POF means that your body lacks sufficient eggs to produce regular ovulation or menstrual cycles. According to many doctors, it is unlikely that anyone with POF will ever become pregnant and carry a fetus to full term.

2.

Our world is besieged with pollutants. Exposure to toxic contaminants cuts across race and class lines, and every being is vulnerable to environmental hazards. In a recent interview, Dr. Elizabeth Guillette, an associate research scientist in anthropology at the University of Florida, told me that the best way to deal with the impact of pollutants on our bodies is to limit our exposure to them.

Yet few working-class and working-poor people of color have any such choice. Typically, we work in industries where we are exposed to environmental toxins as farmworkers, factory workers, domestic workers. The increasing assaults on immigration and decreasing federal worker-protection laws limit our opportunities to deal with our concerns through federal regulatory agencies. Our neighbors are the waterways, power plants, and waste facilities poisoned by the government and corporations. And our exposure to toxins is having disastrous effects on our reproductive systems.

Farmworkers who formerly worked on the North Shore of Lake Apopka—one of the most polluted lakes in Florida and the location of two Superfund sites—have been suffering from chronic health problems ranging from reproductive disorders to lupus since the closing of the farms in 1998.[1] In a 2006 community health survey of former Apopka farmworkers, most of whom were African American, 13 percent said they had a child born with a birth defect, 21 percent had at least one problem pregnancy, and 16 percent had miscarriages. At least three farmworkers who became pregnant while working in the same Immokalee

1. A Superfund site is an abandoned hazardous-waste site targeted by the federal government for cleanup.

labor camp in southwest Florida in 2004 gave birth to children with severe birth defects. The farmworkers contend that they were in the fields during and shortly after pesticides were sprayed—both prior to and during pregnancy.

Yet reproductive health—and the connection between reproductive health and the environment—has not been a top priority of the predominantly white mainstream reproductive rights and environmental movements. Even radical reproductive-justice groups led by women of color have not placed these concerns at the top of their agendas. When we spoke recently, Loretta Ross, director of the national reproductive-justice network SisterSong, admitted that SisterSong lacks a clear policy on the intersection of environmental justice and reproductive justice. To explain, she cited a recent Tides Foundation report about the dearth of funding for women-of-color-led reproductive rights organizations. Only 9 percent of dollars earmarked for reproductive health and reproductive rights funding serve women of color. Even less money goes to groups led by women of color. These groups just don't have the capacity to deal with environmental justice and reproductive health right now.[2] Another concern—and possibly the one that presents more obstacles—is how to come up with a cohesive policy that would not violate existing laws designed to protect workers from sex-based discrimination.[3] Ross says she would like to begin dealing with this topic in the coming year by beginning long-overdue discussions between environmental-justice and reproductive-justice groups.

3.

The trees and sky are zigzagging around me, missing me, avoiding my gaze. It's a perfect spring day. In my doctor's office, holding my partner's hand, I suddenly know it's bad, far worse than anything I could have imagined.

2. SisterSong is a network of organizations, and some of their participating groups are indeed dealing with such issues in their communities. See, for instance, Asian Communities for Reproductive Justice and the Mothers' Milk Project.

3. In the 1980s, the NOW Legal Defense Fund filed and won a sex-discrimination lawsuit against Johnson Controls. Knowing that women in their workplace would be exposed to toxins that would impact their reproductive health, the company wanted, in a supposed effort to protect women's reproductive health, to demand that women show proof of sterilization to continue employment with Johnson Controls.

I say, "So I'm premenopausal." My doctor responds, "No, I'm sorry, you are postmenopausal." I begin to panic. I ask if I will be able to have children. She says no. All of a sudden it's as if something has torn down my throat and picked out my heart. I feel sick and begin to silently cry. I ask again about having children, hoping the answer will be different, and she says, "If you want a child, your only option is an egg donor, which costs about ten thousand dollars, and an in vitro fertilization procedure, which costs about ten thousand dollars—but I could give you a discount and make it seven thousand."

I am astonished. An hour ago, I was a twenty-eight-year-old with choices about becoming a parent. Getting pregnant—being a mother—wasn't even something I necessarily wanted to do (and I certainly don't think it is the inevitable or best path for every woman). Yet I wanted to be the one to make that choice for myself. Now my chances of biological motherhood are reduced to a procedure that is unaffordable and unwanted. I notice the greed in my doctor's eyes. I ask her again if there's any chance at all that I could have my own biological child. She looks at me and says, "No. Besides, even if you could, why would you want to pass this on to your daughter?" And I think, *Well, she has a point.* Wouldn't that make me the worst mother in the world? Isn't that just what my mother did to me?

In 1967, six years after my mother and grandparents left Cuba, my grandmother was diagnosed with ovarian cancer. As recent immigrants to the United States who had fled Castro's Cuba, my family held a privileged position unlike that of other immigrants; we were given gifts like operations and food stamps, and my grandmother received an operation that saved her life. At age fifteen, my mother had her first period. Her cycle was never regular, and at age twenty-one, after marrying my father, she was diagnosed with POF. In order to understand where we are and where we are going, we need to know where we come from.

4.

I grew up in a working-class community where the main roads were lined with one strip mall after another. Every other week, my mother bought us bread and desserts from the Wonder Bread thrift store. She was pleased because on her limited budget she could buy enough bread to make lunches for the two daughters she was raising alone. As a child,

I found the store to be a sugary fantasy of processed bread and sweets. In hindsight, the Wonder Bread store embodies my childhood diet and lack of food security. We bought groceries at the cheapest stores possible. The food we ate was processed and pesticide-laden. We had unlimited access to potato chips, soda, and ice cream. I would cook Cheerios in butter as an afternoon snack when I was in elementary school. In junior high, I ate ice-cream bars for lunch. My mother didn't purposely seek out processed food; she bought food that fit her budget.

Looking back, my mom did what she had to do in order to care for us. She didn't know then what we are learning more and more about processed foods and their connection to endocrine-disrupting chemicals like polychlorinated biphenyls (PCBs), industrial products or chemicals often found in pesticides. The problem for low-income families is that lack of access to whole foods, and misinformation on the part of large agribusiness, means that we will purchase and consume cheaper, processed foods that have been linked to thyroid and other disorders.

Guillette, the research scientist, offers specific advice about what people can do to protect their reproductive health: "Limit your exposure. If you have to live near a dump site or a polluting factory, then you want to eliminate other sources. Follow [the precautionary principle] when preparing foods by peeling certain foods like apples and cucumbers and eliminating foods high in pesticides such as strawberries."

But many recent immigrants and working-poor families cannot provide their families with enough food to survive, let alone choose to avoid certain foods based on potential contaminants. Natalie Freeman, associate professor of environmental health at the University of Florida, was part of a team that conducted another study addressing environmental health issues in and around Lake Apopka. She says that for the families interviewed for the study, concern about environmental issues is an unaffordable luxury. Their immediate concerns are immigration status, lack of basic health and dental care, and neighborhood safety.

Toxins affect all of us, but the ability to deal with the health problems they create is a class-based luxury. Even when we do have access to doctors, it is unlikely that they will ask the right questions. They need to be educated to ask us about the industries we work in and the communities we live in. Still, having access to doctors in our communities is only part of the picture. We need to have grocery stores in our neighborhoods that offer healthy fruits and vegetables, grains and breads without preservatives, and more.

5.

Healing is a radical concept.

In the United States, we are alienated from our own bodies by social and cultural norms. Further, many of us work two or three jobs without benefits in order to survive, few of us have access to adequate health care, and we have little time to care for ourselves and our families. The struggle to survive eclipses all things, and our collective stress is enormous. But we cannot heal ourselves if we are disconnected from the very bodies that we must heal. Thinking about our health holistically requires that we not cut off our physiological selves from our psychological experiences. What we eat, where we live, where we work . . . each of these things plays a part in our mental, physical, and spiritual health.

In the first year after I was diagnosed with POF I was dumbstruck. I retreated deeply into myself. It seemed that everyone knew that I was a twenty-eight-year-old woman who didn't have periods, who couldn't have children, and whose health was deeply compromised. I imagined my reproductive system like a black hole, cold and lifeless. As a survivor of childhood sexual abuse, I was used to feeling betrayed by my body, but this time I felt that I was being punished for my body and its power. Author Joanna Kadi writes, "Child sexual abuse teaches us lessons about power—who has it and who doesn't. These lessons, experienced on a bodily level, transfer into the deepest levels of our conscious and subconscious being, and correspond with other oppressive systems." In our body-memory exists not only painful experiences but the keys to understanding and a map to healing.

6.

I listen to a voicemail from my older sister. In my family, abuse has created fissures, estranged siblings, and drawn lines between us. Like soldiers, we stand on opposite sides; some of us are perpetrator sympathizers, and some of us are part of the truth-teller rebellion. Despite our estrangement, I sense something wrong in my sister's voice. I know that my father is dead.

When we speak later, she sounds sad. Shrouded in her tone is the knowledge that we've been waiting for this moment our whole lives, wondering how we would feel the day it happened. There is a collective feeling among my father's five children that comes from the shared experience of subjugation, abuse, and stolen childhoods. But there is also a knowing that he suffered too, with a childhood possibly worse than ours. I've looked at old photos of my father. As a young child he seems happy, but, somewhere around age ten, I detect a subtle change in the photos: the indifference to the outside world and the wall of violence he put up around him to keep from getting hurt.

At the funeral each of his five children rises to speak. As the last one, I'm reluctant and sad. I'm angry at the damage he did to my family, to my mother, to my siblings. I don't want to get up, and I don't want to say a word. Yet, I find myself at the podium in the small funeral home, looking at the faces of my family members. I meet my godmother's eyes; she cries, as she knows what he did to us. I look at my mother and the tears on her face. She loved him throughout their thirteen-year marriage and twenty-year divorce. I look at my brother. I think about secrets. I begin to tell a story, leaving out some of the details that are important to me. And then I begin to release the fear that I've felt my whole life. It is as if for the first time I can breathe without wondering what will happen next. Later I remember things about my family, my father. And for the first time in my life I decide that I want to be a mother.

7.

Since I was diagnosed with POF in 2002, my period has come and gone many times. Over the years, I have noticed that it coincides with how I'm doing emotionally. In February 2007, two months after my father's death, my period came back. I thought of this as an opportunity to set in motion a real effort to try to get pregnant.

For years, I simultaneously thought about getting pregnant and felt ambivalent about becoming a mother. My relationship with my mother is loaded with mistrust and resentment. When I was eleven years old I swore to myself that I would never be anyone's mother. I grew up knowing about my mother's struggles with infertility, hearing the horror stories of her five miscarriages and one stillbirth. I was told how happy my parents were when they finally conceived me. My father often reproachfully reminded me how much my mother loved me and how hard it was for her to conceive me. I was indebted to them for giving me life.

I don't want that narrative to be the story of my relationship to my child. The conscious decision to become a parent should rest in a larger political context. We have to push ourselves to revolutionize how we approach parenting and the children we choose to raise.

Throughout my life, my maternal grandfather was the one person I completely trusted. He loved me, he thought I was intelligent, and he believed that I could do something more with my life than be a wife to someone like my father. In my home growing up, women were objects to be looked at and showcased. My father's binary, and deeply misogynistic, view of me was that I was either a nuisance or a sexual object. My grandfather was a counterbalance. And, despite her difficulties protecting herself and her children, my mother taught me to rely on myself and to believe that everyone deserves opportunities.

When I think about having a child, I think foremost of my grandfather and the rest of my family. I think about new generations of immigrants in the United States. I think about opening my home for a child who will have options and be empowered to make choices. I imagine that my child will get to learn from a rich community of queer folks, radical people of color, and antiracist white folks.

I am in a process of identifying and unraveling my ambivalence about motherhood. Reckoning with feelings about my sexuality and identity as a queer Latina have been just as important as acknowledging that I have been uncertain about motherhood until now. The foundation of my healing process is the acknowledgment that I know my body better than any doctor does.

For some women, increasing fertility means timed insemination, intrauterine insemination, and a medicine cabinet full of fertility medications. For me, it means figuring out a way to maintain my period for more than one cycle. In February 2007 I began to see an acupuncturist. I changed my diet. I began to tackle issues in therapy about my ambivalence around motherhood. I attended a workshop led by Julia Indichova, the author of *Inconceivable*, who was diagnosed with POF and who, without the use of fertility drugs, was able to conceive. From her I learned to think of conception as something far larger than creating fetuses and children; it is also about rebirthing ourselves.

Nothing concrete happened for months. Yet I felt healthier, more powerful—invincible. In August, after six months, my period came back. It was the first cycle I really tried to conceive a child. Though there have been ups and downs, in the months since I made a decision about healing my body, I have succeeded in having regular cycles. I don't know if this means that I will actually conceive a child. But that isn't the most important thing right now.

8.

For the past four months my blood tests have indicated that my hormones are in the normal range. The doctor says that it's just chance and an opportunity to be seized upon. I agree that it's an opportunity for me to acknowledge how I've healed my body. I am certain of the interconnectedness between what I eat, my current emotional health, my childhood experiences, and the environments I have lived and worked in.

As women whose bodies have yet again become the testing labs of big businesses, we will never get back lost years of reproductive health. No amount of money will diminish the pain of endometriosis or the side effects of PCOS. Nothing can replace the fetuses lost in miscarriages caused by working in hazardous conditions. We cannot undo our painful childhoods, nor can we change the abusive family environments we were born into.

Yet we are not powerless in the face of ubiquitous environmental toxins and the damage they do to our health. In fact, the future of our communities depends on our linking struggles for reproductive health with struggles for environmental justice and struggles against abuse/violence that alienates us from our own bodies. Individually, we can make lifestyle changes. Collectively, we can urge community groups to create grassroots education programs and add these concerns to their policy initiatives. We can support local community-supported agriculture projects in connecting with working-poor and working-class families. And we can influence the larger reproductive rights movement to prominently address these issues.

But instead of counting on the reproductive rights movement to take the lead on this, we should look at the groups already taking matters into their own hands. For fifty years, farmworkers have been toiling the land near Lake Apopka's North Shore, and no one has paid attention to their health—even though international attention was paid to the decline of the alligator population and the massive bird deaths in the late 1990s. In 2006, a report initiated and conducted by former farmworkers and members of the Farmworker Association of Florida was disseminated. The results were astounding, clearly indicating that farmworkers exposed to pesticides suffered from serious health issues, including reproductive problems. This group of former Lake Apopka farmworkers is requesting more oversight from federal and state regulatory agencies, more support for farmworker health and safety education, and access to health-care specialists. The Farmworker Association of Florida is also working with young people from the farmworker community to conduct surveys to better understand the effects on their reproductive health. The multigenerational struggle of the Lake Apopka farmworkers shows us that in order to hold big business and government accountable, more of us will have to take matters into our own hands.

The long-term survival of our communities depends on how we galvanize around the many aspects of reproductive health. If we are armed with information and we push our communities to prioritize these issues, then we can change the outcomes of our individual and collective diagnoses.

Decolonize Your Diet

An Interview with Luz Calvo

By Adela Nieves

Luz Calvo, an associate professor of ethnic studies at California State University, East Bay, founded Luz's Decolonial Cooking Club to reclaim collective ancestral knowledge about food, recipes, and culture among people of color. She lives in Oakland, where she and her partner tend a small urban farm, raising chickens and growing healthy vegetables and herbs.

"Become strong and healthy," she encourages, "so you can fight for justice and liberation!"

AN: What motivated you to start the cooking club?

LC: I teach at Cal State in the Department of Ethnic Studies. Our students are mostly first-generation, working-class, putting themselves through school by working two, sometimes three jobs at a time. I was chatting with a student one afternoon, and she mentioned she didn't know how to cook and was eating mostly fast food. I said, "Why

Originally published in *make/shift* no. 12 (fall/winter 2012/2013)

don't I share some recipes with you? We'll start easy, and I think I could teach you to cook with recipes and good directions."

We started with how to make a pot of beans. Every time I gave her a recipe, she'd make it, bring in a sample of the food, and give her own feedback. It was turning out really good. I wanted a place to post recipes if she couldn't come during my office hours, so I started a cooking class on Facebook.

More students got interested and involved, and after a while I started a special-topics course called Decolonize Your Diet. I felt it was so necessary; many of my students are eating unhealthy foods, doing their best to get by. It expanded from there into cooking demonstrations. Students were required to investigate family recipes and present them to the class, along with samples of the food to share, and their recipes were posted on the website.

What does food mean to you?

I was diagnosed with breast cancer six years ago, and the treatment process was really traumatic. I'd been vegetarian for fifteen years when I was diagnosed, and thought I was really healthy. But breast cancer is an epidemic, and so many people suffer from it. As individuals, we can't control the toxins getting into our bodies, they are so widespread.

It was a struggle to learn what I should be eating to keep the cancer away and heal. I started an organic garden to grow my own food, and began exploring the concept of *la comida medicina* (food as medicine). So I understand "decolonize your diet" as a political statement.

I emphasize what we can do as individuals and families to reclaim those healthy parts of our ancestral knowledge, but recognize we cannot decolonize one family at a time. There has to be a whole social and structural change where we relate differently to our environment and reclaim that native, indigenous epistemological way of thinking. We are not here to exploit Mother Earth, but to live and coexist in harmony, and we're not gonna put this crap in our rivers, our food supply, or our bodies.

There needs to be a bigger political message than "buy organic!" It has to be a bigger movement where we're working on multiple fronts.

I've learned so many little changes that can have a huge impact on my diet. There are so many healing properties in plants, and herbs have amazing vital chemicals. I grow about twenty-five different herbs, and I'll eat them right from the garden. That's medicine: bringing positive, healing nutrients into my body. Every time I cook I grab a fistful of herbs to put in whatever I'm cooking, to add biodiversity to my diet and help me fight disease. Sharing this is important for me. I know in my heart more people will experience this, and I want my students to be able to say, "I knew someone who had the same thing happen to her, and this is how she got through it."

Can you explain "decolonize"?

"Decolonize" means liberating ourselves as people of color from repressive structures—like racism, sexism, homophobia, and more. That's how I understand "decolonize." It doesn't mean going backwards to some preconquest era, which of course would be impossible. But how can we decolonize our minds, and through eating decolonize our bodies? By reclaiming ancestral knowledge, often held by our extended families. Also understanding that knowledge has been squashed and devalued by the dominant culture, which tells us how to eat, presenting "food pyramids" that don't represent our peoples' traditional foods, and that are created to reflect the interests of industrial food producers, which favor meats and dairy, foods pre-Columbian people did not eat in large quantities, or at all.

What about the educational process? Learning how to eat healthy can be difficult, and there are questions of accessibility.

I think it could be easier. If I could teach just one thing, I'd start with a pot of beans. For Mexican folks, beans are essential. But we've been reduced to what I call the hegemony of the pinto bean. Growing up in the '60s and '70s we only ate pinto beans; we were already colonized. And we were presented with false information, that pinto beans are traditional, they're what Mexicans eat. But only two generations ago, our ancestors grew over two hundred varieties of beans. How did we lose that knowledge so quickly, where we're reduced to just one bean?

Every bean has a slightly different nutritional profile. One we learned about in class is the tepary bean, grown in the Sonoran desert; it has a much lower glycemic index than pinto beans.[1] The people of the Tohono O'odham Nation traditionally ate tepary beans; they now have one of the highest rates of diabetes in the world and are starting to reintroduce the bean into their diet. The Tohono O'odham are selling their tepary beans; you can buy them through vendors or online. That knowledge needs to get out.

We don't have to go very far back. I'm in general agreement with the slow-food movement and the general rules of eating mostly plants and distinguishing between real food and processed food. Beans are inexpensive, a slow cooker isn't that expensive, and you can have fresh beans all the time with very little effort. It's good fiber, good protein, plant-based, and you build from there.

Can you talk about traditional assumptions related to gender and cooking?

We've been trying to think about how to advocate cooking without reinscribing traditional gender roles. [Longtime Detroit-based activist] Grace Lee Boggs talks about how alienating work can be under capitalism and patriarchy. She asks, why shouldn't our labor be a creative act? Building a house or making shoes can be a creative activity. But under capitalism labor gets reduced to small tasks routinized, and we lose control because we're doing the labor for someone else. But labor could be creative, generative work, and something you feel good doing. That's how I envision my cooking, as an artistic practice. Food is something I create that is beautiful, tasty, something I give to people I love.

As for getting it outside that gendered, capitalistic framework, I don't have a magic solution for how people can make that happen for themselves—maybe sharing the work with a fair division of labor and appreciation—but it's a good time to reflect about that. About half my class is young men, and they are completely jazzed about cooking, so maybe traditional gender ideas around it aren't as important to the new generation.

---

1. The glycemic index (GI) is a numerical scale used to indicate how fast and how high a particular food can raise a person's blood glucose (blood sugar) level.

You seem to be encouraging your students to find the parallels between food, culture, and tradition. Was that in part due to your own exploration?

I would say so. My family came to the U.S. during the Mexican Revolution. They started selling tacos to farmworkers and packing-plant workers, and eventually opened a small restaurant. In a way, I feel very present with my ancestors when I'm cooking, like, "I know my nana would love this," or thinking she'd probably already know about something I had to research and reclaim.

Quelites (lamb's-quarters, similar to spinach or kale) and *portulacas* (purslane) are two of my favorite foods, and I know my nana knew about both of these. Purslane shows up in the cracks of streets; it's a weed. She used to find it and bring it home and cook with it. *Quelites* and *portulacas* are two of the most nutritious plants in the world, and they are part of traditional Mexican diets. As wild foods, they have not been domesticated, and the tenacity of the plant, that character, transfers to you when you eat it.

Reclaiming that knowledge is so amazing for us and for our ability to survive and fight disease. We have plants that can help us heal and combat disease if we can reclaim them and pass them on to future generations.

What interests your students most about the cooking club?

Some are interested in reclaiming; they get excited seeing things they know their parents and grandparents have done, and now they value them differently because some public person in their lives is now valuing them, instead of devaluing them. But the family and traditional knowledge my students bring to the class from their extended families really blows me away.

Who has inspired your thoughts on cooking and food?

Gloria Anzaldúa's poem "To Live in the Borderlands." There's a line in her poem, "to live in the borderlands means . . . to put *chile* on the borscht, eat whole wheat tortillas." I really appreciate that; decolonizing for me is not about purity or authentic past, it's about reclaiming traditional knowledge to make our present better. And of course we're going to incorporate things from American culture, from Chinese culture, from whatever works for us. It's not about excluding other cultures, but putting things together in a way that is healthy for us.

On the Luz's Decolonial Cooking Club Facebook page, you talk about the "Latino/a health paradox." Can you explain that?

Public health scholars have identified this trend they've named the Latino/a health paradox. The basic concept is Latino/a immigrants who come to the U.S. are, when they first arrive, healthier on all measures—infant mortality, overall mortality, diabetes rates, heart disease, breast cancer—they arrive very healthy, and remain healthy the first couple years here. And that's amazing, considering the stress people are under—racism, undocumented status, lack of access to health care, no financial means, living in crowded conditions. For women who give birth during this time, the infant mortality rate is super low.

How could this be? Health disparities are directly related to lower socioeconomic status, and that's true across the world. But Mexico is an exception to that; poor people in Mexico [who play a big role in the study, though it looks at Latino/a immigrants broadly] have about the same health as rich people. My theory is it's directly related to the diet people were raised on: high in beans, corn tortillas; limited amount of beef, but the beef is raised on *ranchos* and not factory farms; rich in greens and foraged foods; and no butter. That diet protects people, even when they arrive here in the midst of all this social stress.

Unfortunately, the longer they are here they leave that diet, they start eating fast food, and by the next generation, those health benefits have entirely disappeared. It's not genetic; it's the loss of our diet. I just wish people would recognize, "Wow, these Mexican immigrants are bringing this knowledge that could actually save us all!" And give respect for that, instead of devaluing them, their culture, their language, and their labor, and turning them into basically the rest of us, with all our health problems. It's like a shift in how we think about people, how we value people and the cultural knowledge they bring.

Some Monologues on Happiness

Performed by My Friends, Extemporaneously, as I Performed Oral Sex on Them

By T Clutch Fleischmann

Rick

Umm, first thing that comes to mind is certain groups or niches that I may find with people. Like mainly people in Ann Arbor, or my group of . . . my small group of friends here. It's not even like the activities or the things we do or the places we go or anything like that but more like a feeling of . . . um, what's the word, affinities? Having lots of things, core things, that we share that allow me to just be myself and understand . . . I don't know. I like the idea specifically with gay men . . . it makes me happy when I can share something from my past and they sort of already know or have shared a similar experience. Like this idea that there is a we— shared experiences. Coming from a place where everything you do is not mentioned, it's nice to [*deep sigh*], I guess have validation of your experiences. Ummm, and then of course once we're together in these groups, these groups that make me happy, I enjoy kitties—kitties crying at the door. Kitties make me happy and I tell them I love them and I

Originally published in *make/shift* no. 8 (fall/winter 2010/2011)

kiss them and they kiss me. Lesbian relationships make me happy, even though I'm not in them and never will be. I was talking to Arnold last night and I was telling him how I really like the lesbian aesthetic. Like girlfriends. I wish I was a girlfriend and I had cute haircuts and listened to Tegan and Sara while we made lesbian love kind of thing. What else makes me happy? Finding people who are [*laughter*] like T, [*laughter*] as sexually deviant as myself. It makes me happy to find people that I can have more boundaryless relationships with, I suppose. It makes me happy to sort of just exist with them and not have to worry about where our relationship ends or begins, or where they end and I begin [*laughter*]. That's distracting, T. [*Humming*] Should I just let this run and listen to it later? Masturbate to it? [*Deep laughter*] That makes me happy [*more laughter*]. Drugs make me happy [*more laughter*]. Wait, you can't include that. Don't include anything like that. The best way to describe it is, I mean, obviously like car trips and traveling and parks, they all make me happy and bring me joy in that moment. But I think it's more the ahh, the finding community. Being a part of more than one and being able to go in and out of communities where I find a home. Coming off of not being a part of a lot of things it makes me really happy to find groups of people where I can validate experiences. The color green makes me really happy. All shades of green. Chipmunks. [*Sigh*] Yeah.

Rose
Alright—is it started? Okay. [*Laughter*] Ooooo-kay. Happiness. Ahhh . . . last week, on Friday. Okay, so maybe more than a week ago. No, less than a week ago. Anyways. I applied for a job at a health-food store. I felt like I went in there and I was maybe a little bit crazy, and I just, like, answered everything pretty honestly. But they asked me, and I was like, *Is this a serious question?* That's what I thought in my head but I didn't say that to them but they said, What's your idea of success? And I said, Being happy and making other people happy. Like having your happiness and not having that get in anybody else's way of being happy. And then it was really quiet and I realized that they wanted something about stability, and I was just like, *Oh shit*. And they bought it and I got the job, 'cause I guess those are the kinds of people who get to work at health-food stores. I don't know. For what makes me happy. I'm sure

everyone is just going to say my friends, and my family, and that the world's really beautiful. Ahhh. Photosynthesis is pretty much one of my favorite things ever. And not just that it keeps the world as we know it going, because that's only one possible world, just because it's really, really, really pretty great. And I fell in love with it almost as if it were a person when I was in high school [*laughter*]. Ummm, so my friends and family slightly less important than things involving chlorophyll [*laughter*]. Ummm . . . Some of the people that I love make me the happiest. And I've done some stuff that was supposed to be fulfilling work, like when I was working for this nonprofit, organizing people in low-income neighborhoods to come together and stand up and say, "Fuck the man." I just ended up listening to people a lot, and I didn't get them to raise their fists in the air quite so much. So I guess I like listening to people. But again that's just being able to . . . sometimes people don't really have someone to listen to them. I really like reading Allen Ginsberg poems, sometimes to my roommate's cat. Ummm . . . Some of my best friends in the world are people that I really thought I pushed away and realizing that they still cared about me and I need to try a lot harder to fuck things up. Ahhh, I just had one of the best times ever a while ago when I went over to Lansing. The twelfth of June. It was my birthday at midnight and we went out and my friend Tara and I, we just fucking watched *Degrassi* and that made me so happy. I felt like it was, like, the best part of our relationship before that relationship got kind of sour. Not sour, but like, I was in a relationship with a boy that really, really distracted me from caring about some of the people that I love the most. They didn't want me to move to school, to go to some school to be with this kid, and I apparently did, which is why my friend T is going down on my purple strap-on instead of me talking about how I'm a third-string goalie at some college in Minnesota. And yeah. And like, despite all the blowing them off or whatever, I had a really good time with Tara a couple weeks ago.

Miloh
[*Laughter*] Ummm. What makes me happy. Money! makes me happy. Good blow jobs [*laughter*]. Ahhhh [*laughter*]. Ummm, yeah, T sucks great dick [*laughter*]. A lot makes me happy. Damn. [*Moan*] Ummm.

[*Breathing*] Wow, okay. What makes me happy. Ummmm, sex? [*Laughter*] The fact that T gives great head. I've never . . . [*trails off, moans for several minutes*] I can barely talk. [*Laughter*] That makes me happy. [*Laughter; several minutes of moaning and breathing*] God. Oh my god [*moaning and breathing; laughter; several minutes of moaning and breathing*]. Yeah, feels good. T knows . . . [*laughter*] Ummm, yeah [*moaning*]. Damn [*laughter*]. This is a monologue. [*Several minutes of moaning and breathing*] This feels so good. T knows what they're doing. Ahhh. Oh my god. Ahhhh. [*More breathing and moaning*] God that's so good. I masturbated three times today. [*Breathing and moaning*] Are you getting tired? [*More breathing and louder moaning, followed by laughter*] Oh my god. Mmmmmmmm.

Katie Jean Shinkle

What makes me happy is the connections I make with other people. My connections with other people make it worth me doing the things that I do, being open and honest even when I'm not open and honest. [*List of things Katie has done that she later asked I excise*] And I'm not really a bad person, I'm more just finding out who I am and exploring what it is to live here, [*breathing*] in my skin. My connections with other people make me happy because my art wouldn't be what it is without it. It's the reason I get up in the morning. It's the reason I go to bed. It's the reason I eat or don't eat, or sleep or don't sleep, or do cocaine or don't do cocaine, or lose weight or don't lose weight, or see myself as a whole person or not. [*Heavy breathing*] Without my connections with other people I think that I would probably not be alive, I would probably not live, I would probably be a shell and this is what makes me happy. And I don't really know why things manifest the way that they do, and I don't know why my relationships with other people have created what is happening right now in my life, the fact that I'm leaving the place that I've only known and that I write about and that I think about and that I masturbate to and that I love. [*Heavy breathing*] And the people that I love the most are the people that are no good for me. The people that I can't stop talking to are the people that don't love me, and that don't give a shit whether I live or die. And that's okay with me. [*Heavy breathing, some moaning*] Because there's nothing I can do or say that can change other people's perceptions of me. And I don't really want to do that. But it's these perceptions that make me happy, and these perceptions that keep me going. It's those perceptions that I guess I'm really afraid of leaving. It's those perceptions that make it worth it. I think I work really hard at showing a certain thing and making sure everyone knows that certain thing about me. And it's that certain thing that allows the connections in my life to happen. [*Moaning*] This is going to be over really soon, in less than a day. And it makes this breakup worth it. And everything else that I do worth it, because without it there wouldn't be anything. [*Heavy breathing, extended moaning*] I think there's a difference between [*moaning*], difference between going and never coming back, [*moaning*] and I plan on coming back.

Where We Are Not Known

Queer Imagination and the Photography of Kirstyn Russell

By Adrienne Skye Roberts

In the suburban town where I grew up, San Francisco might as well have been as far away as New York. Years later I moved the mere thirty miles across the Golden Gate Bridge and rented an apartment in the middle of the Castro District. This neighborhood—thought of as the center of gravity that all contemporary queers in the United States are expected to orbit around—felt as confining as my homogenous hometown. My imagination began to wander elsewhere.

Kirstyn Russell's photographic series *Where We Are Not Known* makes this search for belonging visible. Russell also grew up in the San Francisco Bay Area, and yet her search for queerness leads her from this queer epicenter to its peripheries and back again. In 2005 Russell planned to photograph gay bars during a road trip to West Virginia. Upon reaching these predetermined destinations she quickly learned that many of the bars were no longer open for business, while others were discreetly located—tucked inside unassuming buildings without any

Originally published in *make/shift* no. 9 (spring/summer 2011)

traditional visual cues to designate queer space. There were no rainbow flags hanging above the door, no pink-triangle signs in the window.

With the absence of these visual markers, Russell projected queerness onto her surroundings. By intentionally reframing everyday, mundane sights, Russell imagines what is barely legible within the landscape. There is a richness to the simplicity of Russell's photographs. Shooting from afar, she creates beautiful fields of color from asphalt or the layers of paint on a building, allowing subtlety and contrast to emerge from within the landscape itself. In Kenosha, Wisconsin, the marquee of a discounted muffler service implies a competitive lesbian sexuality. A grocery store in Medford, Oregon, is recontextualized as a business catering to bisexual customers. Within the context of these photographs, it is the actual queer spaces that appear unremarkable. In Tucson, Arizona, Russell photographed the gay bar Ain't Nobody's Bizness. The image portrays a beige, stucco building foregrounded by three empty parking spaces. It looks more like an abandoned shopping center or office complex than a popular nightclub. Even its name is a coded reference to queerness.

Russell's project utilizes a queer imagination, one that allows for the creation of space for those whose identities are invisible or actively erased within the public sphere. Growing up, Russell projected queerness onto images of tomboys in popular television shows, identifying with the tough, athletic female characters. This recognition provided her with a sense of relief and camaraderie—albeit imagined—in the often alienating experience of growing up queer. This is not an unfamiliar project. With the lack of visibility or representation within mainstream culture, many marginalized subjects create for themselves what is not yet a reality.

There are no people in Russell's photographs: no bar hoppers or customers of local businesses. With this absence of people, the images become backdrops, therefore allowing viewers to project their own stories and fantasies onto these locations. They remove me from my own privileged position within a queer urban locus and unsettle the center-versus-periphery divide. Russell's photographs may as well have been taken in the small suburban town where I was raised. What if I had embodied Russell's queer imagination and was made aware of the possibilities within my seemingly limited environment? Perhaps then I wouldn't have left for a city where queerness is codified and its imagination already defined.

Ain't Nobody's Biz (Gay Bar): Tucson, AZ, 2006

Bimart: Medford, OR, 2010

No Muff Too Tuff: Kenosha, WI, 2010

The Attack on Attachment

Why Love Is the Loser in the So-Called Mommy Wars

By Andrea Richards

I want to posit that the "mommy wars"—from "Tiger moms" to the controversy over attachment parenting to the ongoing lament over women in leadership positions and life/work balance spurred by Anne-Marie Slaughter's July 2012 cover story in the *Atlantic*—are a colossal, complicated act of subterfuge. It's not that the underlying issues aren't important, but, instead of raising them, the media's misdirection plays on private anxieties and sidesteps larger social problems.

First, there is the question of omission: What is not being talked about in these mommy wars? Actual policy: pay inequality, parental-leave requirements, the fraught condition of women's health care, the lack of affordable health care for families, and the rights of domestic and childcare workers. This fascination, which is actually a voyeurism, with motherhood serves no one, certainly not caregivers. (The people supposedly in the trenches of this fake war are not only mothers but anyone who cares for and loves a child.)

Originally published in *make/shift* no. 12 (fall/winter 2012/2013)

What does it matter if you sleep in the same bed as your kid or if you breastfeed them until they're eight if you lose your job because you've taken one too many personal days to tend to sick children (because all children, even breastfed co-sleepers, are petri dishes of disease)? And getting your kid to his cello lesson on time is hardly an issue if you can't afford rent, much less spring for music lessons. What we lovers of children need are not debates about the merits of baby slings and permissive parenting, but resolutions about workplace policies, universal health care, and equal access to quality public education. Private anxieties are trumping public problems. The breastfeeding three-year-old on the cover of *Time* is a skinny little straw man.

But there is another dimension to all these "mommy" debates, something at the heart of the matter of what it means to care for a child—that is, the human heart. I'm talking about love and the fact that American culture is downright anorexic in affection for children. "What?" you say. "This is America, the most child-centered culture there is!" And, as a recent *New Yorker* article states, "Contemporary American kids may represent the most indulged young people in the history of the world." Let's not confuse commerce with care. Indulgence is lazy; affection is work. Hundreds of gadgets are made for getting children to sleep, from infant swings to rotating night-lights to plushies that simulate the sound of the womb. But, as Dr. Sears points out, holding them in our arms usually does the trick—the trouble is it takes time and doesn't support the billion-dollar baby industry.

Caring for a child is inconvenient. Yet, in American culture there is a prevailing idea that children should blend seamlessly into the adult world and our lives be unaltered by their presence, be they newborns or preteens. Their needs, humble as they may be (eat, sleep, and be loved) are constantly being negotiated so that we can trim the amount of time they take. Not because we don't want to be with them but because we *can't*. With questions and comments like these, we have effectively downsized infancy:

"Is she sleeping through the night?"
"Has he started solids yet?"
"Don't hold her too much, you'll spoil her."

Speeding children through "milestones" and measuring them like livestock (the American Academy of Pediatrics' obsession with percentiles) permits workers—caregivers and children—to return to the system as soon as possible. It is inefficient to lollygag in a capitalist economy, but as anyone who has ever tried to get a toddler to preschool on time knows, children are by nature oblique beings. We have to corral their meandering, interrupt their dreaming, and schedule their lives so we can, exhaustedly, get to work on time. As my pediatrician recently said to me with a sigh, "This is a hard place to be a baby."

Our disavowal of children's needs is matched only by our denial of what it takes to be a caregiver. Generally speaking, we expect love to be restrained, to work with our current calendar. We expect that after a night spent caring for a child, we can wake up and resume the same life we had before baby—that we can perform the same job, eat the same breakfast, pay the same bills, enjoy the same conversation at cocktail parties. (For women there is also the pressure to wear the same jeans—who wants to don mom jeans?)

In our caring for children, we think of love as a transaction, an economic one made between two distinct individuals. Love is conditional, controlled, and, by all means, a road to progress: love your children correctly, and they will become productive citizens; "good kids" are investments that yield well. As Alfie Kohn writes in his book, *Unconditional Parenting*, "The laws of the marketplace—supply and demand, tit for tat—have assumed the status of universal and absolute principles, as though everything in our lives, including what we do with our children, is analogous to buying a car or renting an apartment." Capitalist ideals permeate child rearing, and even our emotional connections are required to be productive to be considered worthwhile.

But love doesn't work that way if we really embrace its power; instead, it is the ultimate destabilizing force. Any time you fall in love there is the fragmentation of the self, the vertigo of a fixed identity slipping away. It's exhausting. But then, love *is* exhausting; it pushes us to uncomfortable places, it annihilates our sense of autonomy, identity, and security. It does not progress but circles back, like a snake swallowing its tail. Subjectivities get confused, bodily fluids are exchanged: blood, snot—these are not neat and tidy transactions. Our failure as a culture to recognize this has its price; we have become accustomed to a shallow sort of acceptable love.

I now have two children. When my first came, she arrived like a sea swell and I wrote in my journal: "Will she ever understand the depth of my affection for her? Love like this is frightening; it is an ache, devastation, an annihilation of everything I thought mattered. She is the deepest, darkest part of the ocean and I will always be the half-drunk sailor lost at sea." Having a child freaked me out, not just for all the usual reasons but because of the intensity of the relationship, the bond of a real animal connection if and when I allowed myself to acknowledge it. To get my newborn to sleep, I needed only to breathe in her face. If she stirred, I could, like some Pentecostal preacher, lay my hands upon her and she would still. (I was lucky not to have a colicky baby.)

Becoming a parent—the lover of two miraculous children who beguile me and bring great joy—has forced me to recognize some uncomfortable truths: to really open my heart and mind to the needs of children (not just mine) means a radical revision of the way I've lived my life from the practical—say, working long hours—to the philosophical. Interdependence (about which a great deal has been written, beautifully, in this magazine) is the only option. I cannot raise these children alone, nor should I. We are deeply connected, by necessity, to a larger community of care and to a larger arena of challenges. I do not regret my babies or their demands, but I do feel overwhelmed by the amount that recognizing those demands, rather than diminishing them, requires I reshape my life.

Capitalist society is not working for a lot of people, and we can't "revalue family values" (as Anne-Marie Slaughter asks) without a serious critique of how our economic system is disenfranchising us both economically and emotionally. We need to stop listening to the "mommy wars" and start looking at ways we can really change our society to meet the needs of all kinds of families. Starting from a position of unconditional love—committing ourselves to love our children and each other and to, perhaps, put others' needs above our individual desires, fears, and anxieties. This sounds like heresy, doesn't it? As a feminist I have been taught this is a backward position.

But I'm not talking about being sacrificial because there's nothing left to sacrifice: I no longer buy into the autonomous self. That self dissolved a long time ago—now I move with six arms and three hearts and goodness knows how many souls. Individualism is a myth, no less dangerous than manifest destiny; we are unfinished beings who shape-shift and change with new relationships and experiences. And I, for one, feel more powerful in partiality; I am broken, laid bare, by the intensity of feelings I have for my children, and yet I have never felt so capable, so connected. Thinking for and as a family—however you define "family"—means operating as a collective of disparate interests, aspirations, beliefs but somehow still coming together for no other reason than that you deeply care for one another.

But it's not enough to love only in my private life, just as it's not enough to love only my children—love requires an outward, no less than inward, expression. We must love all children—really love them—in messy, unproductive, and unsettling ways—in public. We must retrain ourselves to give love away for free rather than to make it something children earn by accomplishment, mimicry, or talent. This call is demanding. The truly subversive act is not breastfeeding your toddler on the cover of a magazine; it is kissing, hugging, and holding children's hands during the all-too-few moments we have together in our daily lives.

M/other Ourselves

A Black Feminist Genealogy

or

The Queer Thing

By Alexis Pauline Gumbs

The queer thing is that we were born at all.
I was born in 1982 in the middle of the first term of a president who won by demonizing "welfare queens," in the global context of "population control," a story that says poor women and women of color should not give birth. A story with a happy ending for capitalism: we do not exist. The queer thing is that we *were* born; our young and/or deviant and/or brown and/or broke and/or single mamas did the wrong thing. Therefore we exist: a population out of control, a story interrupted. We are the guerrilla poems written on walls, purveyors of a billion dangerous meanings of life.

And how unlikely that I would love you.
In 1983, Audre Lorde, Black, lesbian, poet, warrior, mother, interrupted the story of a heterosexist, capitalist fashion and beauty magazine called *Essence* with a queer proposition. In an essay on the impact of internalized oppression among Black women, she offered: we can learn to mother ourselves.

*Dedicated to
Mai'a Williams*

*We were never
meant to survive.
—Audre Lorde, "A
Litany for Survival"*

*Mothering. Claiming
some power over who
we choose to be . . .
—Audre Lorde, "Eye
to Eye: Black Women,
Hatred, and Anger"*

Originally published
in make/shift no. 8
(fall/winter 2010/2011)

It's the title of my dissertation and I still don't know what it means. Except that love is possible even in a world that teaches us to hate ourselves, and the selves we see waiting in each other. Except that in a world that says that we should not be born, and that says no to our very beings every day, I still wake up wanting you with a yes on my heart. Except that I believe in how we grow our bodies into places to live at the very sight of each other. We can learn to mother ourselves. I think it means you and me.

You are something else.

The radical potential of the word "mother" is the space that "other" takes in our mouths when we say it. We are something else. We know it from how fearful institutions wield social norms and try to shut us down. We know it from how we are transforming the planet with our every messy step toward making life possible. Radical childcare collectives, mamas who unlearn domination by refusing to dominate their children, all of us breaking cycles of abuse by deciding what we want to replicate from the past and what we need urgently to transform, are m/othering ourselves.

Audre Lorde's essay had an older sister. Ten years earlier, in 1973, Toni Morrison wrote a novel about a dangerous, undomesticated woman, an "artist without an art form" who spurned her own mother's advice to settle down, insisting, "I don't want to make someone else. I want to make myself." *Sula*, the novel that inspired Black feminist literary critics such as Barbara Smith and Mae Gwendolyn Henderson to invent Black feminist literary criticism, is a sacred text about two girls who "having long ago realized they were neither white nor male . . . went about creating something else to be." Sula herself is not a mother type, except for how she creates herself, except for how she creates a context for other people to grow past the norms they knew, except for how in her name contemporary Black feminist literary theory was born and she is how I know how to write these words.

Your mama is queer as hell.

What if mothering is about the *how* of it? In 1987 Hortense Spillers wrote "Mama's Baby, Papa's Maybe: A New American Grammar Book," reminding her peers that mother*hood* is a status granted by patriarchy to white middle-class women, those women whose legal rights to their children are never questioned, regardless of who does the labor (the how) of keeping them alive. Mother*ing* is another matter, a possible action, the name for that nurturing work, that survival dance, *worked* by enslaved women who were forced to breastfeed the children *of* the real mothers while having no control over whether their birth or chosen children were sold away, *worked* by immigrant nannies like my grandmother who mothered wealthy white kids in order to send money to Jamaica to my mother and her brothers who could not afford the privilege of her presence, *worked* by chosen and accidental mentors who agree to support some growing unpredictable thing called future, *worked* by house mothers in ball culture who provide spaces of self-love and expression for/as queer youth of color in the street. What would it mean for us to take the word "mother" less as a gendered identity and more as a possible action, a technology of transformation that those people who do the most mothering labor are teaching us right now?

The queer thing is that we are still here.
We can remember how to mother ourselves if we can remember the proto–queer of color movement that radicalized the meaning of mothering. In 1979 at the National Third World Lesbian and Gay Conference, where Audre Lorde gave the keynote speech, a caucus of lesbians agreed on the statement: "The children of all lesbians are our children," a socialist context for mothering, where children are not individual property but rather reminders of the context through which community exists. This means that "mothering" is a queer thing. Not just when people who do not identify as heterosexual give birth to or adopt children and parent them, but all day long and everywhere when we acknowledge the creative power of transforming ourselves, and the ways we relate to each other. Because we were never meant to survive and here we are creating a world full of love.

That's the queer thing.

Bringing Down

By Jen Benka

On an evening walk in the Village last winter, plodding through more than a foot of fresh snow, I noticed two boys standing near a police van that was plowed in on the corner. One of them was writing something in the snow that covered the windshield of the van. I expected to read "pigs," but then it occurred to me that maybe kids don't call cops pigs anymore. The boys ran down the street, and I stopped to read what they had written: "I love Eric." Further down the block, written in the snow on a car window was, "I love Paul."

How do I say this (imperfectly).

Simonides of Ceos, a Greek poet who lived in the fifth century BCE, invented a way to permanently preserve memories, called the loci method: you convert what you are trying to remember "into vivid mental images and then arrange them in some sort of imagined architectural space, known as a memory palace."

Originally published in *make/shift* no. 5 (spring/summer 2009)

There is a thing that needs to be built (the name for it).

On a trip to Paris a few years ago, I decided to walk over to 27 Rue de Fleurus, where Gertrude Stein and Alice B. Toklas lived. As I turned down their cobblestone street it started to rain. I found their building and looked up to their window, imagining them inside. The shutters opened and a hand emerged. It sprinkled geranium petals down to the sidewalk where I was standing. I picked them up and put them in my pocket. Kiss me. The shutters closed. Kiss me. The rain stopped. Kiss me. Slow then slowly.

Gertrude Stein said love could end the war. And the reporters laughed and laughed and laughed.

PRESIDENT LYNDON JOHNSON: It became clear that if we were prepared to stay the course in Vietnam, we could help to lay the cornerstone for a diverse and independent Asia, full of promise and resolute in the cause of peaceful economic development for her long-suffering peoples.

PRESIDENT GEORGE W. BUSH: We're helping the Iraqis rebuild their infrastructure, and reform their economy, and build the prosperity that will give all Iraqis a stake in a free and peaceful Iraq.

PRESIDENT LYNDON JOHNSON: If we faltered, the forces of chaos would scent victory and decades of strife and aggression would stretch endlessly before us.

PRESIDENT GEORGE W. BUSH: If we were not fighting and destroying this enemy in Iraq, they would not be idle. They would be plotting and killing Americans across the world and within our own borders.

PRESIDENT LYNDON JOHNSON: The choice was clear. We would stay the course. We shall stay the course. (Applause)

PRESIDENT GEORGE W. BUSH: Some critics continue to assert that we have no plan in Iraq except to "stay the course." If by "stay the course," they mean we will not allow the terrorists to break our will, they are right. If by "stay the course," they mean we will not permit al Qaeda to turn Iraq into what Afghanistan was under the Taliban—a safe haven for terrorism and a launching pad for attacks on America—they are right, as well. (Applause)

This could be a memory palace: the space under the Sixteenth Street viaduct where James and the other homeless Vietnam vets slept because they hated the shelter, with its cots and military-issue wool blankets.

Or an airplane-hangar palace. Or a torched-village palace. Or a palace made of rubble. When the quake comes will you reach for me.

It is possible that social, political, and cultural transformation will occur naturally over time. It is possible that we will not wait and that it will come as the result of an organized, nonviolent mass movement led by those outside the dominant culture and ruling class. It is possible that there will be a revolution.

It is not possible that public officials will remember us more than the people who can afford to fund their campaigns for office until we make their forgetting impossible.

Mr. Roger Sherman from Connecticut said he opposed election by the people.

The people, he said, want information and are constantly liable to be misled.

Mr. Elbridge Gerry from Massachusetts did not like the idea of election by the people either. The people do not want virtue, but are "the dupes of pretended patriots." If suffrage were extended to all, the men worried, "the rights of property-owners may be overturned by a majority without property."

Slow then slowly.

The Constitution of the United States was ratified in 1788 and went into effect in 1789. The Thirteenth Amendment, which abolished slavery, was ratified seventy-six years later. African American men were not granted the right to vote for five more years.

The U.S. women's suffrage movement was launched at a convention in 1848. The Nineteenth Amendment, which guarantees women's right to vote, passed seventy-two years later in 1920. For the first 132 years of the United States' existence, women had no formal voice in its democratic government. Elizabeth Cady Stanton and Susan B. Anthony, leaders in the suffrage movement from its beginnings, died in 1902 and 1906, respectively.

It is possible that public policy affording civil rights will be won as a result of litigation. It is possible that elected officials will introduce legislation affording civil rights in response to public demands, and that other elected officials will vote to enact the legislation. It is not possible that they will act on such demands unless the culture has changed first.

"The disruption of the present organization is the first step toward community organization. Present arrangements must be disorganized if they are to be displaced by new patterns . . . "—Saul Alinsky

It is possible that resistance to poetry and resistance to political participation in the United States have been rooted in the same fear, and that this fear has been, in part, one of feeling deeply; and that this fear has been, in part, one of assuming responsibility for the interconnectedness of our lives; and that this fear has been, in part, one of accepting our power.

The reason why is you didn't work hard enough.

The reason why is you were raised by a single mother.

The reason why is you don't have religion.

The reason why is you never finished high school.

The reason why is you got pregnant.

The reason why is you were injured on the job and became disabled.

The reason why is you were exposed to toxic chemicals.

The reason why is you have PTSD.

The reason why is your chronic mental physical mental physical mental physical illness.

The reason why is you are a crack heroin crack heroin crack heroin addict.

The reason why is it runs in your family.

The reason why is it has to be somebody. It's explained in the Bible, he explained to me, Matthew 26:11: "you will always have the poor with you."

The look of lips saying sorry.

Antonio took the train down from New York City to meet me in D.C., where I was for the weekend to participate in the Housing Now march. The march was organized by a coalition of two hundred organizations to draw attention to homelessness and the lack of affordable housing in cities across the country. A small group of us, who volunteered at a meal program in Milwaukee, rented a van and made the long thirteen-hour drive.

"Let's go see the quilt," Antonio said. I had no idea what he was talking about. I was still thinking about why it was that hundreds of thousands of people in the United States were left to survive on the streets. Build houses not bombs. Housing is a human right. Sleeping is not a crime. And then there it was: thousands of colorful fabric panels sewn together and spread out on the Ellipse near the White House—each one made in the memory of someone who had died of AIDS.

We walked between the panels, stopping along the way to read the names and appreciate the painfully short lives they memorialized. The quilt had been displayed in D.C. in 1987, and at that time had nineteen hundred panels. The display Antonio and I saw two years later had more than eight thousand.

I didn't know until he told me, as we were standing in the middle of the quilt, that he had acquaintances that had died from the disease. We were twenty and twenty-one, struggling to accept ourselves as lesbian and gay and coming out to friends, and I felt us fleeting. We didn't have time to count on. Future is a negotiation between greed and justice, and justice was losing. There was no future for us but grief.

A quilted palace. A bathhouse palace. A White House palace.

What are the things I ask myself that I am afraid to repeat to you?

In her 1978 essay, "The Transformation of Silence into Language and Action," Audre Lorde wrote about being diagnosed with breast cancer: "I was forced to look upon myself and my living with a harsh and urgent clarity that has left me still shaken but much stronger." She realized that she "was going to die, if not sooner then later, whether or not I had ever spoken myself. My silences had not protected me." She concluded, "Your silence will not protect you."

The school social worker asked the thirteen-year-old boy to write "your silence will not protect you" on a piece of paper and keep it in his pocket. The next time they called him a faggot, he took out the paper and read it, and read it again.

The woman chanted it to herself while driving to her parents' house where she would tell them that she was in love with another woman.

We painted it on the banner we held up at the protest at a Cracker Barrel restaurant in Kenosha, Wisconsin, where an out gay man was fired.

Activists speaking at rallies demanding more money for AIDS research invoked Lorde's words.

A six-word comfort, a six-word rallying cry. A six-word palace.

Am I too silent? Will I leave no instructions? How do I forgive you without surrendering? Could I ever throw a grenade? How can the way I love be wrong?

And laughed and laughed and laughed.

The people are interested in depersonalization and details. How a body is the same as a rock in red radar. How computers lock a missile on a target. What it feels like to finger the key, the trigger.

In a 1975 interview, Paul Tibbets, the pilot of the *Enola Gay* (named after his mother), which dropped the A-bomb on Hiroshima, said, "I'm not proud that I killed 80,000 people, but I'm proud that I was able to start with nothing, plan it and have it work as perfectly as it did."

I killed 80,000 people.

I'm not proud . . . but I'm proud.

I killed 80,000 people.

I'm not proud . . . but I'm proud.

I killed 80,000 people.

I'm not proud . . . but I'm proud.

Little Boy palace. Fat Man palace. Hiroshima Prefectural Industrial Promotion Hall palace.

It is possible that we will not allow lies to accumulate truth.

It is possible that we will vote for the candidate who will kill the fewest people.

It is possible that in the revision we will have been in love.

when you	I do too
when I	you do too
when they	we do too
when we	they do too

It is possible that we will lay mirrors in the street

to bring heaven down to earth.

NOTES

Joshua Foer, "Remember This," an article about "the archives of the brain," *National Geographic*, November 2007.

Lyndon B. Johnson, "The Anguish and the Hope" (speech, joint session of the Tennessee State Legislature, March 15, 1967), in *Representative American Speeches: 1966–1967* (H. W. Wilson, 1967).

"President Outlines Strategy for Victory in Iraq," as released by the White House's Office of the Press Secretary, November 30, 2005.

Saul Alinsky, *Rules for Radicals* (Vintage, 1971).

Audre Lorde, *Sister Outsider* (Crossing Press, 1984).

A Race for the Ages
/ The Blink of an Aye

An installment of the column
"Centrally Located" by Erin Aubry Kaplan

By the time you read this, the American inauguration of the century will have happened. (Yes, we're only a few years into the century, but sometimes milestones hit early—Jamestown, the Louisiana Purchase, the San Francisco earthquake, World War I, 9/11.) Turns out this was the real event of the political marathon that was 2008. The election that we all dreaded and anticipated in equal measure for so long turned out to be almost anticlimactic—no Florida-style crisis of vote recounting, no court battles dragging on past Christmas, just an unemotional tally of electoral votes that went Barack Obama's way pretty early in the evening. Virginia went, Pennsylvania went, Ohio went, and presto, we have a new—and I mean *new*—president. In some ways the whole affair was utterly unlike these affairs of the last hundred years. Which made it all the more exciting because the system worked for Obama exactly like it worked for all the white men before him. Power changing hands and skin color uneventfully—now *that's* a marvel of

Originally published
in *make/shift* no. 5
(spring/summer 2009)

democracy, even if the thrill turns out to be fleeting. With all the crises that waited for us like fire-breathing dragons on January 21, I suspect that by now that thrill seems fleeting indeed.

So let's continue the reflectiveness occasioned by January and take one last backward look at the entire campaign season, which really started in 2006.

A digression/confession: I never meant to write about politics for this page. I wanted to keep it sacred. I wanted to keep the dirt of the world away from the fresh earth of *make/shift* and write strictly, or primarily, about my inner life and what it might mean; as a Black woman and a writer, that feels far more radical than bloviating, however righteously, about politics and race. That's the usual role for Black journos, and worthy as it is, it isn't all we are. Indeed, I joined the pages of *make/shift* to prove that. But Black people all know that it's often impossible to parse politics from everything else meaningful and illuminating, and this last election, with its naked confluence of politics, bigotry, paranoia, identity crises, and dark nights of the national soul, was one of those times.

The ascendancy of Barack Obama should have been thrilling to me—my troubles with the Democratic Party aside, the sheer, dogged movement of a Black candidate through the thickets of a system that had once been impassable for people of color was historic. It *was* thrilling. But at the same time it was entirely anticlimactic. I felt both things when I first saw Obama at a rally in Los Angeles back in 2006, when he was just gearing up. I came to see what the magic was all about, and he didn't disappoint. On a mild summer day in a park on the edge of South Central, Obama roamed an outdoor stage in a white shirt with rolled-up sleeves, a lanky, handsome man with piercing eyes and a voice that was both soothing and stentorian. He inventoried all the things that were wrong in America, slowly building indignation like a preacher; he counted overpopulated prisons as one of the things wrong, which made him the first presidential candidate I could recall who dared to assail, rather than support, the criminal-justice system and the racial injustice it's come to stand for. He said all this before Black people, white people, teenagers, and senior citizens, and we all drank it in like long-ailing folk finding an elixir we didn't know existed. To get what we actually wanted in a political address rather than pick out what we liked and discard the rest like bones—what we've all been doing the last couple of decades—was heady, giddy, downright sexy.

But I felt even in that buoyant moment that the magic would fall short. The electric promise in Obama sat alongside an equal penchant for compromise that predated this campaign by many years and other election cycles. The urge to do good and do better and be different was real, but no less real than the careful marketing strategy that was evident everywhere in the park, starting with the multiracial choir that opened the Obama show. Yet I bought that Obama was real: he was just like me. Unfortunately, that meant that he was always going to be in the position of having to prove to people not like him (that is, the mostly white voting public) that his Blackness—and the very specific life experiences that entails—does not threaten them, that it makes no difference, that even *he* gives it no consideration at all. This is where I felt Obama was going to lose, even if he won. To effect any change he would have to be himself, to proceed from a point of view fundamentally American but uniquely his. To stand for anything you have to first stand for yourself, and it appeared to me, even on that auspicious afternoon, that this wouldn't be possible for him. The standing would have to be enough.

Of course I hope I'm wrong. I hope we are all in a genuinely better place now, or on the way to one. I hope the settled question is an improvement over the wild uncertainty that's defined the election from start to finish. But I don't know. We won't know for a while.

Social Change through Failure
An Interview with Chris Vargas and Eric Stanley

By Mattilda Bernstein Sycamore

In *Homotopia*, filmmaker Chris Vargas joins forces with direct-action activist and academic Eric Stanley to fuse the politics of political organizing with the techniques of DIY feminist videomaking and, perhaps most surprisingly, the clumsiness of gay relational comedy. *Homotopia* challenges the gay-marriage movement's obsession with assimilation at all costs, yet it does so with a hilarity and a messiness that reveal surprising intersections between gender defiance, failure, and resistance.

Mattilda Bernstein Sycamore sat down with the filmmakers after their recent tour of universities, and got so caught up in the festivities that she neglected to ask why so much of her floral-themed purple coif got cropped out of her cameo in the movie. But on to the rest of the ideas the movie generates . . .

MBS: Let's start with the beginning, where you have a manifesto that ends, "Love Revolution, Not State Delusion." This invocation of revolution seems both critical

Originally published in *make/shift* no. 3 (spring/summer 2008)

and ironic. I wonder if you could talk about that tension between the serious politics and the campy sloganeering?

ES: I think, historically, that people have argued that a camp aesthetic is by definition apolitical—people like Susan Sontag in her "Notes on 'Camp'"—and we started from the belief that camp has been and is a really important political strategy, especially in queer struggles and queer visual cultures. In San Francisco, camp is alive and well in direct-action groups like LAGAI–Queer Insurrection and Gay Shame. LAGAI, for example, had a "First Ever Mass Gay Divorce" back in 1996, complete with the Go Your Separate Ways Travel Agency and a plate-smashing booth.

CV: Yeah, camp is self-critical and also allows a lightness which offers an entry point into some serious political dialogue.

ES: And oftentimes historically, especially in '70s movements, it was all about this masculinist dogma. You know: everyone needs to file in line behind the great male leader, and there's very little room for playfulness or for love or passion or any of those things.

What made you think of using gay relational comedy?

ES: We knew that we couldn't and didn't necessarily want to dabble in the world of realism. And you know there's nothing further from realism than romantic comedies. So I think our intentional distance from any kind of realism opened the space for some kind of comedic effect.

CV: Yeah, we took these potentially serious characters, serious about mobilizing the motley group to crash this wedding that's about to take place, but who are having serious problems amongst themselves. It's poking fun at the icon of the earnest militant. We also didn't want to create one main character, or multiple characters that the viewer absolutely identified with the whole way through the movie whom you were rooting for at the end. It references this kind of feminist-film-theory work which doesn't allow you to get totally lost in the medium but instead foregrounds the apparatus.

Both of you have very conceptual, activist-oriented, theory-based ways of talking about *Homotopia*, but the actual experience of watching the movie doesn't really operate on that level. And so I'm wondering about that sort of choice—I mean, the conversations people have in the movie are not the conversation that we're having here. But simultaneously the movie is stimulating us to have this conversation.

ES: Both Chris and I are fairly theoretical, so it's interesting how much thought it took us to make something so clumsy. Hovering in the background of many shots you can see all sorts of radical books, from Fanon and Mbembe to *That's Revolting!* and *Das Kapital.* We also used shot-for-shot reenactment to reference important films that influenced us like *Battle of Algiers* and *Born in Flames.* . . . [Gay relational comedy is] one of my favorite genres of movie because those kinds of gay movies are so failed in a way, like even though they're not trying to be campy, they're just, like, so, so incredibly failed that they're totally campy.

So, would you say that you're making one of those movies but with the critical engagement actually in the intent?

CV: It seems that one huge difference is that we really avoid this moralistic and/or tightly packaged conclusion that all of these movies like *Shortbus* and *Circuit* try to arrive at, to try and make you think that a sexual liberation, or a really normative kind of love, is going to save you and the world and America.

Speaking of saving the world, this movie appears to be set in San Francisco, and obviously SF in the present day is awash with pro-marriage conversion fever, so it seems a perfect place for a dystopian fable. I thought you got some lovely shots in the gay Castro District that would be hard to plan, like Sing-Along Evita at the Castro Theatre. Or Pride Cleaners. You even managed to include those ghastly "Freedom to Marry" stickers, the ones with the stars and stripes in a heart shape that say, "We all deserve the freedom to marry!"

ES: Those stickers have been a keepsake of mine for some time; that kind of gay nationalism is something that terrifies me, actually—you know, what does it mean when this group of people that has been historically and still is incredibly terrorized by the United States government stands at allegiance with all the warmongers and every other horrible person in the United States?

CV: The rabidness of wanting to be aligned with that kind of colonial patriotism is totally scary.

Yeah, one of the characters in the movie invokes another one of those tired lines when she says, "I would never get married, but I do think other people should have the right to." And then she goes on to point out that marriage gives some people health care, and the other character's response I really liked. She says, "Why should only married people be allowed to live?"

ES: We wanted to recenter the debate and actually talk about basic needs, like health care, like somewhere to live, like food.

I think another thing that the movie keeps coming back to is this notion of a medical industrial complex, whether you're talking about AIDS deaths or pharmaceutical profiteering or marriage.

ES: It was really important to me to rework and rethink what an "AIDS movie" might be—we didn't want to recycle an old, tired narrative about someone dying with AIDS, and their friends rally around. . . . And so I think what we wanted to do is make it really clear that the important things like health care, or universal health care, or access to any kind of health-care situation—historically this is something that has been argued by feminist movements and by early gay-liberation movements and queer movements. And now it's, "We'll work on that in the next four years; after we get gay marriage, we'll come back."

Hillary Clinton's going to do it.

ES: Yeah, Hillary. I think she is. That was in her program.

**Another way you challenge normative ideas of gender is by represent-
ing all of these different sorts of trans, genderqueer, gender-defiant
bodies and identities without defining any of them. And I'm wondering if this is part of the love revolution that you're invoking.**

ES: At one of our showings a person in the audience asked, "Why are
there only white males in your movie?" I mean, to me, obviously there's
tons of people that don't identify as white and tons of people that don't
identify as male and whatever. And I think it was really interesting seeing how different people can either enter it, enter the film, or not at all.
Like, it was just way too much for some people to even get there.

CV: I wanted to say something else about the AIDS genre of movies
that ties in to the transgender genre of movies where there's always this
narrative of disclosure and revelation and then everyone has to come
to terms with it, it becomes everybody's issue. And also in the talking-
head documentary that talks about how I'm dealing with my gender and
how everyone around me is dealing with my gender. But none of those
conversations happen in our movie. Surprisingly, a lot of people didn't
really address the issue of gender presentation on our movie tour; that
was not even talked about. They sort of took everything at face value,
made a lot of assumptions, or were too afraid to ask.

ES: I think a lot of people were totally confused, and I think that was kind
of what we wanted. You know, it wasn't the kind of transitional narrative. . . . We didn't have the before surgery, after surgery; we didn't have—

CV: The sad face before, happy face after, and then the—

The baby pictures . . .

ES: Right, the mom crying about losing her daughter—yeah, there's
none of that. I mean, we had a fair number of people that identified as
trans in a lot of the audiences, and I think even for them, they didn't
really know what to do.

CV: And sometimes they injected their own assumptions about certain
characters' anatomy, especially as it referred to safe sex practices. We

were giving a talk at Smith College, and a person asked why there was not "visible condom use" in the sex scene. This question seemed to assume that a blow job without a condom is unsafe and that both people fucking in this scene were nontrans. These kinds of assumptions about people's bodies, although well intentioned, also need to be placed into question. We recently went back and added a "female condom" in that scene just to secure the gender confusion. We wanted to address safer sex without deciding what that might be for these two characters.

And also in terms of race, you were saying, do you think they were perceiving both of you as being white and nontrans?

CV: Yeah. Actually, in the Northeast, it was really strange to be not legible as trans, and I'm not sure how my race was read at all. Based on that one comment, it seemed they just assumed that we were some regular white dudes up there telling them about something or other. . . .

ES: Yeah, especially since there's a large number of mixed-race people in the movie, and I think that most of them just got read as white.

CV: It's counterintuitive, but for me being in mostly white spaces I often just get read as white and not mixed-race.

And I'm wondering also how you see the medical industrial complex playing a role in trans, genderqueer, and gender-variant lives?

ES: Unfortunately, in trans popular culture there is this push for medicalization. . . . People should feel free to express their genders in any way that they want to—with surgery, without surgery, with hormones, without hormones—you know, there isn't this one way to be trans, or this one way to be genderqueer, this one way to be whatever. And like we were talking about, in the trans genre film, most of the shots are people being pushed into surgery and then they're reborn—it's like Jesus rising from the cave.

CV: It sets up surgery and hormones as the end point—that one moment where one becomes a full-grown man or a full-grown woman. We didn't want to condemn anyone's participation in the medical industrial complex because they want their bodies to look a certain way or their genders to be read a certain way, but also we didn't want to reproduce that commonly understood expectation that one must inevitably do so in order to be legible as the gender one chooses.

You mean challenging that as the one model of success?

CV: Yeah.

And so in some ways do you think that you are invoking failure as a possibility, like maybe this is a place where there is a potential for liberation?

CV: Absolutely. This failure to pass, this failure to participate in oppressive structures—absolutely failure becomes this place of liberation.

ES: Yeah, I think that that's where the revolutionary rhetoric and the camp aesthetic—I think that around failure that's where it becomes really interesting. Because revolutionary rhetoric is all about winning, at-all-costs kind of winning, and camp is about failure, so it's like, what would it mean to create social change through failure as opposed to success? Because success is already so incredibly soaked with every kind of oppression in the world that maybe we need to start thinking about other ways to create change.

Vulnerable and Strong

Manshi Asher on Women Resisting the "Growth Paradigm" in India

By Roan Boucher

Manshi Asher is an environmental-justice activist based in Himanchal Pradesh, a Himalayan state of India. Since 1998, she has been working in alliance with grassroots movements around issues of displacement, environmental justice, and livelihood rights— first with grassroots organizations; then with an organization focused on policy, advocacy, and lobbying; and now as an activist, campaigner, and researcher with Him Dhara, an informal environmental research and action collective. She spoke to me via Skype from her home in the mountains.

RB: Can you briefly describe the work you do?

MA: My current work is supporting local community movements. A large area of this region is forest, and there are a lot of conflicts between local communities, who have a high level of dependence on their natural resources—land, forests, rivers—and large private corporations and the state, which are looking at these natural resources as sources of revenue.

Originally published in *make/shift* no. 9 (spring/summer 2011)

So there have been spontaneous movements arising across the state in which local communities are asserting their rights over these resources. We support these movements in a variety of ways: researching and compiling information so that communities know what's going on and can access decision making; supporting these movements in engagement with the state—lobbying, petitioning, planning public actions, etcetera; writing and media; and building capacities of the local activists to plan, strategize, campaign, and network with other organizations.

You've said that in the past fifty years or so, the ways that environmental degradation and development have happened have been very impacted by neoliberal capitalism and western models of development. Can you describe those impacts?

India is a growing economy, and from the '90s onward has followed a particular path of development focused on deregulation, privatization, opening up of the market for foreign investment, etcetera. If you look solely at economic growth, the growth rate has been improving.

But if you look at the circumstances of the majority of the people, the situation has been declining. Economic growth puts stress on local resources—to support this growth and create the necessary infrastructure, you need to be mining, you need more power plants and dams, you need all of these development projects that both pollute and displace people. People are forced to give up their land if the state wants it for "public purpose." We do have a policy stating that if people's land is being taken away, or their land is being affected by a project, they need to be resettled and rehabilitated with alternative livelihoods, but the government has no accountability. There is absolutely no record of the number of people who've been displaced over the years and whether they have been rehabilitated at all.

The government claims that India's economic growth is leading to increased employment, but what we have seen is that this only applies to "skilled" labor, to the middle class. From the statistics, it is evident that the contribution of agriculture to the growing GDP has steadily been declining—from around 31 percent in 1991 to around 15 percent in the last few years—whereas the agriculture sector supports almost 60 percent of the population, clearly indicating that the growth is happening for a very small percentage of the population. For the working class and those who have agriculture-based livelihoods, increased mechanization and displacement are having a very negative impact on livelihood, and overall poverty is increasing. And there is more environmental degradation, there is more pollution, there is more diversion of forests and rivers toward large projects like roads and mines and dams.

There's a very clear shift of control of resources from the state toward private, and from the local people toward private. People are losing not just their access and control, but their complete livelihoods, their whole economies and economic rights, because of this model of development.

Women are particularly impacted by this model of development and are also on the forefront of many of the grassroots movements that are emerging. Could you talk about what that looks like?

India has a patriarchal society. Women don't have access to or control over property in India, which sustains this patriarchal system; another thing that sustains it is the division of roles, whether in the household or in the community.

In India, women often have very specific roles. For example, in rural communities, it's the women who are putting in sixteen hours of work a day. They start their day at four in the morning, collecting fuel wood, getting water for the family, tending the land. They're providing for the family; they're the ones who have a very close relationship with the land and the forest; they're the ones who are affected when there's a scarcity of water, because they have to walk farther to get access to clean water for their families.

At the same time, women have very little control over resources, and very little public presence, especially in rural areas. And then you have the caste issues, like women who belong to the "lower" castes and those who are from indigenous communities—they are doubly, triply more vulnerable because they face discrimination from a lot of areas.

So women are being impacted by development, and they don't have any recourse. They don't have the choice to say no; they don't have the space in the political arena to determine what kind of development takes place in their village or in their locality.

There's a whole range of issues that affect women when the government and the state follow these kinds of neoliberal policies. There's increasing feminization of labor; women are directly affected by the growing level of impoverishment. If you look at pollution, at the impacts on women and children, it's the women who are most affected: their reproductive health gets affected; their health in general gets affected. Obviously, it is because of this that when a community decides to oppose the government to protect their resources, as is happening in many places in India now, it is the women who are at the forefront of the struggle. Because they know they are going to be the biggest losers.

And obviously, when there is state repression of such struggles, it's the women who get targeted. In the heart of the indigenous area of the country especially, we've seen an enormous amount of state repression targeting women—they're raped, they're assaulted, and they're killed. They are extremely vulnerable, but at the same time they are coming out very strongly in many of these campaigns and movements.

How are these movements for land and livelihood rights connected to broader movements for environmental justice? How do they relate to the global climate-justice movement?

Well, first, any movement in India that is directly contesting this growth paradigm, or directly contesting certain kinds of development—the construction of huge power plants or dams, deforestation—is connected to broader issues. Perhaps the local communities aren't looking at it this way, but many of these can be classified as issues of climate change.

And then there are very specific issues, which are not being taken up so much by communities but more by specific climate activists and campaigners who are more aware of issues at the global level. For instance, you have the carbon credits and the Clean Development Mechanism (CDM), in which governments and companies of the "developed world" are funding and subsidizing projects that supposedly save carbon emissions in the "developing world."

One problem with this is of course the concept itself, which we find severely problematic because it allows the governments of the North to get away without making changes in their own countries, and [they] are instead funding and subsidizing projects in the South; it makes it easier for them to just wash their hands of the responsibility of reducing emissions. But there is another problem, which is that most of the projects that are being funded here are not environmentally friendly or people-friendly at all. Most are actually affecting local people adversely.

Take hydropower projects: they sound good—generating power from water is better than generating power from coal; it's more environmentally friendly. But it isn't that simple; rivers are being diverted for generation of power, and so local communities can't use them, people are displaced, and there is massive deforestation.

Or take windmill projects, which are also being funded by the CDM. Windmills are considered to be so great—they are generating energy—but, for example, in the state of Maharashtra, entire forest is being replaced with windmills, forest that was being used by indigenous communities who completely lost access to it when [a wind-power] company came in to build windmills. And believe me, all the companies were using carbon credits or CDM benefits, and making profits from it. The CDM subsidy just increased their profit margin. So with the CDM, you have these companies profiting from projects that are severely problematic.

So you have all these market-based, quick-fix solutions to climate change. They're all very technocentric solutions, they're market-centric solutions, they're solutions that are being invented by governments who are refusing to deal with the root of the problem, and instead coming up with solutions that are further aggravating the problem.

What impacts are the people's movements having, both on the government and on people's lives?

Well, people's movements have steadily grown over the past ten to twenty years as the amount of corporate projects impacting communities has increased. So the movements are getting more attention in the media. Not as much as is required, of course—media is still focused on catering to a certain [upper-class] population—but many of these struggles are getting highlighted.

Resultantly, there is a greater recognition of the conflicts—between communities on one hand and the state and private corporations on the other—over access to and ownership of resources. That is one of the most concrete impacts of the struggles: they have really raised awareness. People are realizing that they have to fight, that they have to assert their rights in order to keep them. And the media coverage has also helped establish linkages between issues and movements. Many grassroots organizations and activists have realized that these issues cannot be dealt with separately; environmental issues, climate-change issues, issues of livelihood, different regional issues—there are interlinkages across the board. Movements are reflecting that, and are increasingly working together across states and across issues.

And there have been many [laws] passed in response to these movements—[laws] that recognize the rights of communities, or increase communities' access to information about the issues that impact them. We've won a piece of legislation called the Forest Rights Act [passed in 2006], which recognizes communities' claim over the forests where they live. These changes haven't come in a vacuum; they've come as a result of a great deal of organizing. But grassroots resistance has also meant that there is increased state repression and militarization to curb dissent. And this is perhaps one of the greatest challenges that our democracy is facing today.

To All Who Came Before, We Say: Pa'lante!

A Conversation with Nuyorican Activist Emma Torres

By Anna Elena Torres

I grew up hearing all about that day in 1977 when my aunt Emma and her comrades took over the Statue of Liberty, unfurling the once-banned Puerto Rican flag over its face and demanding the release of political prisoners. When I sought out histories of women involved in Puerto Rican liberation movements, I found few stories about their experiences. But just this spring, when Hurray for the Riff Raff released their song "Pa'lante," they offered a new generation of Nuyoricans a way to reclaim that legacy. Sampling Pedro Pietri's classic "Puerto Rican Obituary," singer Alynda Lee Segarra expands the litany of mostly male names in Pietri's poem, calling out to Julia de Burgos and Sylvia Rivera: "To all who came before, we say: 'Pa'lante!' To all who had to hide, we say: 'Pa'lante!'" Hearing the motto of the Young Lords sung by this queer, feminist voice is moving and electrifying.

In that spirit of connection and reclamation, I interviewed my aunt Emma Torres about her experiences organizing with Yuri

Originally published in *make/shift* no. 20 (summer/fall 2017)

Kochiyama, cultural resistance through Spanish, and the history of Puerto Ricans in Native residential schools. She now lives in the mountains of Costa Rica, surrounded by coffee fields.

Anna Elena Torres: How did you get involved with Puerto Rican movements in New York City?

Emma Torres: It was about not only the Puerto Rican struggle, but the people's struggle in general and against the war in Vietnam. My dad always prayed that the war would end after watching the news. By the time I went into Brooklyn College, I had already read about [Puerto Rican independence leader] Albizu Campos. I took a Puerto Rican history class [with Richie Perez]. I had never been part of any group that had to do with *me*. Because of so much racism, and the influence of the Black struggle, you had to find out who you really were. You had whites degrading you, which made you start thinking about color. As time went on, I had to decide what I am and what to affirm.

Tell us about the Statue of Liberty takeover, when your group was agitating for Puerto Rican independence.

The Statue of Liberty takeover, that was in 1977. I was twenty years old. It was in October, in commemoration of [the 1868 uprising against Spain] Grito de Lares. The focus was to free the political prisoners who'd been in jail for twenty-five years by then. We had a whole set of demands—to free the prisoners, to free Puerto Rico, equal access to quality education, retention of open admission, right to equal pay, fair housing access—but most of our motivation was to bring attention to the fact that you still had four Puerto Rican prisoners of war in jail. They were Lolita Lebrón, Rafael Cancel Miranda, Irvin Flores, and Andres Figueroa Cordero. They were our Nelson Mandela. Shortly after that, in 1979, they were freed by Jimmy Carter's administration. I believe that had it not been for that small act, they would have all died in jail.

That morning it was myself, Richard Perez, who was my Puerto Rican studies professor, a friend I would just refer to as Indio, in group number one. There were about six groups making up a total of about thirty people. They were Black, white, and Puerto Rican. We were clear that it would be a peaceful protest. There were more men than women. One person who I would never forget was a Japanese American woman, Yuri [Kochiyama].[1]

I was the youngest and most innocent-looking of the group—or so I was told—so my role was to ask a lot of questions at the front desk until all of the school groups were safely inside and the building had been cleared out. We had to go all the way up about 288 of those winding stairs. It was about going all the way to the top and making sure that Puerto Rican flag was going to look beautiful! No wrinkles from the outside. We had made a decision that when they came in to bust us, we would be together as a group. When someone said, "The bust!" I thought, *Oh my God.* Just because you're fighting for your rights doesn't mean you won't have the human emotion of fear! But principles are stronger than fears. I think I rolled down those stairs so quickly. . . . The men were on one side, the women on the other, since we knew they'd take us out that way. But it took them *nine* hours to get to us.

By the time the SWAT team came along with the federal, state, and local police, we had barricaded the front, but we hadn't destroyed any property. They broke the glass doors. The noise was loud. They were armed and had helmets on. I went to do security at the base of the statue with a Puerto Rican brother, and that's when the helicopters zoomed in. And that's when my parents knew where I was and why I didn't come home that night, which in retrospect was not a good thing at all, to have them worry. But too many Puerto Rican innocent lives had already been lost, both here and on the island, and more lives were going to be lost, so I was willing to take that risk.

When we came down the stairs inside of the statue, it wasn't about gender, it was about justice, and we were in it together, both men and women. Yet I don't think the women's stories have been recorded in any of the history books. Even though on the face of it, you had men and women couples united, there were a lot of problems with some of their relationships. The stress of being involved, under surveillance,

1. Yuri Kochiyama (1921–2014) was a Japanese American political activist who organized with multiracial causes including Asian American liberation, Black nationalism, and Puerto Rican independence. She was present at the assassination of Malcolm X.

some of our people being fired at the university level—what effect does this have on a relationship or a family? But we were defending our rights in our diaspora.

When we were inside the Statue of Liberty, they turned off all the lighting, but we had a small radio, so we could hear what was going on outside of the building. They came in with their helmets, and they were armed, and they used their handcuffs—those new and improved plastic handcuffs—and they escorted us out onto little police boats. But by the time we emerged from the boats, we had all managed to get the SWAT handcuffs off. So we just said, "Thank you, sir" [*mimes returning handcuffs to officers*]. Before entering the police vehicles again, they put the handcuffs back on, this time even tighter—but we managed to remove them again! Pablo Yoruba Guzmán was the first journalist on the scene covering the news. The news went beyond the Iron Curtain.

My friend was arrested with me inside of the statue, and I taught him a little sign language. The guards did not know how the men and women communicated with each other. There was a little window in front of us [in jail], and we could sign to each other!

I visited Yuri Kochiyama a few years ago in Oakland. She constantly cultivated comradeship, corresponding with thousands of people by postcard. She introduced me to every worker in the old-age home—anyone sweeping or cleaning, she shook their hand. What was it like to organize with her?

When I met Yuri, we were inside the Statue of Liberty together. She told me about the [Japanese internment camps during World War II] that her parents were in; because of these experiences, she decided to defend and contribute to the rights of all people. I remember our conversation about Malcolm X, how sad things were inside of the United States, and how much more we had in common. We spoke for many hours. I admired that she was older, and had so many stories and was quite resilient. She passed on her stories, and I listened so intently that the hours passed by quickly.

What were language politics like in the Puerto Rican movement? Was Spanish politicized, and were people organizing bilingually?

My parents taught us to always be proud to speak Spanish, and they never spoke English to us. In kindergarten, people pulled my hair—my mom made us long braids, and our hair was very dark—and they would go "Wooooo" [*imitates stereotypical war whoop*]. There was a lot of violence around speaking another language. Even though being bilingual enhances you, there was never a social context that empowered bilingualism.

A lot of Nuyorican poets at that time were writing in English with Spanish vocabulary.

Language is life; language is always in movement. Code-switching wasn't seen as a historical development of language back then; in fact, when they began to study code-switching, one of the first people studied were the Puerto Rican community. But until a white person wrote about this, it hadn't been valued.

I'd like to hear more about the social and cultural parts of the movement.

There was a lot of salsa, a lot of songs that focused on Puerto Rican pride, open mic on Friday nights. The art was incredible, very vivid colors. One salsa song during that era that I remember was: "Bandera, banderita / A mí mi madre me dijo: el presidente murió." There was another one I really liked: "Qué bonita bandera es la bandera Puertorriqueña." Then we added: "Si tu pasas por mi casa, y tu ves a mi mamá, me le dices que hoy no me esperes que este movimiento no da ni un paso atrás."[2]

When Lolita Lebrón was let out, there was a big celebration.[3] But before that, we would imagine that she was already free. So during the

2. Songs about the island's flag defied the "Gag Law" (Ley de La Mordaza) of 1948, which made it a crime to own or display a Puerto Rican flag, sing patriotic songs, or discuss, write, or assemble in favor of Puerto Rican independence.

3. Lolita Lebrón (1919–2010) was a Puerto Rican nationalist convicted for attempted murder for attacking the U.S. House of Representatives in 1954. She was pardoned in 1979 by Jimmy Carter.

protest, we would say, "Se siente, se siente, Lolita está presente!" It was what we really wanted to see happen, so we turned it into song.

What often gets recognized as activism is militant action, not the action of care. Puerto Rican diasporic movements combined both elements, like building barricades when garbage wasn't getting picked up, urban environmentalism like solar panels, getting people health care through hospital takeovers. . . .

By the time the Puerto Ricans migrated to the United States, we inherited housing in its worst state and didn't have the privilege of getting loans like European immigrants. By the time Puerto Ricans rented the units, there were no longer any services like garbage [collection] and electricity. This [municipal neglect] fed into media stereotypes about Puerto Ricans. I remember my brother telling me that there were no sanitation services before the barricades. This was in the Bronx. Empty lots had been turned into community gardens by people with agricultural skills in all of the boroughs, those from Puerto Rico together with African Americans who'd lived in the South. People were even raising chickens.

Do you have any memories of the Young Lords' hospital takeover in 1970? That confrontation won a lot of services for patients in the South Bronx who weren't well served by the dilapidated hospital.

Specifically about Lincoln Hospital—they were fighting to set up acupuncture clinics to treat drug addiction. Finally, after the takeover, they were able to set up that kind of clinic so people wouldn't be dependent on methadone.

A few years ago, we learned that your grandmother was among the Puerto Ricans taken from the island and sent to the Carlisle Indian Industrial School in 1905.[4] Government papers categorized her as

4. Established by Captain Richard Pratt in 1879, the United States Carlisle Indian Industrial School was the first federal boarding school established to culturally assimilate Native students. See Pablo Navarro-Rivera, "Acculturation under Duress: The Puerto Rican Experience at the Carlisle Indian Industrial School 1898–1918," *Centro Journal* 18, no. 1 (2006): 222–59; and the work of archivist Barbara Landis.

"full-blood Porto Rican." It's a racial paradox: official records claimed the Taínos were wiped out, but at the same time, some Puerto Ricans were listed as "full-blood" into the twentieth century. The contradictory logics of the state don't negate each other! So we're looking for traces of that disrupted history in state archives, in family oral history, in each other's faces. And the archives themselves are a fraught space: those photos were tools of surveillance, of violence—yet it's the material that relates Carlisle students' experience.

I had always heard that my grandmother was Taína. She was from Mayagüez, where some of the Taínos had been forcibly removed and taken to Carlisle. I heard about [new research on Carlisle], and I would like to read more about it, but there's a lot of pain attached. It's not that I don't want to know, but [Pratt's] motto, "Kill the Indian, save the man"—that's very, very painful to me. Some of the indigenous people at Carlisle, their spirits couldn't be broken. I think my grandmother was one of them.

In the United States, the newly elected administration poses a profound danger to our collective health and the environment. How do we cultivate and sustain resistance in the face of this?

To all my Black and Puerto Rican, Palestinian, Mexican, white, Jewish, and Latino friends inside of the U.S., remember to nurture peace when in a war. You are much more effective out of jail than in jail. If you see or are offered any weapons all of a sudden from anyone or a group that you don't know, beware: it's a set-up. Don't fall for it. When public school is no longer a viable tool, keep reading, do research, and set up study circles. Learn from history. Choose food that will keep you strong and healthy if you can. Stay vigilant and prepare your mind, body, and soul to defend your children and elderly first. Living in community is loving in community. Stay away from words or plans that do not serve life. Think about the potential consequences. Real heroes don't seek media attention. Keep up your spiritual traditions. They will strengthen you.

About the Authors

Jessica Hoffmann (coeditor/copublisher of *make/shift*) is an editor, writer, community organizer, and museum administrator. She is a member of *POOR Magazine*'s Solidarity Family, sings in a choir that specializes in Eastern European folk music, and loves being an aunt.

Daria Yudacufski (coeditor/copublisher of *make/shift*) is the executive director of Visions and Voices, the arts and humanities initiative at the University of Southern California. She is grateful to be part of an incredible community of people who have contributed to *make/shift* over the past decade and are working toward creating a more just world. She finds hope for the future in her daughter, who challenges gender norms and kicks ass in jiujitsu, whose favorite song is David Bowie's "Rebel Rebel," and who makes her smile with her punk rock awesomeness every day.

About the Contributors

Stephanie Abraham (StephanieAbraham.com) was a member of the editorial and publishing collective that founded *make/shift*.

Jen Benka is the author of two poetry collections and the executive director of the Academy of American Poets in New York City.

Roan Boucher is an artist, facilitator, and parent living with his queer family in Carrboro, North Carolina.

Heather Bowlan is a writer and editor based in Philadelphia.

Iris Brilliant lives in Oakland, California. She organizes young people with wealth to support social justice and is a singer-guitarist in a band.

brownfemipower can be found on twitter under @RustBeltRebel. Her website is sundaymorningeasy.com.

Ching-In Chen (www.chinginchen.com) is the author of *The Heart's Traffic* and *recombinant*.

Celina R. De León gets marginalized voices seen, heard, and published. You can follow her at @celvoz.

Lisa Factora-Borchers is a Filipina American writer and poet and the editor of *Dear Sister: Letters from Survivors of Sexual Violence*. She was previously a front-of-book editor and member of the social-media team at *make/shift*.

Sam Feder is a filmmaker and advocate. Their films center trans lives.

T Clutch Fleischmann is the author of *Syzygy, Beauty* and *Time Is the Thing*.

Alexis Pauline Gumbs is the author of *Spill: Scenes of Black Feminist Fugitivity* and *M Archive: After the End of the World*, and a coeditor of *Revolutionary Mothering: Love on the Front Lines*. She runs an intergalactic educational center and archive based in Durham, North Carolina. She was *make/shift* magazine's poet in residence.

Conner Habib is an author, sex workers' rights activist, and host of the podcast *Against Everyone with Conner Habib*.

Sharon Hoshida is a political organizer and community activist active in the peace movement, and an advocate of feminist society and environmental justice.

Lailan Sandra Huen is a Chinese American community organizer whose family came to California's Bay Area in the 1850s.

Jessi Lee Jackson is a psychotherapist who lives in Vancouver, unceded Coast Salish territory.

Randa Jarrar is the author of *A Map of Home* and *Him, Me, Muhammad Ali*.

Javon Johnson is a poet, performer, and professor of African American and African diaspora studies at UNLV.

Erin Aubry Kaplan is a journalist, essayist, and author based in Los Angeles who writes about life as an American of color.

Nomy Lamm is a fat queer white jewish disabled artist who lives on Nisqually, Squaxin, and Chehalis lands with their partner Lisa Ganser and other beloved animals.

Jessica Lawless is an artist and writer. She attributes her organizing skills to her love of herding cats. The rest is just about paying off debt.

Stacey Milbern is a disability justice thoughtleader based in Oakland, California. She is a mixed-race disabled queer woman of color.

Mia Mingus is a writer, educator, and community organizer for disability justice and transformative justice.

Courtney Desiree Morris (courtneydesireemorris.com) is a visual artist and assistant professor of African American and women's, gender, and sexuality studies at Penn State University.

Yasmin Nair is a writer and activist. Her work is archived at www.yasminnair.net.

Jennifer New (jennifernew.wordpress.com) is a writer, yogi, administrator, and mother.

Adela Nieves is a mixed media maker, traditional community health and healing arts practitioner, and mama.

Christine E. Petit is a community organizer and writer living in Long Beach, California.

Leah Lakshmi Piepzna-Samarasinha is a queer disabled Sri Lankan writer of *Dirty River*, *Bodymap*, and other books.

Andrea Richards is an author, editor, and enthusiast. She is a member of the Narrated Objects collective.

Adrienne Skye Roberts is from the Bay Area and is involved in movements to end criminalization.

Mariana Ruiz Firmat is a poet, writer, auntie, and organizer living in Brooklyn.

Raia Small is a writer and organizer living in Northern California.

Mattilda Bernstein Sycamore (mattildabernsteinsycamore.com) is most recently the author of *The End of San Francisco* and *Sketchtasy*. She edited *make/shift* magazine's reviews section.

Dean Spade is an associate professor at the Seattle University School of Law, founder of the Sylvia Rivera Law Project, author of *Normal Life: Administrative Violence, Critical Trans Politics and the Limits of Law*, and maker of the documentary *Pinkwashing Exposed: Seattle Fights Back!* (free online at pinkwashingexposed.net).

Anna Elena Torres is a professor of comparative literature at the University of Chicago.

Jessica Trimbath (aka Davka) lives, writes, and works as a jeweler in Ojai, California.

Index

Editors' Note: In preparing this book, it became clear to us that a conventional approach to subject-matter indexing is at odds with the ideas of intersectionality, in that it fails to fully capture the relationships between topics that are at the core of an intersectional view. Further, standard information-science categories for sociological and other groups do not always reflect the ways the contributors to this book define ourselves, our identities, and our communities. And finally, how could we limit terms like "sexual violence" (as just one example) to a short list of page numbers, rather than recognize how this topic is threaded through so many different discussions here? We know there are radical librarians and others building an intersectional-feminist approach to indexing, and we are reminded of how important that work is. Meanwhile, in the interest of providing a reference tool that might be useful for people who may not read this book in its entirety, we have included an index of proper nouns, since these can more easily be tied to specific page numbers and offer a way to cite people, projects, and places who appear in the book.—JH and DY

"Passim" (literally "scattered") indicates intermittent discussion of a topic over a cluster of pages.

AK Press is small, in terms of staff and resources, but we also manage to be one of the world's most productive anarchist publishing houses. We publish close to twenty books every year, and distribute thousands of other titles published by like-minded independent presses and projects from around the globe. We're entirely worker-run and democratically managed. We operate without a corporate structure—no boss, no managers, no bullshit.

The Friends of AK program is a way you can directly contribute to the continued existence of AK Press, and ensure that we're able to keep publishing books like this one! Friends pay $25 a month directly into our publishing account ($30 for Canada, $35 for international), and receive a copy of every book AK Press publishes for the duration of their membership! Friends also receive a discount on anything they order from our website or buy at a table: 50% on AK titles, and 20% on everything else. We have a Friends of AK ebook program as well: $15 a month gets you an electronic copy of every book we publish for the duration of your membership. You can even sponsor a very discounted membership for someone in prison.

Email FRIENDSOFAK@AKPRESS.ORG for more info, or visit the Friends of AK Press website: HTTPS://WWW.AKPRESS.ORG/FRIENDS.HTML.

There are always great book projects in the works—so sign up now to become a Friend of AK Press, and let the presses roll!